Country Music
Goes to War

Country Music Goes to War

Edited by
Charles K. Wolfe and
James E. Akenson

THE UNIVERSITY PRESS OF KENTUCKY

Publication of this volume was made possible in part
by a grant from the National Endowment for the Humanities.

Scholarly publisher for the Commonwealth,
serving Bellarmine University, Berea College, Centre
College of Kentucky, Eastern Kentucky University,
The Filson Historical Society, Georgetown College,
Kentucky Historical Society, Kentucky State University,
Morehead State University, Murray State University,
Northern Kentucky University, Transylvania University,
University of Kentucky, University of Louisville,
and Western Kentucky University.

Editorial and Sales Offices: The University Press of Kentucky
663 South Limestone Street, Lexington, Kentucky 40508-4008

09 08 07 06 05   5 4 3 2 1

Library of Congress Cataloging-in-Publication Data

Country music goes to war / edited by Charles K. Wolfe and James E. Akenson.
    p. cm.
  Includes bibliographical references (p.   ).
    ISBN 0-8131-2308-9 (hardcover : alk. paper)   610²   Renfro Valley Barn Dance (Mt.Vernon) ky
    1. Country music—History and criticism. 2. Country music—Social aspects.   600' Lair, John
  3. Music and war. 4. Political ballads and songs—History and criticism.
  I. Wolfe, Charles K. II. Akenson, James Edward, 1943-
  ML3524.C695 2005
  781.642]1599--dc22   2004020806

This book is printed on acid-free recycled paper meeting
the requirements of the American National Standard
for Permanence in Paper for Printed Library Materials.

Manufactured in the United States of America.

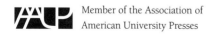

Member of the Association of
American University Presses

Contents

Introduction

In her definitive anthology of country song lyrics, *Sing Your Heart Out, Country Boy,* Dorothy Horstman devotes one of her keystone chapters to the heading "War and Patriotism." She explains, "A country audience likes nothing better than a tragic song, and what better setting for it than a war? It has all the elements of drama—separation, loneliness, betrayal, danger, disfigurement, and death—and hillbilly songs about the experience have managed to cover them all." Although the popularity of war songs naturally ebbs and flows depending on the political climate and the actual existence of military conflict, a surprising number of such songs have entered the standard country repertoire and are still sung on a regular basis—"The Soldier's Last Letter," "Silver Dew on the Blue Grass Tonight," "Each Night at Nine," "At Mail Call Today," and "God Bless the USA," to name a few. Similarly, more than a few of the old British and Scottish ballads (the "Child ballads") that provided some of the roots for country music are full of stories about war and battle.

Events of the last ten years have brought to the nation a new sense of patriotism and a renewed interest in songs that reflect on these difficult times. New versions of patriotic standards such as "The Star-Spangled Banner" and "America the Beautiful" have been recorded by major modern stars like Aaron Tippin, Lyle Lovett, and Toby Keith. New songs by Keith, Darryl Worley, Charlie Daniels, and the Dixie Chicks have not only found homes on the airwaves, but often have become newsworthy items of their own. Tippin, for example, has said of his song "You've Got to Stand for Something," "I hope it will help our country heal." Such a climate suggests that now is an appropriate time to explore the tradition of war-related country music and to assess the impact of such songs.

Thus the fourteen essays presented here as the second volume in a new series of thematic anthologies about country music. The essays range from Civil War songs to the tragedy of 9/11 to the war with Iraq; they cover a geopolitical spectrum that ranges from Northern Ireland to Australia. The writers approach their subjects from a wide range of perspectives: history, English, folklore, education, political science, and popular culture. And precisely because of this diversity, *Country Music Goes to War* cannot be read as a full and complete history of the subject. We readily admit that country music addressing World War II and the cold war seems to attract more academic interest than songs of the Vietnam era (which is complex enough to merit a full-length book of its own), songs in Hollywood films, the impact of technology (like the Armed Forces Radio Network) on spreading wartime music, or the use of country war songs in political campaigns. We would have preferred to have essays on these topics, but none were forthcoming (perhaps because some of the topics have received little academic study).

All the diverse essays, however, address one common concern: What different functions do these songs play in different societies? Once the question of function has been asked, numerous others arise: Do the songs inspire, motivate, rally, console, or simply cause the listener to reflect? How does the social and political function of a song shift over the years and within different settings? As a full-fledged commercial art form, is country music still able to project the sincerity and honesty that once marked the classic old ballads? We may not answer all of these questions, but we hope this first gathering of studies about this powerful genre will stimulate further research and discussion.

This marks the fifth anthology of country essays edited by Charles Wolfe and James Akenson, and the second thematic volume. We are hoping to explore in a future book the world of country music and the movies, and we invite interested parties to contact us, Dr. Wolfe at cwolfe@frank.mtsu.edu, or Dr. Akenson at jakenson@tntech.edu.

Charles K. Wolfe and James E. Akenson

1

The Civil War in Country Music Tradition

Andrew K. Smith and James E. Akenson

Introduction

Fig 1. Cannon on ridge of Louisiana position at Vicksburg. (Photo by James E. Akenson.)

Despite lasting only four years—from 1861 to 1865—the American Civil War continues to fascinate the public and scholars in the United States and around the world. In recent years, Ken Burns's Public Broadcasting Service documentary series generated intense interest. Annual reenactments at Civil War battlefields such as Shiloh and Chickamauga continue to attract thousands of spectators, and popular magazines such as *Civil War Times* may be found in Wal-Mart, as well as in supermarkets and gas stations. The July 2003 *Smithsonian* magazine featured "Making Sense of Robert E. Lee," an article by Roy Blount Jr. Books such as Tony Horwitz's *Confederates in the Attic: Dispatches from the Unfinished Civil War* (1998) and Jim Cullen's *The Civil War in Popular Culture: A Reusable Past* (1995) provide evidence of the general public's interest in all things Civil War. In addition, the remarkable number of Web sites devoted to the conflict, such as the American Civil War Homepage (Hoemann 2003), reflects a strong popular appetite, not to mention continued scholarly activity and controversy of a voluminous nature. Even the daily news points out that the Civil War lives on. One need only look to newspapers to see controversies over the Confederate flag's appearance in school dress (Smith 2003), on license plates (de la Cruz 2003), and in school presentations (Alligood 2003). Of all the historical events that live on in the public consciousness, the Civil War surely ranks as one of the prominent. William Faulkner believed that "The past isn't dead. It isn't even past." The country music tradition provides a case in point about the enduring legacy of the Civil War, for, as Conway Twitty sang, it is indeed "a bridge that just won't burn." During the 140-plus years since its conclusion, the Civil War has made, and continues to make, its way into country music in a remarkable number of ways.

This essay focuses on Civil War–era material in the country music tradition, Civil War themes in individual songs, Civil War concept albums, and Civil War references in songs not overtly about the conflict; also considered are visual references on album covers and CD booklets. From Alabama, Dave Alvin, David Olney, Steve Earle, Claude King, Shenandoah, Johnny Horton, Brother Phelps, Tracy Lawrence, and Hank Williams Jr. to Jimmy Arnold, Johnny Cash, Jimmy Driftwood, Tennessee Ernie Ford, and fortunately obscure releases by Ku Klux Klan sympathizers, the Civil War does indeed live in the country music tradition. The examples provided are extensive, but not exhaustive, owing to the remarkable number of recordings by mainstream artists as well as artists who never made any visible impact on the mainstream or even alternative country music market.

Music during the Civil War

According to Wiley (1978b, 151), "[P]erhaps the favorite recreation of the Confederate Army was music." Although new songs were written during the war—as evidenced by the large number of songbooks published between 1861 and 1865—the small list of camp favorites was largely made up of melodies familiar before the war. Among the favorites were "Home, Sweet Home," "Lorena," "All Quiet along the Potomac Tonight," "Annie Laurie," "The Girl I Left behind Me," "Her Bright Eyes Haunt Me Still,"

"Listen to the Mockingbird," "Just Before the Battle, Mother," "Dixie," "The Bonnie Blue Flag," and "Maryland, My Maryland."

The lyrics were occasionally altered to reflect the times and circumstances. Thus, Confederate soldiers retreating from Tennessee after John Bell Hood's unsuccessful December 1864 attempt to take Nashville most likely sang "The Yellow Rose of Texas" with these new words:

> You may talk about your Beauregard
> And sing of General Lee
> But the gallant Hood of Texas
> Played hell in Tennessee.

Fiddle music was especially in demand, to the extent that the price of fiddles escalated dramatically during the war. Popular tunes included "Hell Broke Loose in Georgia," "Billy in the Low Ground," "Arkansas Traveler," "Money Musk," "The Goose Hangs High," "When I Saw Sweet Nellie Home," "My Old Kentucky Home," "Oh Lord Gals One Friday," and "Dixie."

The Confederate commander James Ewell Brown ("JEB") Stuart enjoyed banjo music so much that he had Sam Sweeney, the younger brother of Joel Sweeney (a blackface minstrel said to be the "inventor" of the five-string banjo), transferred to his command. Sweeney, unfortunately, died of smallpox during the winter of 1864 (Thomas 1988, 280). With Sweeney playing banjo, Stuart would often sing songs such as "Her Bright Smile Haunts Me Still" (sung by Eleazer Tillett and Martha Etheridge, the song was later "collected" by Anne and Frank Warner in 1951), "Lorena," and "Jine the Cavalry" (Davis 1994, 69–70). Stuart may well have had a greater appreciation of music than Gen. Ulysses Grant, who disliked marching bands and claimed he could recognize only two tunes: "'One was "Yankee Doodle,"' he said; the other wasn't" (Ward, Burns, and Burns 1990, 280).

Music was also popular in the Union Army; however, unlike the fiddle music favored by the Southern troops, "the music enjoyed most was that made by the soldiers' own voices. Yanks went to war with songs on their lips" (Wiley 1978a, 158). Northern music publishers produced numerous songsters during the war. The most popular Northern song, "John Brown's Body," received new lyrics when Julia Ward Howe wrote "Battle Hymn of the Republic" in 1861, but soldiers apparently preferred the original song. Other popular Union songs were "Happy Land of Canaan," "The Battle-Cry of Freedom," "The Star-Spangled Banner," "When This Cruel War Is

Over," "The Girl I Left Behind Me," "Johnny Fill Up the Bowl," "Tenting on the Old Camp Ground," "When Johnny Comes Marching Home," "Johnny Is Gone for a Soldier," "Tramp, Tramp, Tramp," and "Just Before the Battle, Mother" (160–62).

Like their Southern counterparts, Union soldiers were adept at changing the words to songs. "Just Before the Battle, Mother" was sometimes parodied as

> Just before the battle, mother,
> I was drinking mountain dew,
> When I saw the Rebels marching,
> To the rear I quickly flew. (Commager 1978, 1:568)

One of the most contentious songs of the Civil War to Southern ears was Henry Clay Work's "Marching Through Georgia," which celebrated Sherman's destructive passage through the South after the sacking of Atlanta. The song became so well known that it was played by the Japanese when they entered Port Arthur, Manchuria, sung by the British in India, and played and sung by Allied forces in World War II (1:570).

Of the war's artistic output, music (and not poetry or literature) may well have been the most enduring legacy. This is certainly true from a Northern perspective. Paul Johnson notes "how little impact the Civil War made upon millions of people in the North. When Edmund Wilson came to write his book on the conflict, *Patriotic Gore: Studies in the Literature of the American Civil War* (1962), he was astonished by how little there was of it. There were hymn-songs, of course: 'John Brown's Body,' Julia Ward Howe's 'Battle Hymn of the Republic,' to rally Northern spirits, Daniel Decatur Emmett's 'Dixie' to enthuse the South. . . . It was quite possible to live in the North and have no contact with the struggle whatsoever" (1997, 406).

Johnson surmises that the difference between North and South was "that it would have been far less likely for a Southerner to be unaffected by the war, owing to the relatively larger impact the war had on the South." Factually, this rings true; except for two forays by Lee (at Antietam in 1862 and Gettysburg in 1863) and Jubal Early's Washington Raid (1864), the North was free from large-scale invasions by the South. In contrast, the Confederacy was both blockaded and invaded. In particular, Sherman's march to the sea, in which he essentially waged war against civilians—aspects of which were described by one British writer as "brigandage" (Boatner 1959, 511)—had a profound, demoralizing effect on the South.

The Civil War and Country Music

Peterson and Davis (1975) identify the "Fertile Crescent" of country music as a Southern-based hearth of culture; within this region, interest in the Civil War manifested itself over time in country music. The Civil War's impact on Southerners helps to explain why songs of the war lingered in their memories long after the conflict ceased, and why they were later recorded by country musicians as early as 1920. "Dixie," for example, was recorded at least ten times between 1924 and 1936 by Uncle Am Stuart, Doc Roberts and Edgar Boaz, Gid Tanner and His Skillet Lickers, Earl Johnson, the Kessinger Brothers, Red Foley, and others (Meade, Spottswood, and Meade 2002, 344), including Boxcar Willie (Lecil Martin). Canadian Ray Griff, who performed several times at the Jimmie Rodgers Memorial Festival, also recorded "Dixie" (no date [n.d.]). "Just Before the Battle, Mother" was recorded four times between 1935 and 1945 (462–68), and Marty Robbins recorded it again in 1963. Meade et al. list six pre-1939 versions of "The Vacant Chair," which Kathy Mattea also recorded more recently on *Songs of the Civil War* (1991). "Faded Coat of Blue," one of the most memorable Civil War songs in country music, was recorded by Welby Toomey, Buell Kazee, the Carter Family, and David Miller, Frank Welling, and John McGhee. Bill Clifton (1963), Betsy Rutherford (n.d.), Jay Ungar and Molly Mason (1993), and Suzanne Thomas (1998) have also recorded it.

"Lorena" also persisted from the 1860s to the era of recorded country music: the Blue Ridge Mountain Singers recorded it in 1930. Later, John Hartford (who recorded it at least three times), the Osborne Brothers (1994), Robert and Claudene Nobley (1975), and the bluegrass group East Virginia (n.d.) had versions similar to the original. Johnny Cash (with versions in 1959, 1970, and 1972), Waylon Jennings (1994), and even Australia's Kevin Shegog (n.d.) sang a later variation of the Civil War favorite. Another plaintive song about a dying soldier, "Write a Letter to My Mother," was recorded by Charles Nabell, Roy Harvey, Charlie Poole and the North Carolina Ramblers (1930, reissued 1998), J.E. Mainer's Mountaineers (1935, reissued n.d.), and as "Not a Word of That Be Said" by Wade Mainer (1980) and Hazel Dickens, Carol Elizabeth Jones, and Ginny Hawker (1998).

Over the years, country and bluegrass fiddlers have recorded many tunes played during the conflict. For example, Fiddlin' John Carson and Gid Tanner and His Skillet Lickers recorded "Hell Broke Loose in Georgia," a tune that may well have been inspired by Sherman's capture of Atlanta and his subsequent march through Georgia and South Carolina. "Billy in the Low Ground," "Arkansas Traveler," "My Old Kentucky Home," and other Civil War tunes have been played as instrumentals by country musicians for decades. Russell suggests that old-time bands such as the Skillet Lickers, with repertoires reaffirming Southern attitudes, such as "Run, Nigger Run" and "Dixie," would have been warmly welcomed in any Southern port of call (1970, 21). More recently, Jim Taylor has recorded at least two thoroughly annotated albums of fiddle tunes that were played during the Civil War.

Country musicians also recorded songs of plantation life, though not all of these were written before, or during, the war. Among these recordings are "Gum Tree Canoe," "Uncle Ned," "Massa's in the Cold, Cold Ground," "Ella Rhee" (better known as "Sweet Allalee"), "Darling Nellie Gray," "Poor Old Slave," "Kitty Wells," "Year of Jubilo," "Down in the Cane Brake," "Those Cruel Slavery Days," "I'm Going from the Cottonfields," "Little Log Cabin by the Stream," and "No More the Moon Shines on Lorena" (Meade, Spottswood, and Meade 2002, 462–68). Because these songs were sung from a Southern perspective, perhaps not surprisingly many of them offer a somewhat sanitized depiction of antebellum plantation life at odds with abolitionist portrayals of slavery. "My Pretty Quadroon" (The Browns, 1960), for example, may well disguise a "massa's hot intentions towards the estate's little octoroons" (Russell 1970, 20), although the lyrics focus on "gardens and bowers, and flowers that were always in bloom," and "flowers that faded too soon." Similarly, Mac Wiseman's 1966 recording of "Darling Nellie Gray" only hints of the forced separation of slave couples (a common occurrence in the prewar South). A few songs, however, describe the cruelty of slavery: Fields Ward and His Buck Mountain Band were unequivocally damning in their recording of Ward's "Those Cruel Slavery Days" (1929), with its references to slaves being sold "for silver and gold" and to "those agonizing cruel slavery days."

Some of commercial country music's earliest performers had tangible links with the Civil War. Uncle Dave Macon's father, John Macon, for example, was a captain in the Thirty-fifth Tennessee Infantry Regiment and fought at Shiloh, Perryville, and Murfreesboro (Wolfe 1995b, 4). A more tenuous link involved Gilliam Banmon Grayson's uncle, Col. James Grayson, who captured Thomas Dula ("Dooley") in Tennessee in 1866. Dula, fleeing after murdering Laura Foster, had been a member of the Forty-second North Carolina Regiment during the Civil War. So when Gilliam Grayson and

Henry Whitter recorded "Tom Dooley" in 1929, the lines "Hadn't a-been for Grayson / I'd a-been in Tennessee" may well have had personal meaning for Grayson (Curry 2003). Frank Proffitt, who sang "Tom Dooley" for Frank Warner in 1938, had a grandfather who had fought for the Union and a great-uncle who sided with the Confederacy. Eck Robertson and Henry Gilliland recorded twelve sides for Victor in New York on June 30 and July 1, 1922, after attending an old Confederate soldiers reunion in Richmond (Wolfe 1995a, 668). Fiddlin' John Carson, a member of the Ku Klux Klan, performed at a 1914 fiddlers convention organized by the United Daughters of the Confederacy (Wiggins 1987, 114, 49), and probably played at Confederate reunions as far back as the late nineteenth century. Carson also played for Confederate veterans as late as 1941 (136). Land Norris was associated with the nephew of Fiddlin' Ira Sisson, a Confederate veteran who is supposed to have won a world's fiddling championship in the late nineteenth century. Given the popularity of fiddle music with Confederate soldiers, it is probably not a coincidence that conventions of old Rebel soldiers and fiddlers sometimes went hand in hand (Bill Malone briefly touches on this and other aspects of the links between country music and the Civil War [1983, 17—22; 2002, 157–58, 223–24]). More recently, country singer Stonewall Jackson traces his ancestry to his namesake, the Confederate commander Thomas "Stonewall" Jackson.

As well as singing songs from the Civil War itself, country artists have recorded songs about the war that were composed after 1865. One of the most potent images of the link between modern country music and the Civil War is captured in photographs, taken in July 1959, of Johnny Horton singing the Merle Kilgore tribute to soldiers of the South, "Johnny Reb," to a bedridden 116-year-old Confederate general, Walter Williams, who "tapped his crippled hand defiantly in time with the music" (LeVine 1982, 136–37). Tex Ritter (1948, reissued 2000) and Johnny Cash (1972) have both recorded Abraham Lincoln's eloquent Gettysburg Address as recitations. Cash also sang "God Bless Robert E. Lee" (1983). In 1959, Lefty Frizzell recorded Harlan Howard's "The Ballad of the Blue and Grey" (reissued 1992). Frank Proffitt sang "Poor Soldier" (1968), which he learned from his aunt, and the Boys from Indiana wrote and recorded "Atlanta Is Burning" (1974). One of the most popular bluegrass songs about the Civil War is Charlie Moore's "The Legend of the Rebel Soldier" (1976), based on the experience of Private James Smith, a Confederate prisoner of war. The song, which appears to be a variation of an Irish song about a member of the IRA (Wiseman n.d.), was also a hit for the Country Gentlemen, who recorded it in 1971 (reissued 1998). Flatt and Scruggs recorded "The Legend of the Johnson Boys" (1962), as well as "Poor Rebel Soldier" (1970); the Dry Branch Fire Squad sang of a soldier from Georgia whose dying plea was that "Someone Play Dixie for Me" (1985); and Joan Baez recounted the Band's "The Night They Drove Old Dixie Down" (1976). Steve Earle has recorded two Civil War–related songs: "Dixieland" (1998), about a volunteer of the Twentieth Maine at Little Round Top, Gettysburg, and "Ben McCulloch" (1995).

Concept Albums

During the early 1960s, probably to celebrate the centenary of the war, several Civil War "concept" albums were recorded by Jimmy Driftwood (1960, reissued 1991), Tennessee Ernie Ford (1961), and Don Reno and Red Smiley (1961). These concept albums vary in their thematic arrangements. Tennessee Ernie Ford's album contains Civil War songs, yet fails to exhibit a connective tissue beyond the Civil War itself. Ford's songs about the South include "Stonewall Jackson's Way," "Lorena," "Riding a Raid," "Maryland, My Maryland," and "Goober Peas." Likewise, Jimmy Driftwood's discontinuous selection includes "Won't You Come Along and Go," "Billy Yank and Johnny Reb," "How Do You Like the Army," "When I Swim the Golden River," as well as "Git Along Little Yearlings" and "The Rock of Chickamauga"; the final song chronicles General Thomas's stand, which prevented General Longstreet from routing Federal forces. Reno and Smiley's album describes the war and its battles. Some tracks, such as "Shiloh" and "Antietam," are recitations, replete even with specific historical facts and detailed figures of battle losses. Others, like "Stonewall's Brigade," are accompanied by military drumming—typical of saga songs of the day.

Concept albums, however, continued to emerge after the 1861 centennial. Jimmy Arnold's *Southern Soul* (1983), described by Bill Malone as "the best country concept album" (2002, 359), also lacks an overt cohesion beyond the Southern orientation as he presents selections such as "The Rebel Soldier," "Sail Away Ladies," "My Home's Across the Blue Ridge Mountains," "Lorena," and "General Lee." Shawn Camp released *Stone Grey Day: Songs about the Confederacy* in 1992. *Songs of the Civil War* (1991) includes Kathy Mattea's versions of "The Southern Soldier Boy," "Somebody's Darling," and "The Vacant Chair," as well as cuts by Hoyt Axton, Waylon

Fig. 2. Rocks of Chickamauga. (Photo by James E. Akenson.)

Jennings, and John Hartford. Within the bluegrass tradition, Sonny Osborne comments in the liner notes to *When the Roses Bloom in Dixieland* (1994) that "I thought it would be an interesting theme to record a CD of Civil War era songs. I didn't know so many albums had been done using that idea." Other bluegrass musicians have written and recorded numerous songs about the Civil War. In 2001, Rebel Records released *Last Day at Gettysburg,* an album comprising songs about the war. Dave Mathews released two Civil War albums: *Shades of Blue & Gray* (1989) and *A Nation's Broken Soul* (1992). Marijohn Wilkin's *Battle of the Blue and Gray* (n.d.) also has numerous songs with both Confederate ("When Johnny Comes Marching Home") and Union ("Slavery Chain Done Broke at Last") perspectives. Several other albums by the likes of Bobby Horton (1985), Wayne Erbsen (1995), and the interracial couple Rhonda and Sparky Rucker (1992) possess Civil War content, but do not represent artists with aspirations to, or visibility in, the alt.country or mainstream country music industry; however, their music may be found at Civil War sites such as the Vicksburg, Mississippi, National Battle Field.

Paul Kennerley's *White Mansions: A Tale from the American Civil War*

1861–1865 (1978), which features Waylon Jennings, Jessi Colter, and others (including members of the Ozark Mountain Daredevils), is bound together by a connected story line, unlike the concept albums discussed above. *White Mansions* recounts the Civil War from a predominantly Southern perspective, yet reflects a tenor that adds complexity and interpretation beyond nostalgia or pro-Confederate romance. Both the album cover, a stately antebellum mansion framed by the arches of tunnel-like mighty oaks leading to the mansion's front entrance, and the CD graphics, a Southern mansion with four white columns, two stately trees on either side, and finely clad planter and wife on the grounds out front, suggest an uncomplicated view of the conflict. The romantic, stereotypical representation, however, belies the complexity of the *White Mansions* story line.

A booklet accompanying the original *White Mansions* album offers a combination of period photographs, idealized photographs of story characters, commentary, and lyrics. The characters include Matthew J. Fuller, a twenty-three-year-old son of a wealthy Georgia cotton planter who joins a Georgia infantry regiment as a captain, and Matthew's sweetheart, Polly Ann Stafford, who, as the daughter of a wealthy nearby landowner and diplomat, attends the wounded in a hospital. Caleb Stone, the "white trash," symbolizes a class of poor Southern whites who have no profession, land, or property. Despite being an overseer and Confederate army enlistee, Caleb feels hostility for the plantation owner. The Drifter, whose voice is supplied by Waylon Jennings, narrates the album, providing a rather balanced view through both Confederate and Union perspectives. Finally, slaves make their way into the story.

The story line moves from the excessive optimism of the early days in "Join Around the Flag"—with its tag line that "we're going to whip their ass . . ."—to a concluding "Dixie, Now You're Done," which sadly recognizes that it is time for the South to "hang your head and cry . . ." and that the end has come: "oh Dixie, you're done." In between, *White Mansions* offers pro-Confederate loyalties as well as conflicting perceptions of the desirability of and the actual opportunity for victory. *White Mansions*, which reflects Cullen's (1995) observation that the Civil War mirrors the times of those who study it and their fascination with the Civil War as it impacted the South, goes to neither romantic nor unreconstructed Rebel extremes—all the more remarkable because Kennerley, an Englishman, was living in Britain when he wrote the album's songs. The production and content of *White Mansions* are of sufficient quality for Desi Fisher to list *White Mansions* on

"Desi's Top Ten Country Albums" on his BBC Web page for McLean's Country BBC Radio Foyle (2003) and for other committed fans such as Steven Hull (2003a, 2003b) to maintain Web pages about the album. Even Waylon Jennings's Web site maintains a full page for *White Mansions*, and amazon.com offers *White Mansions* for sale.

Paul Kennerley also wrote *The Legend of Jesse James* (1979), which features Levon Helm along with Johnny Cash, Emmylou Harris, Rodney Crowell, Rosanne Cash, and Charlie Daniels. Jesse James's career as a criminal evolved from his Civil War experience and ended with an unsuccessful bank robbery in Northfield, Minnesota. *Jesse James* ranges from "Ride of the Redlegs" and "Quantrill's Guerillas" through "Northfield: The Plan" and "Northfield: The Disaster" to "The Death of Me," "The Plot," and "One More Shot." Both *White Mansions* and *The Legend of Jesse James* are marketed on the Band's Web site.

In 1990, Ken Burns's documentary series *The Civil War* aired on television. The nine-part story of the Civil War, with its haunting music (including the Jay Ungar composition "Ashokan Farewell"), revived interest in the war. A book and album of Civil War music (*The Civil War: Music from the Original Soundtrack* [1990]) accompanied the series. Although this album generally couldn't be considered "country," Burns later released another album of songs from the Civil War, sung by country and folk artists (*Songs of the Civil War* [1991]). Subsequently, Jay Ungar's haunting fiddle tune "Ashokan Farewell," which is featured on the soundtrack, became a part of the repertoire of some country and bluegrass artists, including the Osborne Brothers (1994).

The Civil War: The Nashville Sessions (1998), a more recent, late-twentieth-century concept album based on the Broadway musical *The Civil War*, includes Charlie Daniels, Travis Tritt, Deana Carter, Trace Adkins, Tracy Lawrence, Amy Grant, Kevin Sharp, John Berry, and Trisha Yearwood. The musical itself reflects the need for multicultural balance in the national arena, while the album reflects changes in attitudes of many southerners in the late twentieth century. Even the very conservative Charlie Daniels found it desirable and appropriate to participate in a project that also includes Bebe Winans. Proclaiming that Fort Sumter began the "bloodiest conflict in American History . . ." and deeming the war the nation's "most defining experience . . . ," Daniels delivers the "Prologue," which includes Walt Whitman quotations. In a manner similar to that of *White Mansions,* John Berry delivers "Last Waltz for Dixie," which admits defeat, but claims "of the sons of the gray not one turned away . . . ," with the ending line of "That's the Dixie in me." Even more balanced in its content than *White Mansions,* the album offers a strong, extended slave voice through "River Jordan." Deana Carter presents the perspective of a Union soldier's wife in "Missing You (My Bill)"; Kevin Sharp sings of a dying Union infantryman's wish to "Tell My Father" that he fought with honor and "upheld the family name"; and Trisha Yearwood extends the Union widow's grief in "The Honor of Your Name." Even Charlie Daniels's rendition of the ambiguous "In Great Deeds" can appropriately be assumed by either side as "reverent men and women" realize that the "power of their vision shall pass into their souls." Thus, *The Civil War: The Nashville Sessions* exhibits even less of the extreme highs of Southern optimism than *White Mansions* and even more of the suffering experienced by both sides.

Civil War References

References, both verbal and visual, to the Civil War continue to work their way into country music. The use of visual or verbal references offers a more subtle, and acceptable, reminder to the country music audience and artists of Civil War connections. Civil War references run the gamut from subtle to outlandish. Conway Twitty's *Southern Comfort* (1982) album depicts Twitty standing with a young woman in a long white dress, her hand on his chest and her head on his shoulder. The two are framed by a V formed from white railings and two massive columns on a front porch. The back cover of *Southern Comfort* shows Twitty in the foreground, the two-story antebellum mansion in the background, with the young woman sitting on the porch railing gazing toward Twitty.

Rhett Akins's *Friday Night in Dixie* (2001) makes significant use of the Confederate battle flag and Civil War–era references throughout the packaging and labeling of the compact disc. The Confederate battle flag provides the background for the liner booklet; the four triangular fields of the central St. Andrews Cross create the red background for the white lettering "Friday Night in Dixie," and a peach overlaid with the red initials "RA" appears on the thirteenth white star at the cross's center. Eleven of the twelve pages have bold Civil War content: three use a Confederate battle flag with the names Mechanicsville, Frazier's Farm, Manassas, and Harpers Ferry at the outside edges of the red triangles created by the cross; four display the Confederate battle flag in all four corners; one, the back page, shows a

Fig. 3. Confederate positions on Lookout Mountain. (Photo by James E. Akenson.)

portrait of Akins with an oval CSA belt buckle at the bottom and handwritten script in the background with the date 1861 clearly visible; and the two center pages of the booklet feature the Confederate battle flag of the Thirty-eighth Regiment of Alabama volunteers, with "Chickamauga" and "Lookout Mountain" lettered in white in the lower triangle of the cross. Beneath and beside the Confederate battle flag are the original Confederate Stars and Bars and a flag with a magnolia blossom in the center and the inscription "Any Fate but Submission." In addition to a list of persons "I would like to thank," the address and phone number of "The RhettNecks" (the Rhett Akins International Fan Club) are provided.

Akins's photo is further defined by four Confederate battle flags, as well as three rough-hewn timbers, an open wooden gate, and a pathway that lead the eye to his portrait. Lest one doubt Rhett's roots, the inside back page shows a map of Georgia over which the state seal is embossed in the lower quadrant. Four rough-hewn timbers and four Confederate battle flags in the corners frame the scene. Most of the northern half is overlaid by a prominent group photo in which Akins, who is flanked by musicians involved in the project, holds a Charlie Daniels sweatshirt. Daniels himself stands directly behind Akins's left shoulder.

Only one page does not contain obvious Civil War references. A rural scene with a dirt road leading to a farm house is the work of Viola Eaker, Akins's great-aunt. The dedication creates the final Civil War connection:

Fig. 4. The current state seal of Georgia. (Courtesy of the State of Georgia.)

"This album is dedicated to the Akins and LaHood families and the artwork was inspired by my love of Southern history and my Great, Great, Great, Grandfather, James Nelson Akins who fought in the Civil War, Company G 63rd Georgia Infantry." The final visual link to the Civil War appears on the CD itself. The Georgia state seal provides the background for the entire disc, and ribbons proclaiming wisdom, justice, and moderation connect three Corinthian columns that are capped by an arch inscribed with the word "constitution"; immediately beneath the arch is the date 1861.

Despite all the visual references in the accompanying booklet and on the disc itself, Rhett Akins makes only one overt Civil War reference in the lyrics of *Friday Night in Dixie*. The title song, "Friday Night in Dixie," offers a hell-raising good time involving the county sheriff, four-wheel drives, blue-eyed girls, moonshine, references to country music, and, finally, a "Rebel yell." Akins's lavish use of symbolic Confederate images borders on a resistance to mainstream sensibilities that somewhat resembles the overt resistance of the Atlanta Redneck Underground (discussed below). Akins's obvious propensity for the Confederate battle flag came at a time when the state of Georgia struggled, as it continues to struggle, with the divisive issue of the content and meaning of the state flag. Outside Interstate 285, the inner ring of the metropolitan Atlanta region, strong sentiments exist toward efforts that resulted in a compromise Georgia flag; the compromise removed the singular, dominant Confederate battle flag and replaced it with one small Confederate battle flag set alongside the other flags of Georgia. Even into 2004, controversy continued. Sonny Perdue, elected in 2002 as the first Republican governor since 1872, benefited from a coalition of discontent. Three groups—teachers, opponents of additional roadways around Atlanta, and rural whites disgruntled over the state flag change—contributed to the defeat of Democratic governor Ray Barnes. The splinter Southern Party of Georgia expressed feelings that are often felt outside metropolitan Atlanta: "Roy Barnes followed the dictates of the Atlanta Chamber and Downtown Establishment to an unprecedented degree. Republicans have an affinity, too, for corporate fat cats. . . . It's hard to imagine Perdue's administration will be much different than Barnes' in dealing with the establishment and its agenda. Even though he was elected in part because of growing public opposition to downtown Atlanta's agenda" (2003). Although the Southern Party's views may be more extreme than those of most conservatives, rural white Georgians indeed voted against the assault on the Confederate flag and helped elect Sonny Perdue. Their actions at the ballot box buttress John Shelton Reed's view that the enduring South may have urban enclaves of northern migrants and urban attitudes that have little impact on southerners outside the enclaves (1993, 132). Somewhat like the ability of the human body to isolate a sliver or bullet from infecting the entire system, southerners like Georgian Rhett Akins, immune from the Atlanta metroplex, can continue to show their allegiances.

A less mainstream but almost more intriguing example may be found in the album covers of B. Bob Akers, "The Ole Rebel." Akers's *Gettin' Down in Dixie* (n.d.) features Akers in full Confederate uniform, hands clasped, in front of a Confederate statue, with a courthouse in the background. The back cover features six photos of Akers in front of the Confederate statue and the Hernando County Courthouse in Florida. One photo, captioned "Did we really lose?" shows a dejected Akers seated, chin in hand, on the statue's base. Another pose features Akers leaning against the flagpole, head bowed, Confederate hat in hand, with the title "O.K., O.K., so Lee surrendered." While not a multicultural statement, the album itself features a variety of songs by Akers, including "Walking the Dog" (authored by Memphis blues artist Rufus Thomas), a pop standard "Love Letters in the Sand," and a variety of country music standards, such as "Walkin' the Floor over You," and southern-oriented statements such as "Dixie When I Die," "Dixie on My Mind," "If Heaven Ain't a Lot Like Dixie," and "South's Gonna Do It Again."

Gettin' Down in Dixie provides some insight into Akers and a set of interrelated perceptions about country music. The album sleeve tells the

Fig. 5. B. Bob Akers on the cover of his album *Gettin' Down in Dixie.*

"Ole Rebel" story, but says nothing overtly related to the Civil War beyond the U.S. and Confederate flags juxtaposed beneath the title. The message proclaims that B.B. Akers is a "rebel with a cause: preaching the gospel of pure country music and giving country music back to the people!" Although Akers doesn't use the term "empowerment" and probably never read Paulo Friere, he clearly sees country music in the context of battles over authenticity and notions that somehow corporations have wrestled control of the music from the ordinary fan (Akenson 2003). Akers follows with a personal history that includes his youthful accompaniment of Ernest Tubb, Bob Wills, and Hank Williams records with his mail order guitar, as well as his being paid $25 for two of his songs at age thirteen. The death of Ernest Tubb prompted him first to write a tribute song that had "no crossover appeal" and then to invest in Rebel Records of America over $200,000 of his own money, with further contributions invited from interested fans. Akers states that he wishes to provide a "new concept that offers the people an opportunity to profit from distribution, wholesale record purchases, concert tours, talent and song discoveries. . . ." The Civil War packaging thus includes a mixture of populism, workers controlling the means of production, and capitalism in a fascinating blend.

Other album covers reflect the southern roots of country music artists and serve related functions. The Boys from Indiana's *Atlanta Is Burning* album (1974) features a burning Confederate flag. Alabama's early covers such as *My Home's in Alabama* (1980), *Alabama* (1981), and *Mountain Music* (1982) depict the Confederate battle flag. *Pictures* (1984), by the short-lived group Atlanta, features the band in white suits with a U.S. flag in the foreground and the Georgia state flag and the Confederate battle flag in the smoky background. The cover of the landmark *Will the Circle Be Unbroken* (1972) similarly references the Civil War: three Confederate battle flags on the left and three U.S. flags on the right sit within a framed engraving of a Civil War officer. The record sleeve, which lists production and other credits, includes an engraving of slaveholder Andrew Jackson's Hermitage mansion, replete with six white columns. The southern roots of Confederate Railroad are made obvious both by the band's name and by the cover of their self-titled release (1992). The latter features a Confederate battle flag waving to the left and right of the steam locomotive pushing through a red circle upon which "Confederate Railroad" is written in white. Stars from the St. Andrews Cross of the battle flag flank both sides of the title circle. The band's Web site features a Confederate battle flag as well.

Like visual Civil War references, country music lyrics refer to the war in a variety of ways, often with sexual innuendo. The most intriguing direct reference to the conflict comes from the Redneck Underground scene associated with Little Five Points in Atlanta, Georgia (Dechert and Lewis 2002). The Bubbapaloooza festival, presented at the Star Bar, spawned Deacon Lunchbox's "Loweena, the Urban Redneck Queen" (1995). Lunchbox dedicates the song to "some girls I'm in love with, the Dixie Hickies" and then tells that Loweena caught his eye down at the flea market, where she was purchasing Elvis Presley memorabilia. Loweena is "all decked out in micro leather and sporting Confederate paraphernalia." The narrator's come-on to Loweena combines a classic mixture of white southern symbols. He approaches her by asking if "Robert E. Lee would have won that damned Civil War" if Elvis Presley, Richard Petty, and the Hell's Angels had been born one hundred years earlier. The over-the-top, anti-Nashville stance of the Redneck Underground community makes explicit references to the Civil War even more desirable and appropriate than what could be produced and marketed to please mainstream sensibilities.

References to the Civil War fit nicely with sexual innuendo based upon heat and burning. Alabama metaphorically and literally used the Civil War in "Burn Georgia Burn" (1981), which mentions that "Atlanta was on fire," as was the woman the previous night. "The roaring of the guns" was out of control, like their love affair, which took place "while the world was falling down around them." The narrative forces the male to leave and become a casualty—"how the war had taken toll"—with only memories for the woman and a passion that makes "Georgia Burn." Similarly, "See the Embers, Feel the Flame" proclaims that in the heat of passion, just like the South, "we're gonna rise again." Conway Twitty offered a different song titled "Burn Georgia Burn (There's a Fire in Your Soul)" (1982). The group Atlanta made obvious use of sexual innuendo in "Atlanta Burned Again Last Night," which chronicles the passionate romance of a couple repeatedly giving into sin. In a bit of role reversal, the male is but seventeen and the woman over thirty and "in her second marriage. . . ." References are made to a "red hot Georgia night," which means that "Atlanta burned again last night." The band also offered "Blue Side of the Gray," which not only refers to the Civil War through the catchy title, but also tells a story that finally reveals that "Bugles rang on both sides of the river" and at "Shilo [sic] the young man lost his life." A Union slant becomes clear, as the soldier was with "ten thousand sons of freedom" and sleeps on the "blue side of the gray." The song ends with lines from "The Battle Hymn of the Republic."

Other lyrics referring to the Civil War include Alabama's "Song of the South," which asserts that there "ain't nobody looking back again." Such a reference, made within the context of "Dixie," provides a positive statement about the future. Conversely, Hank Williams Jr. adopted a strident tone in songs such as "If the South Would Have Won," whose lyrics provide a tour of southern states while snippets of "Dixie" play in the background. According to the song, a Confederate victory would have restored the capital to Alabama, and "We would have it made." The lyrics propose special holidays honoring important southerners such as Lynyrd Skynyrd, Elvis Presley, Hank Williams Sr., and Patsy Cline. No African Americans are mentioned, and the desire to designate a national holiday for Patsy Cline stands in obvious contrast to a holiday for Martin Luther King Jr. Similarly, Hank Jr.'s "Dixie On My Mind" (1992) disparages New York City in a number of ways, including the lamentation that the radio stations don't sign off with "Dixie" "the way they do in sweet home Alabam'."

More subtle references to the Civil War appear in Tracy Lawrence's ode to past pleasures "If the World Had a Front Porch" (1995), which contains lines very similar to some poetry by Tennessee Poet Laureate Maggie Vaughn. Lawrence proclaims that with a front porch the custom of treating one's neighbors like family wouldn't "be gone with the wind." The Country Gentlemen used the title "Dixie Look Away" (n.d.) for a bluegrass collection on the Starday label. Such a reference offers a subtle, easily understood reminder of the Civil War as a touchstone of white southern identity. John Conlee's version of the Mickey Newberry–penned classic "An American Trilogy" (1983) demonstrates a softening of ideology, subtly blending "Dixie," "The Battle Hymn of the Republic," and the slave narrative "All My Trials" into a powerful, somewhat multicultural blend capable of balancing late-twentieth- and early-twenty-first-century sensibilities.

Brother Phelps, a spinoff of the Kentucky Headhunters, offered historically detailed content in "Lookout Mountain" (1995), which depicts the inability of Confederate forces to resist the Federal assault up the steep slope of Lookout Mountain. (The episode also appears in similarly titled songs by obscure artists such as Otto Bash [n.d.], Wayne Henderson [n.d.], and June Lou [n.d.].) The Bellamy Brothers expressed less detailed, albeit clearly defined, sentiments related to the Civil War in "You Ain't Just Whistlin' Dixie" (1982); the explicit musical reference to the Civil War is accompanied by lyrics mentioning Robert E. Lee and the fact that the band's members are Sons of the Confederacy. Ultra-hip Dwight Yoakam charted with "I Sang Dixie" (1988), in which the narrator proclaims that old times were never as terrible as they were on the streets of Los Angeles when he held a dying southern expatriate in his arms.

Finally, mention must be made of an unfortunate class of records, even though they did not widely reach a mainstream country music audience. Typical of the class are the Sons of the Confederacy's "Stokely Who" and "Mohammad Rabbit" (n.d.); the Coon Hunters' "We Don't Want Niggers (In Our Schools)" and "Nigger, Nigger" (n.d.); and the Confederates' "Black Bear" (n.d.). Reb Rebel Records provided a failed country music artist with opportunities to record hate-infused music: "[I]n the late 1960s, [C.J.] Trahan began to record and release music for the late Jay 'J.D.' Miller's Reb Rebel Records in Crowley [Louisiana]. Trahan was now going by a new name: Johnny Rebel. His first songs were 'Lookin' for a Handout' and 'Kajun Klu [sic] Klux Klan.' He followed with more singles, among them 'Nigger, Nigger,' 'Some Niggers Never Die (They Just Smell That Way),' and 'In Coontown.' He set his lyrics to the twangs of the era's swampbilly craze, backed by a studio band" (Pittman 2003, l).

The Reb Rebel release *For Segregationists Only* (n.d.) included songs such as "Lookin' for a Handout," "Dear Mr. President, and "Voice of Alabama" and prominently displayed the Confederate battle flag on either side of the label. Trahan no longer performs as Johnny Rebel, but his recordings may be found on white power Web sites.

Conclusion

In an obscure DOT release, Johnny Slate proclaims "I Don't Believe Ole Dixie Ever Died" (n.d.). Indeed, the research of John Shelton Reed (1993), Peter Applebome (1996), and others suggests that for all the changes, the South still endures. Because of its strong southern cultural roots, country music often includes verbal, auditory, and visual references to the Civil War, an epic event that helped define the United States. Although Civil War themes have never dominated country music, past or present, one need not verbalize or visualize connections to an event, region, or belief system during each moment, or each performance, to communicate important touchstones of a communal past. The changing present will most likely influence the manner in which Civil War references make their way into country music. The genre may well be national and international in scope, but a southern cultural engine still provides its drive, heart, and soul. We should not be surprised to find visual, auditory, and verbal reminders of the Civil War in country music songs, CD booklets and covers, or performances in the future.

References

Akenson, James E. 2003. An afterword: Australia, the United States, and authenticity. *Outback and urban: Australian country music,* 1:187–206.

Alligood, Leon. 2003. Confederate flag salute in program upsets parents. *The Tennessean.* May 14.

Applebome, Peter. 1996. *Dixie rising: How the South is shaping American values, politics, and culture.* New York: Harvest Books.

Blount, Roy, Jr. 2003. Making sense of Robert E. Lee. *Smithsonian* 34 (4):58–68.

Boatner, Mark. 1959. *The Civil War dictionary.* New York: David McKay Co.

Commager, Henry. 1978. *The Blue and the Gray.* Vol. 1. Canada: Bobbs-Merrill.

de la Cruz, Bonna. 2003. Battle flag on Confederate tag design. *The Tennessean.* July 3.

Cullen, Jim. 1995. *The Civil War in popular culture: A reusable past.* Washington, D.C.: Smithsonian Institution Press.

Davis, Burke. 1994. *Jeb Stuart: The last cavalier.* Princeton, NJ: Random House.

Dechert, S. Renee, and George H. Lewis. 2002. The drive-by truckers and the

Redneck Underground: A subcultural analysis. In *Country music annual*, ed. Charles K. Wolfe and James E. Akenson, 151–60. Lexington: University Press of Kentucky.

Horwitz, Tony. 1998. *Confederates in the attic: Dispatches from the unfinished Civil War.* New York: Pantheon.

Johnson, Paul. 1997. *A history of the American people.* Great Britain: Weidenfeld and Nicolson.

LeVine, Michael. 1982. *Johnny Horton: Your singing fisherman.* New York: Vantage Press.

Malone, Bill. 1983. *Singing cowboys and musical mountaineers.* Athens: University of Georgia Press.

———. 2002. *Don't get above your raisin'.* Urbana: University of Illinois Press.

Meade, Guthrie, Richard Spottswood, and Douglas Meade. 2002. *Country music sources: A biblio-discography of commercially recorded traditional music.* Chapel Hill: University of North Carolina Press.

Peterson, Richard, and Russell Davis. 1975. The Fertile Crescent of country music. *Journal of country music* 6:19–27.

Reed, John Shelton. 1993. *My tears spoiled my aim and other reflections on southern culture.* New York: Harvest Books.

Russell, Tony. 1970. *Blacks, whites and blues.* New York: Stein and Day.

Smith, Bruce. 2003. Confederate flag shirts stir controversy. *Herald Citizen* (Cookeville, TN). May 3.

Thomas, Emory. 1988. *Bold dragoon: The life of J.E.B. Stuart.* New York: Vintage Books.

Ward, Geoffrey, Ric Burns, and Ken Burns. 1990. *The Civil War: An illustrated history.* New York: Knopf.

Wiggins, Gene. 1987. *Fiddlin' Georgia crazy: Fiddlin' John Carson, his real world, and the world of his songs.* Chicago: University of Illinois Press.

Wiley, Bell I. 1978a. *The life of Billy Yank: The common soldier of the Union.* Baton Rouge: Louisiana State University Press.

———. 1978b. *The life of Johnny Reb: The common soldier of the Confederacy.* Baton Rouge: Louisiana State University Press.

Wolfe, Charles. 1995a. Eck Robertson. In *Definitive country*, ed. Barry McCloud, 688–89. New York: Perigree.

———. 1995b. *Uncle Dave Macon.* Murfreesboro, TN: Rutherford County Historical Society.

Web Sites

The Band. http://theband.hiof.no/albums/legend_of_jesse_james.html.

Confederate Railroad. http://www.confederaterailroad.net/front.html.

Curry, Peter. 2003. The Kingston Trio Place presents "Tom Dooley": The ballad that started the folk boom. http://home.att.net/~kingstontrioplace1/tdooleydoc.htm.

Fisher, Desi. 2003. http://www.bbc.co.uk/northernireland/radiofoyle/mcleans country/desi.shtml.

Hoemann, George C. 2003. American Civil War homepage. http://sunsite.utk.edu/civil-war.

Hull, Steven. 2003a. http://seaghull.home.texas.net/OzarkIntro.html.

———. 2003b. http://seaghull.home.texas.net/white_mansions.html.

Jennings, Waylon. 2003. http://www.waylon.com/Music/white_mansions.htm.

Pittman, Nick. 2003. Johnny Rebel speaks. http://www.bestofneworleans.com/dispatch/2003–06–10/news_feat.html.

Southern Party of Georgia. 2003. http://www.spofga.org/Updates/2003/.may/sonny_purdue.phtml.

Discography

Note: In many cases, reissue albums are cited and not the original 78 rpm issues.

Akers, B. Bob. *Gettin' Down in Dixie*. Rebel Records of America 202. N.d.

———. *The Old Rebel*. Rebel Records of America 201. N.d.

Akins, Rhett. *Friday Night in Dixie*. Rhett Akins. 8062–6–81069–2–8. 2001.

Alabama. *Alabama*. RCA AHL-3930 LP. 1981.

———. *Mountain Music*. RCA AHL 4229 LP. 1982.

———. *My Home's in Alabama*. RCA AHL 1–2644 LP. 1980.

Arnold, Jimmy. *Southern Soul*. Rebel Records of America 1621. 1983.

Atlanta. *Pictures*. MCA-5643 LP. 1984.

Baez, Joan. "The Night They Drove Old Dixie Down." *The Essential Joan Baez from the Heart—Live*. Karussell 550129–2. 1976.

Bash, Otto. "Lookout Mountain." RCA Victor 47–6426. N.d.

The Bellamy Brothers. "You Ain't Just Whistlin' Dixie." *The Bellamy Brothers Greatest Hits*. MCA/Curb MCAD-3102. 1982.

Blake, Norman, and Tony Rice. "Lincoln's Funeral Train (The Sad Journey to Springfield)." Rounder 0266. 1990.

Boxcar Willie. "Dixie." *Two Sides of Boxcar*. MCPS GRF151. N.d.

The Boys from Indiana. *Atlanta Is Burning*. King Bluegrass KB 530. 1974.

Brother Phelps. "Lookout Mountain." *Anyway the Wind Blows*. Asylum 61724–2. 1995.

The Browns. "My Pretty Quadroon." *Our Favorite Folk Songs*. RCA LPM-2333. 1960.

Camp, Shawn. *Stone Grey Day: Songs about the Confederacy*. Jasper JR CD 101. 1992.

Cash, Johnny. *Johnny 99*. CBS SBP 237953. 1983.

———. "Lorena" and "The Gettysburg Address." *America: A 200-Year Salute in*

Story and Song. Columbia/Legacy 5053992000. 1972. (Cash recorded "Lorena" in 1959, 1970, and 1972.)

The Civil War: Music from the Original Soundtrack. Elektra Nonesuch 7559–79256–2. 1990.

The Civil War: The Nashville Sessions. Atlantic 830909–2. 1998.

Clifton, Bill. *Soldier, Sing Me A Song.* Starday SLP 213. 1963. (Reissued on *Around the World to Poor Valley.* Bear Family BCD 16425 HK. 2001.)

Confederate Railroad. *Confederate Railroad.* Atlantic. 1992.

The Confederates. "Black Bear." BBB 6500. N.d.

———. "Dixie." BBB 6500. N.d.

Conlee, John. "An American Trilogy." *In My Eyes.* MCA 5434. 1983.

Country Gentlemen. "Dixie Look Away." *Various Artists.* Starday 45–408. N.d.

———. *The Early Rebel Recordings 1962–1971.* REB-4002. 1998.

Coon Hunters. "Nigger, Nigger." N.d.

———. "We Don't Want Niggers (In Our Schools)." N.d.

Dickens, Hazel, Carol Elizabeth Jones, and Ginny Hawker. "Not a Word of That Be Said." *Heart of a Singer.* Rounder CD 0443. 1998.

Driftwood, Jimmie. *Songs of Billy Yank and Johnny Reb.* RCA LSP-2316. (Reissued on *Americana.* Bear Family BCD 15465 CH. 1991.)

Dry Branch Fire Squad. "Someone Play Dixie for Me" and "Walking Back to Richmond." *Tried and True.* Rounder 11519. 1987.

Earle, Steve. "Ben McCulloch." *Train A Comin'.* Cortex CTX026CD. 1995.

Earle, Steve, and the Del McCoury Band. "Dixieland." *The Mountain.* E Squared 1064–2. 1998.

East Virginia. *The Major Years.* Major MBR-5376. N.d.

Erbsen, Wayne. *Southern Soldier Boy: 16 Authentic Tunes of the Civil War.* Native Ground 005. 1995.

Flatt, Lester, and Earl Scruggs. "The Legend of the Johnson Boys." *Folksongs of Our Land.* Columbia CS 8630. 1962.

———. "Poor Rebel Soldier." *Breaking Out.* Columbia C 30347. 1970.

Foley, Red. "Dixie." Decca 9–27810. N.d.

For Segregationists Only. Reb Rebel Records. N.d.

Ford, Tennessee Ernie. *Tennessee Ernie Ford Sings Civil War Songs of the North.* Capitol ST-1539. 1961.

———. *Tennessee Ernie Ford Sings Civil War Songs of the South.* Capitol ST-1549. 1961.

Frizzell, Lefty. "The Ballad of the Blue and Grey." Reissued on *Life's Like Poetry.* BCD 15550 LI. 1992.

Griff, Ray. "Dixie." Royal American RA 19. N.d.

Hartford, John. *Gum Tree Canoe.* Flying Fish 4588. 2001.

———. *Live from Mountain Stage.* Blue Plate Music BPM 401. 2000.

Henderson, Wayne. "Legend of Lookout Mountain." Larkwood 1105. N.d.

Horton, Bobby. "Songs of the C.S.A." Homespun. ISN 1–882604–15–6. 1985.

Jennings, Waylon. "Lorena." *Back in the Saddle*. HADCD 181 (Aust.). 1994.

———. *White Mansions: A Tale from the American Civil War, 1861–1865*. A & M Records AMLX 64691. 1978. CDA&M Records 75021 6004. 1989.

Last Day At Gettysburg: Songs about the American Civil War. Rebel REB-CD-7501. 2001.

Lawrence, Tracy. "If the World Had a Front Porch." *I See It Now*. Atlantic CS 4–87119 AL82656. 1995.

Lou, June. "Ballad of Lookout Mountain." Process 101. N.d.

Lunchbox, Deacon. "Loweena, the Urban Redneck Queen." *Bubbapalooza*. Vol. 1 of *Chronicle of the Redneck Underground*. Sky Records. 1995.

Mainer, Wade. "Not a Word of That Be Said." *Old Time Songs*. Old Homestead OHS 90123. 1980.

———. *We Will Miss Him*. Bluebird BB B 8042. 1939.

Mainer's Mountaineers. "Write a Letter to My Mother." *J.E. Mainer's Mountaineers*. Vol. 1. Old Timey LP 106. N.d.

Mathews, Dave. *A Nation's Broken Soul*. Laserlight 12 355. 1992.

———. *Shades of Blue & Gray*. Laserlight 12 354. 1989.

Moore, Charlie. *The Fiddler*. Old Homestead OHCD 90052. 1975.

———. *The "Original" Rebel Soldier*. Wango 114. 1976.

Nobley, Robert, and Claudene Nobley. "Lorena." *Lamp Lighting Time: Old Time Songs*. Davis Unlimited DU-33020. 1975.

Osborne Brothers. "Lorena" and "Ashokan Farewell." *When the Roses Bloom in Dixieland*. Pinecastle PRC 1026. 1994.

Poole, Charlie. "Write a Letter to My Mother." Reissued on *The Legend of Charlie Poole*. Vol. 3. County CD-3516. 1998.

Proffitt, Frank. "Poor Soldier." *Memorial Album*. Folk-Legacy FSA 136. 1968.

———. "Tom Dooley (Dula)." *North Carolina Songs and Ballads*. Topic 12T162. 1996. (Originally issued on Folk Legacy.)

Reno, Don, and Red Smiley. *Folk Songs of the Civil War*. King 756. 1961.

Ritter, Tex. "The Gettysburg Address." Reissued on *High Noon*. Bear Family BCD 16356 DI. 2000.

Robbins, Marty. "Just Before the Battle, Mother." Reissued on *Country 1960–1966*. Bear Family BCD 15 655 DI. 1995.

Rucker, Sparky, and Rhonda Rucker. *The Blue and Grey in Black and White*. Flying Fish FF 70611. 1992.

Rutherford, Betsy. "Faded Coat of Blue." *Traditional Country Music*. Biograph RC-6004. N.d.

Shegog, Kevin. "Lorena." *Greatest Hits*. WG 25/1991 (Aust.). N.d.

Slate, Johnny. "I Don't Believe Ole Dixie Ever Died." DOT DOA-17445. N.d.

Songs of the Civil War. Columbia CK 48607. 1991.

Sons of the Confederacy. "Mohammad Rabbit" and "Stokely Who?" BBB 101. N.d.

Taylor, J. *The Falls of Richmond.* PearlMae 001B. 1989.

————. *Little Rose Is Gone.* PearlMae 002CW. 1991.

Thomas, Suzanne. "Faded Coat of Blue." *Dear Friends & Gentle Hearts.* Rounder CD 0423. 1998.

Tillett, Eleazer, and Martha Etheridge. "Her Bright Smile Haunts Me Still." *Her Bright Smile Haunts Me Still: The Warner Collection.* Vol. 1. Appleseed APR CD1035. 2000.

Twitty, Conway. "Burn Georgia Burn (There's a Fire in Your Soul)." *Dream Maker.* Elektra/Asylum 60182. 1982.

————. *Southern Comfort.* Elektra/Asylum El-60005 LP. 1982.

Ungar, Jay, and Molly Mason. "The Faded Coat of Blue." *Civil War Classics: Live at Gettysburg College.* Fiddle and Dance Records FDCD 102. 1993.

Ward, Fields, and His Buck Mountain Band. "Those Cruel Slavery Days." *Early Country Music.* Historical HLP 8002. N.d. (Although this was recorded in 1929, it was not issued on an album until the 1970s [?].)

Wilkin, Marijohn. *Battle of the Blue and Gray.* Columbia CS 8441. N.d.

Williams, Hank, Jr. "Dixie on My Mind." *Hank Williams Jr.'s Greatest Hits.* Elektra/Curb 60193. 1992.

Will the Circle Be Unbroken. United Artists. UAS 9801 LP. 1972.

Wiseman, Mac. "Darling Nellie Gray." *Sincerely.* Hamilton HLP 130. 1966.

————. "The Legend of the Irish Rebel." *Mac Wiseman Sings at the Toronto Horseshoe Club.* MACW105. N.d.

Yoakam, Dwight. "I Sang Dixie." *Buenas Noches from a Lonely Room.* Reprise 4–27715 CS. 1988.

2

"Bloody War"

War Songs in Early Country Music

Charles K. Wolfe

During the earliest years of commercial country music, which historians generally date from 1923, singers were seldom able to create their own repertoire and often had to rely on the nineteenth-century folk and vaudeville traditions in which the new music was rooted. Thus many early country singers performed songs about the Civil War that were embedded in these old traditions; pioneer singers like the McCravy Brothers recorded "The Vacant Chair," and blind Kentucky street singer Charlie Oaks recorded a strong rendition of "Just Before the Battle, Mother." Kentucky old-time singers seemed especially fond of the 1865 ballad "Faded Coat of Blue," which was recorded by Welby Toomey, Buell Kazee, and others—including the Carter Family. By the 1920s, though, Civil War songs and stories were receding into the misty past and becoming a part of the "Old South" imagery that pervaded so much of the new commercial country music—which, after all, was actually called "Old Familiar Tunes," "Old Southern Tunes," and even "Tunes from Dixie."

The war songs that made the first direct impact on country music were songs about much more recent conflicts: mainly the turn-of-the-century Spanish-American War and World War I, which the United States entered in 1917. And, curiously, the man who is acknowledged as the first country singer to record, Georgia mill hand Fiddlin' John Carson, developed one of the larger bodies of World War I songs. One of his best known was a 1914 comic vaudeville piece, "I'm Glad My Wife's in Europe," a familiar nagging wife song set in wartime America. Carson sings:

My wife, she taken a notion,
That she would cross the sea,
And then war broke out in Europe,
And she can't get back to me.

I'm glad my wife's in Europe,
And she can't get back to me,
If she gets back from Europe,
She's gonna have to swim the sea.
I'm glad that she's in Europe,
And she can't get back to me.

Another Carson favorite was the one he called "Tipperary," a comic song that started life in 1912 as a British music hall song. Rather than commenting directly on the hardships of trench warfare, the lyrics celebrate the buffoonery of an Irishman who goes to war. More commonly known as "It's a Long Way to Tipperary," Carson's version was also extremely popular with British troops. A number of string bands, including Gid Tanner and the Skillet Lickers, followed Carson's lead and recorded the tune in the late 1920s.

One of the few songs addressing America's direct involvement in the war was Carson's 1924 recording of "Dixie Division." This was in tribute to the Thirty-first Division of the U.S. Army, which trained at Macon before shipping out overseas in late 1917; nearly all its members were from the South, and the song was apparently written by its bandsman A.C. Mitchell, a friend of John Carson's son Clarence (one line of the song read "They're all from Dixie, hurrah for Dixie"). Although the song celebrates the fighting spirit of the Thirty-first, the division, in the words of one member, "got all busted up"; gradually its members either merged into other forces or trickled back to the South one or two at a time. During the war, though, the song remained one of Carson's most popular, and another popular early duo, Tom Darby and Jimmie Tarleton, recorded a related song called "The Rainbow Division" in 1928.

Though American troops spent less than two years overseas, they suffered some 116,500 fatalities. Surprisingly, few country music songs were written to memorialize the wartime losses. One that ignores the bitter price, but chronicles the war in a sarcastic, off-the-cuff way is "The Kaiser and Uncle Sam." This ersatz history of the war was popular enough that three major first-generation country singers all recorded it in 1924: Virginia carpenter Henry Whitter, Virginia singer Ernest "Pop" Stoneman, and Charlie

Oaks. Oaks's version, which he probably also sold as a printed ballad card, is probably the closest to the folk tradition of which the song was becoming a part. Sung to the general tune of the white blues "All Night Long," it begins:

> The Kaiser said to his soldiers,
> Come on boys, let's go,
> We'll conquer all of Europe
> And the world will be our foe,
> But we want to keep peace with Uncle Sam.

It continues to tell the story of the war in a fairly chronological manner, referring even to the coming of unrestricted U-boat warfare on Allied shipping.

> Then they began sinking.
> The best of the good old USA,
> Then Woodrow said to the Kaiser,
> This game we'll help you play,
> You can't run a bluff on Uncle Sam.
> (Vocalion 15104)

If "The Kaiser and Uncle Sam" appears to take a sardonic view of armed conflict, another popular war song from the 1920s takes an unabashedly comic stance. Known variously as "Bloody War," "That Crazy War," or "The Battleship of Maine," the song deals not with World War I, but with the Spanish-American War of 1898. The first recorded version was made by Ralph Peer in Charlotte, a few days after he had discovered Jimmie Rodgers and the Carter Family in the famed Bristol field sessions. The artists were Red Patterson and his Piedmont Log Rollers; a textile mill worker from North Carolina, Patterson was a banjo player and singer. His opening verses give a taste of the song's attitude toward what many Americans considered a war trumped up by the Hearst newspaper syndicate.

> McKinley called for volunteers,
> Then I got my gun,
> First Spaniard I saw coming,
> I dropped my gun and run.
> It was all about that battleship of Maine.

At war with that great nation Spain,
When I get back to Spain I want to honor my name,
It was all about that battleship of Maine.

"Why are you running?
Are you afraid to die?"
"The reason I am running,
Is because I cannot fly."
It was all about that battleship of Maine.

The chronicle of misery and misfortune continues through the lively string band setting.

The peas they was greasy.
The meat, it was fat,
The boys was fighting Spaniards,
While I was fighting that.
(Victor 20936)

The song, recorded several times during the early days, was popularized on the radio over *National Barn Dance* by Lulu Belle and Scotty. In later years, during the Vietnam protest movement, it became a favorite with the folk revival (especially as done by Mike Seeger and the New Lost City Ramblers). Even the Grand Ole Opry comedian Stringbean did an updated version, "That Crazy Viet Nam War."

Throughout the 1930s country music became increasingly professional, attracting performers who were able to make a full-time living from singing on the radio, on records, and at concerts in theaters, schoolhouses, and various clubs. It also began to attract a growing corps of songwriters who specialized in country themes—writers like Carson Robison, Bob Miller, Grady Cole, and Fred Rose. Thus, by the time World War II broke out, war songs began to develop as a genre unto themselves.

The first documented song about the war, "Cowards over Pearl Harbor," was recorded by an ersatz cowboy singer named Denver Darling on December 22, 1941, barely two weeks after the attack on Pearl Harbor. If the Decca Records files are to be believed, the song was actually released the same day it was recorded. Darling was part of a cadre of country singers who were basing their operations not in Texas or Nashville, but in New York City. A native of Illinois, Darling settled in New York in 1937, where he soon became a favorite over stations WOR and WNEW and performed regularly at the Village Barn, a country music nightclub. He had just signed a contract with Decca and had been recording for barely a month when he was recruited to record "Cowards over Pearl Harbor," written by veteran songsmith Fred Rose, who had created many of Gene Autry's songs and was now in Nashville preparing to start a historic company with Roy Acuff, Acuff-Rose. The tone of the song, neither bellicose nor angry, is sad and resigned. Singing in a soft, well-mannered radio voice, Darling begins by describing "peaceful Pearl Harbor"; then out of the sky come "hawks of destruction," and "cowards dropped death and destruction." The conclusion is remarkably restrained—"what will they do on that great judgement morning?" he asks. "Some day they'll pay."

Written in a slow waltz meter, the song quickly caught on with radio singers (among whom were Wilma Lee and Stoney Cooper) and apparently spread like wildfire. On February 18, Decca rushed Darling back into the studio to cut four more war songs: "We're Gonna Have to Slap the Dirty Little Jap (And Uncle Sam's the Guy Who Can Do It)"; "Get Your Gun and Come Along (We're Fixing to Kill a Skunk)"; "Mussolini's Letter to Hitler"; and "Hitler's Reply to Mussolini."

For a time, Darling appeared to be on the verge of winning the dubious distinction of being the first country singer to base his recording career on war songs. Throughout 1942 and 1943, he continued to record sessions every few months, usually including at least two war songs in each session. Most were not especially popular, bearing titles like "I'm a Pris'ner of War (On a Foreign Shore)," "Care of Uncle Sam," "When Mussolini Laid His Pistol Down," and a song suggested by a fan letter from a soldier, "Send This Purple Heart to My Sweetheart." Decca thought enough of his efforts that they grouped four of his war song records into a special 78 rpm album that seemed to sell fairly well. After the war, Darling continued to record—mostly cowboy songs—but gradually tired of the New York scene and returned to Illinois.

The first real hit of the country music war scene was a savage parody by veteran songwriter Carson J. Robison, "1942 Turkey in the Straw." A native of Kansas who worked as a studio man and songwriter in the New York studios through the 1920s and 1930s, Robison had been responsible for Darling's "Get Your Gun and Come Along." Now he crafted a jaunty parody about a monkey and a baboon (the Axis powers), which he sang himself, accompanied by a banjo-driven string band. Released on Victor's popular Bluebird label, Robison's composition hit the best-seller charts on April 4, 1942. Soon covered by Darling and others, the song began blaring from jukeboxes around the country.

As Americans suffered defeat after defeat in the early days of 1942 and began to realize the war might be a long, costly affair, the smug self-confidence and simplistic optimism of the early songs gave way to more somber and self-reflective works. Their popularity was compromised, however, by a recording ban imposed by the Musicians' Union from August 1942 until November 1944. Union musicians could not go into a studio during this time, and record companies had to rely on backlogs of material recorded earlier for their releases. A shellac shortage brought about by the lack of raw materials from occupied countries also discouraged the companies from releasing and pressing as many sides as they normally would have. Consequently, the newer, more introspective war songs often had to wait until late 1944 to find their way onto records.

One of the exceptions was the 1942 effort by Bob Miller and Paul Roberts, "There's a Star Spangled Banner Waving Somewhere." The song, which won for its singer, Elton Britt, the first gold record in country music, is important enough that it is discussed in a separate essay in this volume (see chapter 3). This superb merging of an evocative lyric and a haunting melody continues to be played and recorded even today.

To be sure, songwriters continued to generate songs that dealt with the war in broad, patriotic terms and explored the conflict on the national level (such as "Praise the Lord and Pass the Ammunition" and Opry star Zeke Clements's Armageddon-like "Smoke on the Water" [1943]). But soon following was a second generation of songs that dealt with the war on a personal level by reflecting the anguish of families separating and suffering loss on a firsthand basis. Dealing with these archetypal themes had always been something country and folk music handled well, and while pop music was offering pablum like "Don't Sit Under the Apple Tree," country singers sang of loss, separation, and loneliness.

One of the first and most enduring of these new songs was Floyd Tillman's "Each Night at Nine" (1944). "This was a song born in a barracks," the composer recalled. The title refers to the "lights out" time in the barracks, when the bugle softly plays. The speaker is a soldier "a thousand miles" from his wife and children. "Gee, but it's lonely these army nights, / Go tell the kiddies I'm doing fine." He closes by promising to say a prayer for them, and asks that she think of him "each night at nine." Tillman recorded it on Decca; he told Dorothy Horstman, "[I]t got a lot of play on network radio, but was hard to buy because of the shellac shortage."

The same sense of separation, but from the woman's view, occurs in one of the biggest wartime hits for Bob Wills, the haunting "Silver Dew on the Blue Grass Tonight" (written 1943, recorded 1945). In it a lonely girl writes to her sweetheart, "I pray you'll come through the fight" to return to see the "silver dew on the blue grass." Film and radio comedienne Judy Canova ended her popular network programs with a wistful song called "Goodnight, Soldier." Ernest Tubb's powerful "Soldier's Last Letter," a song about a boy who didn't come through the fight, was one of the most popular of all war recordings, rising to number 1 on the *Billboard* charts and staying on the charts for an incredible twenty-nine weeks. Written by Pee Wee King's singer, Redd Stewart, then a sergeant in the army, it starts with a mother receiving a letter from her son, who is fighting overseas. At first she is overjoyed, but then she reads on: "The Captain just gave us our orders," he says, and he will finish the letter when he returns. But the letter is unfinished, and suddenly she realizes "that her darling had died."

As the war wound down and the magnitude of its cost in casualties became more and more apparent to the average American, the songs became even more personal and more graphic. In 1945 Bob Wills, featuring Tommy Duncan's singing, had two number 1 hits with "Stars and Stripes on Iwo Jima" and "White Cross on Okinawa." On the Grand Ole Opry, the plaintive harmony of the Bailes Brothers framed "Searching for an Unknown Soldier's Grave."

The image of a widow or mother searching for her soldier's grave in the aftermath of the war is a stark and bitter contrast to the type of war song country music first generated in its own innocent years. The carefree, back-woods boaster mentality of songs like "Bloody War" may have been well suited for an audience who initially saw the First World War as yet another remote example of European folly. But country music, like the rest of America, outgrew the carefree Ragtime era and Roaring Twenties, and soon found itself having to reflect new hardships, new challenges, and new realities. Relying on its honest folk tradition, and its essential humanity, it found itself up the task.

3

"There's a Star Spangled Banner Waving Somewhere"

The Story behind Its Success

Louis Hatchett and W.K. McNeil

On December 7, 1941, the Japanese bombed Pearl Harbor, thereby bringing the United States into World War II. Coinciding with the nation's entry was the American music industry's attempt to cash in on the conflict and, at the same time, aid the war effort. The resulting songs, of course, ran the gamut from such memorial pieces as "Remember Pearl Harbor," with its admonition to remember the Pearl Harbor attack "and go on to victory," to sentimental items like "Dear Mom," to silly titles like "Good-bye, Mama, I'm off to Yokohama," to slapstick comedy, like "Der Fuehrer's Face," to jazzed-up pieces of nostalgia, like "Don't Sit Under the Apple Tree" ("with anyone else but me"), whose melody was merely a variation of Thomas Haynes Bayly's "Long, Long Ago" (1839).[1] Other war songs commented on such matters as "He Wears a Pair of Silver Wings" or memorialized phrases such as "Praise the Lord and Pass the Ammunition," while some, such as "We're Gonna Have to Slap That Dirty Little Jap," commented on the enemy's ethnic background.

Commercial country songs generally focused on tragic events, even if they were only fictional, such as "Soldier's Last Letter," or on nostalgic scenes, such as "Silver Dew on the Blue Grass Tonight." Among the exceptions, however, were "Smoke on the Water," with its apocalyptic vision of war's result, and "There's a Star Spangled Banner Waving Somewhere," whose story presented history, religion, and bravery while celebrating heroism and patriotic self-sacrifice as qualities shared by almost every male, even a crippled mountain boy.

Fig. 1. Elton Britt, the first country music artist to be awarded a gold record. (Author's collection.)

The latter song, recorded by Elton Britt, became a smash hit—for the first time, a country music artist was awarded a gold record. The piece was attributed to Paul Roberts and Shelby Darnell, Darnell being a pseudonym for Bob Miller. Although Miller (1895–1955) did write a number of songs that were all examples of what he called "main street music"—such as "Twenty-One Years," "Eleven Cent Cotton and Forty Cent Meat," "Rocking Alone in an Old Rocking Chair," and a song about the death of Huey Long written before Long was assassinated—he probably did not write "There's a Star Spangled Banner Waving Somewhere."[2] It was the work of Paul Roberts, the stage name of Paul Roberts Metivier, who was born on March 30, 1915, in Dorchester, Massachusetts, and spent most of World War II in the U.S. Army. He and his wife previously had toured the United States in vaudeville, singing his songs, and had then gone on to work as a radio team. In addition to his biggest hit, Roberts wrote several other songs, such as "She Taught Me How to Yodel" and "If I Could Only Learn to Yodel," but none were very successful. (Although one of his songs was titled "New England Is the Place for Me," he, like a lot of other East Coast northerners, moved to Florida when he retired.) Rumor has it that the character in his wartime hit was based on an actual person. If so, Roberts has never divulged who that individual was; he has, in fact, been somewhat reluctant to discuss at all his most famous song.

But if Bob Miller didn't write the song, he certainly had a lot to do with its recording and marketing. The song was first recorded by Britt in New York City, March 19, 1942, along with three others that day: "Buddy Boy,"

"I Hung My Head and Cried," and "When the Roses Bloom Again." None of the others did much, except for the third, which was the flip side of the Roberts song. Britt was joined by Mac Ceppos on fiddle, Tony Gattuso on guitar, Lester Braun on bass, and William Graham on the toy trumpet; the trumpet—Miller's idea—provided the recording with its distinctive sound.

Britt's recording caught on almost instantaneously and, according to Miller, was 1943's biggest seller in both sheet music and records, a real rarity by the 1940s.[3] In the early twentieth century, hits were measured by sheet music sales, but as mid-century approached, record sales became the gauge. So, if Miller's claim was true, the song was a double-barreled hit. The number of records sold is a matter of some dispute, with estimates generally ranging from just over one million up to four million. The latter number seems a bit high, but may represent the actual number sold during the entire time the song was in the RCA Victor catalog. Britt recorded the song twice more, first with unnamed accompaniment for a transcription around 1944 and then with Zeke Manners's band for ABC in 1959.[4]

Miller, never one to let records go unpromoted, had definite ideas about how to properly showcase songs. Sometimes he took steps that many people considered counterproductive. According to Doron K. Antrim, writing in *Collier's* magazine in 1946, "With Miller, it's either a hillbilly or it isn't, and no compromise. He tries to confine his offerings to authentic outlets and this has caused him some embarrassment."[5] Thus, when "There's a Star Spangled Banner Waving Somewhere" proved to be successful, he placed an ad in *Variety* pleading with big-name bandleaders not to play it. Then, when it made *Your Hit Parade,* an achievement most song publishers coveted, Miller didn't like the way the song was performed—and threatened to sue if it was repeated as played.

As crazy as Miller's actions seemed to some, for him it was simply a matter of maintaining his reputation as a writer and publisher. His feeling was that the song, and others like it, were for the common man and thus must have the "common touch." Such a number required the artistry of a "true son of the soil" like Elton Britt. Miller, Antrim reported, also stipulated that it required traditional accompaniment, "not the symphonized setup of a popular radio band." To present it in the latter way was, to Miller, a matter of breaking faith with his clientele. Except for the toy trumpet, the fiddle, guitar, and bass backing up Britt on the recording were fully traditional.

In considering the number's appeal, one can't discount the lyrics, which refer to a variety of icons from American history. One sentence alone mentions the names of Abraham Lincoln, an assassinated president; George Armstrong Custer, the general who died with his entire cavalry unit at Little Bighorn; George Washington, the revered first president and Revolutionary military leader; Oliver Hazard Perry, the American naval officer who defeated the British at the Battle of Lake Erie; Nathan Hale, the American Revolutionary patriot whom the British hanged as a spy; and Colin Kelly, an early hero of the Second World War who gave his life to prevent a Japanese attack. This touch of history emphasizes martyrdom and heroism, since all of the men mentioned gave their lives in service to their country, and all were heroes. Images of George Armstrong Custer gallantly, albeit somewhat foolhardily, going to his death in Montana and Nathan Hale at age twenty-one gladly being hanged for serving his country are intentional devices designed to conjure up wartime audiences' pride in America's past. Added to these images are those of the American flag and fundamentalist Christian ideas of heaven, all of which add meaning and weight to the images of martyrdom and heroism enunciated in the song. The lyrics achieved the desired results: the number became popular with people not just in the South, traditionally thought of as country music's domain, but throughout the nation.

Also key to the song's success are the protagonist and his patriotic statements. The boy, not only from the mountains, but crippled as well, is an unpromising hero, or an underdog, one of the main characters in folktales throughout the world.[6] Because many listeners identify with the familiar figure of the underdog, the narrator finds a receptive audience that makes him their favorite. Certainly, if a crippled mountain youth with legitimate reasons for keeping out of military action still wants to contribute to the war effort, how much more should a healthier person be willing to give? Audiences of the time responded sympathetically to the narrator's statement that "God gave me the right to be a free American, / And for that precious liberty I'd gladly die." Indeed, the sentence summarized the patriotic feelings of most Americans during World War II.

The artist who recorded "There's a Star Spangled Banner Waving Somewhere" played an equally significant, if not more important, role in the number's success as Bob Miller's promotion, the images evoked by the song's lyrics, and the narrator and his comments. Like many entertainers, Elton Britt became famous under a stage name. Unlike most others, though, he wasn't named at all until he was over a year old; he was what is now known as a "blue baby" and wasn't expected to live. So his parents, James and Martella Baker, delayed naming him for over a year after he came into the world on June 27, 1913, in Zack, Arkansas, a tiny community nine miles from the nearest town of Marshall.[7] Then they dubbed him James Elton Baker—James after his father and Elton in honor of Dr. Elton Wilson, who managed to keep him alive the first year of his life.

Being sickly, and the youngest of six children, Elton grew up thinking of himself as the "runt of the litter" and developed a certain toughness because of this attitude. It probably didn't help that his mother and family members called him "Cute." He was always ready to engage in fights, either with pocket knives or fists, and he also demonstrated his toughness by a love of snakes; as a child he kept a collection of them in a rain barrel in the yard at home. It didn't seem to matter to him whether the reptiles were poisonous or not. Once, as a prank he picked up a copperhead and threw it at his sister, nearly giving her a heart attack.[8] In most respects, though, Elton's youth was typical of that of most Ozark farm boys of his era.

Ironically, despite being prankish and somewhat pugilistic by nature, young Baker essentially was a private person. Nervous about performing in public, he eventually developed duodenal ulcers, but also formulated a stage persona to disguise his timidity. Yet, even though he achieved fame as a singer, he was always a somewhat reluctant entertainer. He was happiest doing things that could be accomplished in private, such as walking in the woods or hunting.

Britt started singing at an early age. His interest in music was not surprising, considering his family's background: His mother loved to sing old ballads, and his father was an excellent old-time fiddler who was said to have once won the Oklahoma state championship.[10] Their children also enjoyed music, and sons Arl and Vern were excellent self-taught instrumentalists. Elton himself first started singing at age ten when he managed to save $4.95 from working in the fields, with which he bought a guitar by mail order from Montgomery Ward. He picked up songs from his mother, Martella, and from the few records he was able to hear. He was especially impressed with Jimmie Rodgers and managed to obtain several of his 78s, playing them frequently on an old windup Victrola that the Bakers owned. Elton taught himself to yodel by listening to these records and became well known for an ability to sustain his yodel for an unusually long time. A form of relaxation he enjoyed as a child helped him accomplish this feat. He loved swimming and liked to stay submerged underwater for several minutes at a time; the breath control learned in this manner later enabled him to maintain his long yodel.[11]

Elton's rise to fame began when Glen Rice and Raymond R. MacMillan,

Fig. 2. Elton Britt developed a stage persona to overcome his reluctance to perform in public. (Author's collection.)

of MacMillan Petroleum Company, came to Zack, Arkansas, looking for talent for a radio show. MacMillan was the owner of radio station KMPC in Los Angeles, and Rice was his station manager. Why they came to the Ozarks is a matter of conjecture, but probably had something to do with the nature of the show for which they were seeking singers. One of the star attractions on the station was a country band called the Beverly Hill Billies, which sprang into existence as the result of a rather interesting publicity stunt.

One day late in March 1930, Rice excitedly interrupted the station's programming to tell an unusual story. According to him, he had gotten lost while out riding in the Malibu mountains and accidentally stumbled on a small community of hill people who had been out of contact with civilization for more than a century. These folks lived in log cabins and had one small church, a blacksmith shop, and various other buildings typically found in small backwoods hamlets, circa 1850. Rice asked these hillbillies if they would come to Los Angeles and appear on his radio station. They were somewhat leery about such a venture but gave him a qualified "maybe." For the next several days Rice kept this tale before his radio audience, promising each day that the "newly discovered hillbillies" would arrive soon.

On Sunday, April 6, 1930, Rice announced that he was certain this would be the night. "As a matter of fact, I think they are coming up Wilshire Boulevard right now. Yes, yes, I see them getting off their mules, and here they are. Ladies and gentlemen, may I present the Hill Billies."[12] This group soon became known as the Beverly Hill Billies and became one of the most popular acts on KMPC. Having fabricated these "hillbillies" from whole cloth, Rice then found it necessary to keep them in the spotlight with new publicity stunts. One of his schemes was to bring a young yodeler from the Arkansas Ozarks, the nearest region that was stereotyped as a home to backward hillfolk. One of these was Hubert Walton, the stage name of fourteen-year-old Hugh Ashley, who spent six weeks in Los Angeles beginning in June 1930. Because the boy was so young, his parents would not allow him to stay longer than the six-week stint. Then Rice and MacMillan headed back to the Ozarks and young Elton Baker. They had known about him all along and had even tried to recruit him when they hired Ashley, but he had stubbornly refused to sing for the men.[13]

Rice and MacMillan, successful on their second attempt, persuaded Elton's mother to let him go to California. Before they arrived they changed his last name to Britt, which they considered a more suitable stage name than Baker. When they arrived in California their plane was greeted by a large crowd that newspapers estimated at ten thousand, but one thousand is probably a more accurate figure.[14] He was even posed playing a fiddle despite having never performed on the instrument. Britt became a hit with the radio audience and went on to have a recording career that lasted almost forty years. When he became associated with RCA Victor and Bob Miller in 1939, he began the most fruitful portion of his career. Miller was a good person to have on his side, but theirs was a somewhat bittersweet relationship; Britt had a stubborn streak in him and sometimes resented Miller's dictation of which songs to sing, how to record them, and so on.

Ironically, Britt, one of country music's greatest yodelers, noted for his triple yodels and ability to hold notes for an incredibly long time, wasn't called on to use these talents in his best-remembered song. Additionally ironic is the fact that near the end of his career, probably because he covered "I Left My Heart in San Francisco" and "MacArthur Park," he became regarded as an uptown singer and fared poorly with the revival and reissue circuits: he was considered too sophisticated for revival audiences and too modern for hard country fans. As a result his talents have been underrated in recent years.

Fig. 3. Elton Britt. (Author's collection.)

Such was not the case in 1942 as Americans listened to Britt's mellow voice make "There's a Star Spangled Banner Waving Somewhere" his own. He had a real feeling for the ballad's sentiments, Christian fundamentalism, ideas of heaven, patriotism, bravery, and even pathos, and it showed. Moreover, an Ozark farm boy who had done his share of plowing, he met Miller's requirement of being a "true son of the soil" who could connect with his audience. Also, unable to enter the military due to his congenital heart problems, he most likely identified with the song's crippled protagonist, who couldn't join the fighting men.

Thus, it seems fair to say that the song and Britt were a perfect fit for each other, and they were matched at just the right time. Roberts's song coincided with the mood of the country, but without Britt's expert reading it probably would not have been a hit. Bob Miller's promotion also aided in establishing this song, which marks the beginning of the war song genre. True, every war since the beginning of American history has brought forth a number of songs, but Britt's hit set the standard. From 1942 on, patriotism and a willingness to give one's life for America, even in the face of extreme obstacles, have been spelled out overtly. Britt himself followed with a Red River Dave song expressing many of the same sentiments, titled "I'm a Convict with Old Glory in My Heart."[15] Other songs, such as Ernest Tubb and Redd Stewart's "Soldier's Last Letter" (1944) and Loretta Lynn's "Dear Uncle Sam" (1965), promote patriotism and a willingness to give one's life for his or her country, but lack the unpromising hero aspect. In this regard, Britt's hit of "There's a Star Spangled Banner Waving Somewhere" led the way as the nation and its music industry struggled with the awful realities of war.

Notes

1. "Remember Pearl Harbor," words by Don Reid, music by Don Reid and Sammy Kaye. Republic Music Corp., 1941. "Don't Sit Under the Apple Tree," one of the favorite songs of World War II, was popular with both servicemen and women and with civilian audiences. The words were by Lew Brown and Charles Tobias, and Sam H. Stept arranged the music. Glenn Miller and the Andrews Sisters had the best-selling recordings of the song, which was also featured in the 1943 movie musical *Private Enckaroo*.

2. Although most sources, including Miller's obituary, credit him with cowriting this song, Elton Britt's third wife, Mary Ellen "Penny" Baker, in an interview with W.K. McNeil in Tulsa, Oklahoma, on August 19, 1990, insisted that Miller had nothing to do with writing the piece. The possibility that he merely put his own pseudonym on it as a means of splitting royalties is certainly believable, since the economic move was not unknown to Miller, or other publishers, then or now.

3. Miller's claim is reported in Sigmund Spaeth, *A History of Popular Music in America* (1948; reprint, New York: Random House, 1967), 540.

4. The 1944 transcription has been reissued on *Riding with Elton*, Soundies SCD-4121.

5. Doron K. Antrim, "Whoop-And-Holler Opera," in Linnell Gentry, *A History and Encyclopedia of Country, Western, and Gospel Music,* 2nd ed. (Nashville: Clairmont Corp., 1969), 44. Originally published in *Collier's* 117, no. 4, January 26, 1946, 18, 85.

6. Numerous references to the unpromising hero motif appear in Stith Thompson, *A Motif-Index of Folk Literature,* vol. 5 (Bloomington: Indiana University Press, 1957), 8–16 (category L100–L199).

7. Most sources give Marshall as Britt's birthplace, presumably because it is the closest town, but his family members indicated that this is inaccurate.

8. Greta Sanders, interview with W.K. McNeil, Zack, Arkansas, March 2, 1984.

9. Biographical information regarding Baker is from interviews with numerous family members, including his sister and his former wife.

10. Elton's relatives, particularly Zona Baker, provided ballad and folk song collector Theodore R. Garrison with his largest cache of material for his pioneering volume on Searcy County folk songs. Garrison's work was originally done in 1944. (See Theodore R. Garrison, *Forty-Five Folk Songs Collected from Searcy County,* ed. W.K. McNeil, in *Mid-America Folklore* 30, nos. 1 & 2 [2002].) The story is often told about Elton's father winning the fiddling contest, but the authors have been unable to verify when it took place. Since there are rarely standards about such things, almost anyone can call any contest the state championship. James Baker definitely played the fiddle and probably won some contest called the state championship, but whether or not it was certified as the Oklahoma state championship is another matter.

11. This information appears, among other places, in an untitled biography of Britt by his third wife, Mary Ellen "Penny" Baker, 11.

12. Ken Griffis, "The Beverly Hill Billies," *JEMF Quarterly* 16, no. 57 (spring 1980): 5.

13. Information about Baker's refusal to sing for the talent scouts comes from several informal conversations with Hugh Ashley.

14. The figure of ten thousand appears in, among other places, an undated newspaper clipping from an unidentified paper that was in possession of the late Patsy Montana.

15. "I'm a Convict with Old Glory in My Heart" was recorded November 22, 1944, in New York City.

4

Gene Autry in World War II

Don Cusic

In the summer of 1939, while Hitler was planning his Blitzkreig of Poland, Gene Autry was touring the United Kingdom and Ireland. During the next several months Autry performed in a number of cities, including London, Liverpool, Glasgow, and Dublin, in theaters filled with people who had seen his movies. Accompanied on his appearances by his horse, Champion, the singing cowboy star was mobbed just as later rock stars would be.

When Hitler sent his army across the German border into Poland on September 1, 1939, causing Great Britain and France to declare war on Germany, Gene Autry was in Liverpool. "The signs of war were everywhere, unmistakable," said Autry. "And the people talked about it. They talked of little else. In their hearts they knew it was only a question of time. But no one seemed to be preparing for it." Autry remembered a newspaper headline that read "Hitler Says He Is Losing Patience," and underneath, "Cowboy Takes Liverpool."

In Dublin, Gene Autry rode down the streets on his horse while 300,000 cheered. In his second-floor dressing room of the city's Theater Royale for his last performance on the tour, Autry heard people outside chanting "We want Gene." Finally, a microphone with loudspeakers was put together on the fire escape, and Autry performed a few songs for people who couldn't get tickets for his shows. "I went outside and sat down on the fire escape and told them how much I loved Dublin, and all of Ireland, and how great it had been, and how grateful I was. Then the crowd sang to me. First a few voices, then more, until it seemed all of them had joined in and you could hear it for blocks, the words of 'Come Back to Erin.'" Autry cherished this treasured memory until he died, "one of the most touching, one of the purest moments of my life."

Backstage in Dublin, Autry first heard the song "South of the Border," written by Michael Carr and Jimmy Kennedy, two Brits who had never been to Mexico. About five years previously Autry had recorded "Ole Faithful," which Carr had written with Hamilton Kennedy, Jimmy's brother. Jimmy was a well-known British songwriter, having written "Red Sails in the Sunset," "Harbor Lights," "Roll Along Covered Wagon," "My Prayer," and "Serenade in the Night." As a military captain, he had been performing "South of the Border" for British armed forces at the front, and the tune had proven popular with the troops. "South of the Border" would become a major hit in America for Gene Autry.

The Dublin date would also lead to Autry's network radio show. P.K. Wrigley, owner of the Wrigley Chewing Gum Company, had wanted to sponsor a radio program to advertise Doublemint gum. He was in Dublin during Autry's tour, and when the singer returned to Chicago, Wrigley called his advertising agency, J. Walter Thompson, and told them he wanted to explore the development of a radio program starring Autry that would advertise Doublemint.

During the time Autry was in Britain, several of his films were released; *Colorado Sunset* costarred Patsy Montana, and *In Old Monterey* costarred Stuart Hamblen, Ken Carson, Sarie and Sallie, and the Ranch Boys. Earlier that year four Autry movies had been released, *Home on the Prairie, Mexicali Rose, Blue Montana Skies,* and *Mountain Rhythm,* and Autry had recorded his first cut of "Back in the Saddle Again." The song was written by Ray Whitley, who, in 1938, received an early-morning call from a movie executive telling him they needed another song for a movie Whitley was to sing in that starred George O'Brien. Whitley had to come up with a song in two hours, and he remarked to his wife, "I'm back in the saddle again." When she commented that was a good title, he sat down and composed the song quickly. The song was first performed in the movie *Border G-Man* and later recorded by Whitley with his group, the Six Bar Cowboys, for Decca in 1938. Autry wanted to use the song in his movie *Rovin' Tumbleweeds;* he paid Whitley for the copyright and received cowriting credit on the song, which he altered slightly from Whitley's original version.

In September 1939, after Autry returned to the United States, he went into a Chicago recording studio and recorded "South of the Border," the rights to which Republic purchased for use in a movie. *Rovin' Tumbleweeds*, originally titled *Washington Cowboy*, was released in mid-November, and *South of the Border* was released in December. The latter movie and song were so successful with audiences that Republic made plans for a second movie, *Down Mexico Way*, the title coming from the second line in the song.

Gene Autry wasn't the only singing cowboy between 1935 and 1940, but he certainly led the pack. Autry, Roy Rogers, and Tex Ritter were the most famous singing cowboy stars, although the Sons of the Pioneers were also featured prominently in a number of movies and their "sound" was influential in country music.

The year 1940 began with the *Melody Ranch* radio program on CBS, premiering on January 7. In March *Rancho Grande* was released, and Autry hit the road to promote the picture. In Oklahoma he met up with the Jimmy Wakely Trio and encouraged the band's members to move to Hollywood. Known originally as the Bell Boys, they had made their first trip to Hollywood in 1939, where they recorded some transcriptions and Wakely appeared in a Roy Rogers film, *Saga of Death Valley*; failing to find more movie work, the group returned to Oklahoma. In May 1940 the group returned to Hollywood, and Wakely managed to appear in some western movies before Autry returned from some out-of-town engagements. Autry arranged an audition with his radio show sponsor for the group, but the advertising agency turned them down. Autry decided to put them on the show for two weeks anyway. In September, the Jimmy Wakely Trio joined Autry on the thirty-minute program as regulars; one member, Johnny Bond, would be an integral part of Autry's organization for the next twenty years, playing guitar and accompanying Autry on tours. That spring and summer four Autry movies were released: *Shooting High*, *Gaucho Serenade*, *Carolina Moon*, and *Ride, Tenderfoot, Ride*.

On September 29, 1940, Gene Autry turned thirty-three years old. He had been a movie star for six years, and a recording star for ten. "Observing him in person," noted Johnny Bond,

one got the impression that he had just stepped out of a steam bath . . . both his person and his form fitting costumes were always spotless. His ten-gallon Stetson was always solid white with the traditional 3 1/2 inch brim. . . . Almost everything that he wore was tailor made for him, even his boots. He didn't go for the "loud" cowboy clothes except for those occasions when the script called for it. For street wear, he would have a conservative Western suit made with just enough trimming to show that it was Western only after close inspection. The suits, too, were always immaculately cleaned and pressed.

In October of 1940, Gene Autry made his first appearance at the big Madison Square Garden Rodeo in New York. Several aspects of this booking would play a role in Autry's career. First, Republic wanted to promote him in large cities; next, Autry saw the rodeo as good exposure that fit with his cowboy image; and finally, the rodeos needed a boost in terms of entertainment. Previously, they had featured clowns and amusements like donkey basketball games and trick roping for their entertainment between events. Having a movie cowboy star appear at a rodeo would provide a definite entertainment boost.

On Saturday evening, December 4, Autry appeared in a benefit organized by Cowboy Association for British War Children's Relief to help young victims of Nazi bombing raids. The event was broadcast live around the world and was distributed to radio stations on transcriptions. In addition to Autry, Roy Rogers, Tex Ritter, Jack and Tim Holt, Buck Jones, Bill Boyd, and other cowboy stars appeared in the show, which featured "hold-ups" at various places around the Los Angeles area to raise money.

In January 1941 *Ridin' on a Rainbow* was released; one of the songs in that movie was "Be Honest with Me," which would be nominated for an Academy Award that year. In February Autry appeared at the rodeo in Houston, then at rodeos in Hershey, Pennsylvania; New Haven, Connecticut; Pittsburgh, Pennsylvania; and Washington, D.C. While in Washington, Autry and Bond drove past the Washington and Lincoln monuments and went to the Smithsonian. During the drive around Washington, Autry surprised Bond by asking, "So what do you think of all that's happening?" Bond was stumped and asked what he meant. "I believe we're headed towards a war," replied Autry.

In March *Back in the Saddle* was released, marking the third time that Autry performed that song in a movie. In August *Under Fiesta Stars* was released; in September he was in a Hollywood recording studio putting down four songs, including "Amapola" and "Maria Elena"; and in October Autry once again performed at the Madison Square Garden Rodeo and managed to attend some of the World Series games that year. Also in October his movie *Down Mexico Way* was released. The next month his fiftieth movie, *Sierra Sue*, was released.

During the first week in November, Autry began a two-week series of performances at the Boston Garden for the rodeo there. After his last performance in Boston, Autry traveled to Berwyn, Oklahoma, population 227, which was changing its name to "Gene Autry, Oklahoma." At two in the afternoon on Sunday, November 16, the "Berwyn" sign was replaced by one reading "Gene Autry." Autry then performed his *Melody Ranch* radio show live before the 35,000 in attendance, broadcasting the event all over the country.

On Sunday morning, December 7, 1941, the Autry troupe rehearsed for their radio show at the CBS studio. The band consisted of the same lineup that accompanied him on his rodeo tours during 1940 and 1941: Jimmy Wakely on guitar, Dick Reinhart on bass, Johnny Bond on guitar, Carl Cotner on fiddle, Frankie Marvin on steel, and Paul Sells on accordion. The group was working on a movie with Autry tentatively titled *Deep in the Heart of Texas*. This would be the only movie that the Jimmy Wakely Trio performed in with Autry, although the group traveled with him and were regulars on his radio show.

Both Autry and Bond remembered that there was a buzz around the studio that something big had happened, although most found it hard to believe. About twenty minutes before air time, the troupe took their places on stage. Then, about ten minutes before the show was scheduled to begin, Autry came out, told a few jokes, and was interrupted by a voice over the speakers saying that a special announcement would be coming from the CBS newsroom in New York. Instead of Gene Autry singing "Back in the Saddle," the cast, crew, and audience stood on the stage and heard the announcement that the Japanese had bombed Pearl Harbor. Bond recalled that "It goes without saying that each of us, Gene included, was stunned. We looked at our room full of people while they sat motionless looking up at us on stage. Autry made no comment but began his theme song upon cue from our director." Autry remembered that

we had to put on a show as though nothing had happened. No one told us the control room had received word that "Melody Ranch" was to be delayed for a special report from the CBS newsroom in New York. At the moment our theme usually began, the report was piped into the studio. Those of us on the stage—and the hundred or so seated in the audience and the millions riveted to their radios across the land—listened numbly to the details of the attack on Pearl Harbor. For the next vacant seconds the people in the studio were like figures in a wax museum. No one stirred. Or spoke.

Then the director gave a cue, my theme came up, and almost by reflex, we started the show. . . . One of the most awkward of my life. We sang. Joked. Went through our lines. And when it was over the audience got up and walked out in a silence that was like leaving a tomb.

After the show, Autry and the Jimmy Wakely Trio finished up their movie, which had to be retitled *Heart of the Rio Grande* because Universal had purchased the rights to the title song of the movie, "Deep in the Heart of Texas." On the Saturday following Pearl Harbor, Autry went into the studio and recorded four songs; among those he recorded was "I Hang My Head and Cry."

Gene Autry reportedly made over $600,000 in 1941. Although Autry was always friendly and outgoing, he kept many of his plans to himself; also, he moved in several groups of people, and one group might not know about the other. Johnny Bond remembered that "Gene was not in the habit of revealing everything about his personal plans and movements, but we did get rumors from sources close to him that he was preparing to enter the service in some manner. We knew that he was taking flying lessons when various strangers in uniform began to appear upon the scene either at rehearsals or some other gathering."

On April 29, 1942, Gene Autry was ordered to report for an army physical and was immediately classified 1-A, which meant he was eligible for the draft. Married, without children, and thirty-four years old, Autry knew he had to decide what his role in the war would be. A few days later his movie *The Singing Hill* was released.

Gene Autry completed four movies in the first six months of 1942; in January *Cowboy Serenade*, a movie he finished in 1941, was released. In February 1942 Autry took a huge cast and crew to Houston for a two-week appearance at the rodeo there. Among the actors in the giant production were colorfully costumed square dancers who performed under newly installed strobe lights that gave a fluorescent glow. The show also featured appearances in the arena by historical reenactors such as Buffalo Bill (played by Tex Cooper), Teddy Roosevelt (played by Eddie Dean), Kit Carson, Davy Crockett, Sitting Bull, Annie Oakley, and General Custer. Although the show was a colorful addition to the rodeo, Autry mounted it only once because of production costs and the impending possibility that he would be entering the armed services.

In March *Heart of the Rio Grande* was released; in April *Home in Wyoming* was released; and the next month *Stardust on the Sage* came out. On

July 4, 1942, Autry and his troupe performed at Soldier Field in Chicago. The next day, with media in tow, he went down to the recruiting station and signed up for the army, although he would later be sworn in during a broadcast of *Melody Ranch*. If Autry had to serve in the army, he wanted some publicity mileage out of it—and so did the army, which used the publicity as a recruiting tool.

Rather than waiting to be drafted, Autry preferred enlisting, because doing so would give him some say in his job with the army. "I wanted to get into something that I know a little bit about and I had a pilot's license at that time," he told an interviewer some years later. Autry had gone to Washington before his Chicago appearance and arranged with military chiefs of the Army Air Corps to enter the army with a rank of sergeant. He had originally been offered an officer's commission, but a committee headed by Senator Harry Truman investigating favoritism by the military toward Hollywood celebrities had caused that offer to be withdrawn. However, Autry did negotiate with the army to allow him to finish one more movie, *Bells of Capistrano*, which began production on July 6.

The *Hollywood Reporter* noted that "Enlistment of Gene Autry in the Army Air Force automatically halts all preparations for his 1942–43 film program, which had been set up as the most important of his career." Autry was scheduled to star in eight pictures, four of which would be top-budget musicals. At the time of his enlistment, the cowboy star had three unreleased pictures in the can. His movies were scheduled to be released every six weeks, but because of the war, that schedule would have to be altered.

The fact that other actors could enter the service further threatened Republic's schedule. Don Barry, who starred in a series, was scheduled to enlist in the military, while the status of Roy Rogers was uncertain, although he held a deferred classification because he had two children. The Three Mesquiteers series was a little safer because Tom Tyler and Bob Steel were both too old for the draft; however, the newest member of the trio, Jimmy Dodd, was waiting to hear from his draft board.

In an interview at that time, Autry stated, "I think the He-men in the movies belong in the Army, Marine, Navy or Air Corps. All of these He-men in the movies realize that right now is the time to get into the service. Every movie cowboy ought to devote time to the Army winning, or to helping win, until the war is over—the same as any other American Citizen. The Army needs all the young men it can get, and if I can set a good example for the young men, I'll be mighty proud." Not all the movie cowboys took his advice; Roy Rogers eventually received a deferment because of his children, while John Wayne received deferments engineered by Republic Pictures. Herbert Yates's determination to keep Wayne at Republic stemmed in part from his anger over Autry's decision to refuse the studio's offer to obtain draft deferments on his behalf so he could continue making movies.

On July 24 Autry finished production of *Bells of Capistrano* and on July 26 was sworn into the Army Air Corps on his *Melody Ranch* broadcast. On August 1 he reported for duty at Fort Bolling, Washington; he then transferred on August 17 to the airbase at Santa Ana, California, for basic military training. By this point, he had logged over two hundred hours as a civilian pilot and wanted to fly. However, the army preferred he perform shows for the troops. "They put me in Public Relations and Special Services," remembered Autry later. "And I said 'Look, I've been doing that kind of stuff for so long and I want to do something else. I want to get in the flying end of it.' So I was transferred to the Air Transport Command."

After Gene Autry started basic training, *Call of the Canyon*, his fifty-fifth movie, was released. Autry's musical director, Carl Cotner, entered the service about the same time, but Smiley Burnette stayed in Hollywood and costarred in movies with Roy Rogers, Bob Livingston, and Sunset Carson. The Jimmy Wakely Trio split up, with Dick Reinhart moving back to Texas and Wakely pursuing a solo career in the movies, and Johnny Bond elected to stick with Autry. Fred Rose moved back to Nashville, where, in October 1942, he formed Acuff-Rose Publishing Company with Roy Acuff. Although Autry's enlistment gave Rose a convenient reason to move back to Tennessee, in truth Rose's wife was tired of Hollywood and wanted to return to Nashville, where her family lived.

Autry and Cotner were soon transferred to Luke Field in Phoenix, but they continued the *Melody Ranch* broadcasts. Gene and his wife, Ina Mae, stayed together in Phoenix, but on the weekends they caught the Southern Pacific train back to Hollywood for the radio show. Autry kept up with Hollywood news by having the *Daily Variety* and *Hollywood Reporter* forwarded to him in Phoenix.

After Autry and Cotner completed basic training, the J. Walter Thompson Agency informed them of arrangements between the military and Phil Wrigley to send them on a tour of bases, where they would perform daily shows for servicemen. Performing with Autry would be Johnny Bond, Eddie and Jimmy Dean, and Carl Cotner, who would play fiddle and continue his duties as orchestra director for the radio program. CBS arranged for Chicago staff musicians and radio engineers to go wherever Autry was performing for the radio broadcasts. During this period Autry broadcast from Denver, Casper (Wyoming), Indianapolis, Louisville, and Birmingham. On the regular shows, a local officer at the base would introduce Autry, who would sing several of his hits.

"I had mixed feeling about doing camp shows," wrote Autry in his autobiography.

> It was soft duty. For the cut in pay I had taken, I felt I was entitled at least to get shot at. I didn't want to play show-and-tell, or beat the drums for war bonds or the Red Cross or WAC enlistment drives. I knew how to fly. . . . But I had a problem. My age was against me. I had flown only small aircraft, so just to get into flight school I needed a higher rating—so many hours flying [with] so much horsepower. I found a private field in Phoenix and, on my own time, at my own expense, I started checking out bigger aircraft, the Stearman and Fairchild 84 and the AT-6.

"I flew two or three times a week for six months and, finally, I was accepted for flight school at Love Field, in Dallas," remembered Autry.

> Believe me, when you are competing with nineteen-and-twenty-year-old boys, trying to match their reflexes and their stamina, it is mighty tough. But I had no intention of washing out. And I guess I should make it clear. Being Gene Autry had nothing to do with that. Didn't help, didn't hurt. I didn't take any hazing, either. Anyone who cared to look could see I was earning my way. That's why I considered it a break, not coming in on a cushion, as an officer. Gene Autry's name and reputation meant little. But love of flying did. And I was hooked on those clouds.

Autry was finally accepted as a flight officer in 1943 and assigned to the Air Transport Command, or Cargo Division, ferrying supplies to India, China, Cairo, and throughout the Middle East. During the war he flew the C-109, which carried 10,000 gallons of gasoline to bases. One of his proudest moments was flying over "The Hump," the Himalayas in the China-Burma-India theater. It was a dangerous flight—the clumsy plane was heavily burdened with cargo that could explode and burn.

Gene Autry did not completely relinquish his entertainment career or the comforts of home. He continued his radio show until 1944, when he had to stop because of his active work as a cargo copilot. But because the

Musicians' Union had called a strike for recording musicians that lasted from August 1, 1942, until the end of 1944, Autry could not have made any recordings even if he had been in Hollywood at the time.

In October 1943 Autry performed at the Madison Square Garden Rodeo. Herbert Yates came backstage and spoke angrily with him after insisting Roy Rogers should have Autry's dressing room. Yates told Autry, "Well, you wouldn't cooperate and I'll break you if it's the last thing I ever do. And I'll make Roy Rogers the biggest thing that ever happened in this business."

In September 1943 Republic had re-released *Man from Music Mountain*, an Autry picture that had debuted in 1938. Although Republic would also reissue some of Autry's other movies during the war, the studio reacted to Autry's departure by heavily promoting Roy Rogers as the "King of the Cowboys." The war would give Rogers, who stayed in Hollywood making movies, a big career boost.

Comparing Gene Autry and Roy Rogers may lead one to conclude that Rogers was a better actor, but Autry, who consistently took care with his recordings, was better when it came to selling records. Rogers, who was never comfortable as a solo performer, neither paid as much attention to his recording career nor sold as many records as Autry did. Instead, Rogers was busy starring in movies and making personal appearances, so it is understandable that he let the musical part of his career slide. However, his formation of the Sons of the Pioneers and the early recordings he made with them constituted a major contribution to country music. The harmony sound—especially with the yodels—would influence several generations of country singers. But Gene Autry, who sought out new songs to record and put together a traveling show, found more success as a recording artist.

In January 1944 *Billboard* magazine, the music trade journal, began a "folk" chart that included country songs. On January 29 the chart listed Autry's recording of the old Carter Family standard "I'm Thinking Tonight of My Blue Eyes"; on April 29, his recording of "I Hang My Head and Cry" was listed. That same year, Republic released Autry's first serial, *The Phantom Empire* (filmed in 1934), as a two-part feature that was titled *Men with Steel Faces* and *Radio Ranch*. Autry was certainly concerned about his career as a movie star during the war. In March 1944 he confided to Johnny Bond that he felt if the war lasted much longer, he would be too old to be a cowboy star. Gene Autry would turn thirty-seven that year.

During the late spring and early summer, Autry was in a Hollywood recording studio, creating a good stock of records to release after his discharge, which came on July 17, 1945. No longer would he collect a paycheck for $135 per month as a sergeant. He had one perk while in uniform—he was allowed to wear cowboy boots—and one idiosyncrasy: he refused to salute female officers.

After his discharge, Autry immediately arranged to do a USO tour for troops in the Pacific. Beginning in August 1945, when he flew into Saipan, he spent ten weeks going from island to island with Rufe Davis, Will and Gladys Ahern, Marjorie Alden, and Sandra Shaw, playing approximately eighty-five shows for GIs on a USO Camp Shows trip arranged by the Hollywood Victory Committee. "Everywhere we went the first thing the boys said was: 'where's your horse,'" Autry told a reporter after he returned. "And I sure could have used Champ on those islands. I walked up hills and down hills and into Jap caves, until I had walked off 22 pounds. The only time I got to ride was on Guam, where they gave me a water buffalo." The troupe covered 35,000 miles, performing at Guam, Saipan, Tinian, Kwajelein, Angar, Peleliu, and Iwo Jima.

"We were on Iwo Jima when the news came that the Japs were going to give up, and I never saw a bunch of men go quite so crazy," said Autry shortly after he returned. "Most of them were Marines who were getting ready for the next invasion, and that news meant that a lot of them would not have to die."

"We never had less than 3,500 in the audience and a lot of times we played to an entire division of 15,000 men in a day," related Autry. "The boys are a wonderful audience and next to wanting to go home, they want entertainment, and they will continue to want it as long as they are overseas."

In his autobiography, Autry told the story of having a drink with General Ramey on August 4, two days before the *Enola Gay* took off to drop the atomic bomb on Hiroshima. Autry and the troop were in Tinian on August 6 when the bomb went off. "All over the islands, the news touched off a wild celebration," wrote Autry. "The kind that ends at four in the morning with people trying to hold each other up and sing barbershop harmony. There was no question of what we felt then. Pride. Relief. In all the moral agonizing that has taken place in the years since, we sometimes seem to forget how few doubts anyone had at the time that decision—Harry Truman's awesome decision to use atomic power—was the right one."

The Japanese surrendered about a week later, and within hours Autry and the troupe were on a plane headed back to the United States. "I had gotten up close to a very wide screen, had felt a lot of emotions I probably would never feel again," remembered Autry. "But it was behind me now. Somewhere over the blue Pacific, a few hours outside of Honolulu, it occurred to me that I was a civilian again. More than that, I was a free agent. The way I had it figured, my contract with Republic had run out while I was in the service. From my seat I could see the metallic blur of the plane's propellers. They were turning no faster than the thoughts turning in my mind."

However, once again, Herbert Yates, head of Republic, did not see things the same way Gene Autry did.

In September 1945, the *Melody Ranch* radio program went back on CBS but, due to a crowded schedule, was only fifteen minutes long until the spring of 1946, when it resumed its thirty-minute schedule. Carl Cotner remained on the show, playing fiddle and directing the band, as did Johnny Bond, who played guitar for Autry; however, the new show included some changes in the lineup. The Cass County Boys were the featured trio; Fred Martin played accordion, Jerry Scoggins played guitar, and Bert Dodson played bass. The Pinafores—Beulah, Eunice, and Ione Kettle—had also joined the show.

The fight to get out of his Republic contract occupied most of Gene Autry's time and attention during the fall of 1945. He had signed a seven-year contract in September 1938 and then joined the service in July 1942. Autry, who had long wanted to own his own movie production company, reasoned that the contract would have expired by September 1945, allowing him the freedom to pursue an independent movie production deal. Herbert Yates and Republic argued that Autry, by joining the service, had not fulfilled his contract, which was thus "suspended" during the time he was in the service. According to their logic, when he returned from the war, he was obligated to three more years, or twenty-one more movies for that studio. Autry appealed to patriotism, arguing that the duty he owed to his country surpassed his duty to Republic during the war, and also pointed out that Republic had not paid him anything during his service years.

When Autry enlisted in the armed services, five movies remained to be filmed under the third option of his five-year contract, which, if it ran the full five years, would terminate on March 6, 1945. However, on May 11, 1942, before Autry enlisted, he and Republic agreed that one more year would be added to the 1938 agreement, obligating him to appear in eight more movies for $15,000 each. Republic picked up his fourth option, notifying Autry on March 3, 1944, even though Autry was in the service. But on June 17 of that year, Autry served Republic "a notice of termination of the agreements and employment thereunder by reason of military service." On June 27 he filed his case against Republic.

Autry based his case on a California law (the "Shirley Temple law") that states no contract can run more than seven years. He hired attorney Martin Gang, who had used the same legal basis to win a case for Olivia de Haviland against Warner Brothers. Autry's suit was decided in Republic's favor in February 1945 (although not entered on the court records until March 20), and Autry appealed. On November 7, 1945, the case went before Judge Louis Palmer of the Los Angeles District Court; Autry spent a week on the stand testifying. The court ruled in Autry's favor, but Republic appealed the decision. This fight would continue into the next year, when Autry agreed to film several movies for Republic before signing an agreement with Columbia Pictures, where he began filming in 1947.

At the end of World War II, the phrase "country music"—then called "folk" in the trades and "hillbilly" in conversations within the music business—was an umbrella covering a fairly wide variety of music. "Western swing," led by Spade Cooley, Tex Williams, and Bob Wills and the Texas Playboys, was the most commercially popular "country music"; it was basically big bands performing with fiddles, doing a mixture of country songs with jazz arrangements. The "mountaineer" image and string band sound was popular, led by Roy Acuff at the Grand Ole Opry in Nashville; the string band sound had emerged as "bluegrass" when Bill Monroe hired Lester Flatt and Earl Scruggs, whose three-fingered style of banjo playing would increasingly define bluegrass, at the end of 1945. Gospel still had an important place in country music, with most performers including gospel in their shows, while comedy, either through comedic routines or funny, novelty-type songs, was also important.

"Western" music was alive and well thanks to the singing cowboys, but increasingly the "western" came from the clothes they wore, not necessarily the songs they sang. The "honky-tonk" songs that evolved from the Texas and California barrooms, led by Ernest Tubb, Ted Daffin, Floyd Tillman, the Maddox Brothers and Rose, and others would later be called "traditional" country music after Hank Williams wrote and recorded standards in this genre. Finally, a smooth, pop-type sound, later called "countrypolitan," was emerging, led by "crooners" Red Foley and Eddy Arnold. This particular sound was an attempt to take the "twang" out of country, to make it more palatable to urban ears and give it some middle-class respectability.

Gene Autry was still a singing cowboy; he certainly dressed the part. But he increasingly recorded pop songs and sought a more pop-sounding backing in his recordings after World War II. This would be the direction that country music would increasingly take in the coming years, although that was not so obvious when World War II ended.

Sources

Adams, Les, and Buck Rainey. *Shoot-Em-Ups: The Complete Reference Guide to Westerns of the Sound Era*. Waynesville, NC: World of Yesterday, 1978.

Arentz, B. "Gene Autry: Businessman, Pilot." *Flying*, December 1949, 30–31, 62.

Autry, Gene, with Mickey Herskowitz. *Back in the Saddle Again*. Garden City, NY: Doubleday, 1976.

"Autry Leads the Herd in Rep's Western Pix," *Variety*, December 18, 1940, 22.

"Autry Still Tied to Rep," *Variety*, February 6, 1946, 2.

"Autry to Head Own Rodeo; Pic Unit Waits," *Variety*, November 14, 1945, 9.

Block, Alex Ben. "Salute to Republic Entertainment," *Hollywood Reporter*, October 24, 1995.

Bond, Johnny. "Gene Autry: Champion." Archives, Country Music Foundation, Nashville, TN.

———. Interview. March 1975. Oral History Music Project, Country Music Foundation, Nashville, TN.

———. *Reflections: The Autobiography of Johnny Bond*. Los Angeles, CA: John Edwards Memorial Foundation, 1976.

Buscombe, Richard. *The BFI Companion to the Western*. New York: Atheneum, 1988.

"Campaign to Make Big Cities Autry-Minded." *Variety*, October 23, 1940, 2.

Cusic, Don. *Cowboys and the Wild West: An A to Z Guide from the Chisholm Trail to the Silver Screen*. New York: Facts on File, 1994.

"Film Cowboys, Yodelers to Air Four-Hour Show for British War Kids," *Variety*, December 4, 1940.

"Gene Autry Home," *Los Angeles Citizen-News*, September 6, 1945.

"Gene Autry Twirled a Mighty Fetching Lariat," *Variety*, October 4, 1950.

George-Warren, Holly. *Cowboy: How Hollywood Invented the Wild West*. Pleasantville, NY: Reader's Digest Books, 2002.

Goodwin, Doris Kearns. *No Ordinary Time: Franklin and Eleanor Roosevelt; The Home Front in World War II*. New York: Touchstone, 1994.

Green, Douglas B. "Gene Autry." In *Stars of Country Music*, ed. Bill C. Malone and Judith McCullough, 116–31. Urbana: University of Illinois Press, 1975.

———. *Singing in the Saddle: The History of the Singing Cowboy*. Nashville: Country Music Foundation Press and Vanderbilt University Press, 2002.

Haslam, Gerald W. *Workin' Man Blues: Country Music in California*. Berkeley and Los Angeles: University of California Press, 1999.

Haynes, Dick. Interview with Gene Autry. Broadcast on KLAC (Los Angeles, CA), February 20, 1974.

Horstman, Dorothy. *Sing Your Heart Out, Country Boy: Classic Country Songs and Their Inside Stories by the People Who Wrote Them.* New York: Dutton, 1975.

Hurst, Richard Maurice. *Republic Studios: Between Poverty Row and the Majors.* Metuchen, NJ: Scarecrow Press, 1979.

Kingsbury, Paul, ed. *The Encyclopedia of Country Music.* New York: Oxford University Press, 1998.

Kingsbury, Paul, and Alan Axelrod, eds. *Country: The Music and the Musicians.* New York: Abbeville Press, 1988.

Knauth, Percy. "Gene Autry, Inc." *Life*, January 28, 1948.

Loy, R. Philip. *Westerns and American Culture, 1930–1955.* Jefferson, NC: McFarland & Company, 2001.

Malone, Bill C. *Singing Cowboys and Musical Mountaineers: Southern Culture and the Roots of Country Music.* Athens: University of Georgia Press, 1993.

Malone, Bill, and Judith McCullough, eds. *Stars of Country Music.* Urbana: University of Illinois Press, 1975.

McCloud, Barry, ed. *Definitive Country: The Ultimate Encyclopedia of Country Music and Its Performers.* New York: Perigree, 1995.

Roberts, Randy, and James S. Olson. *John Wayne: American.* New York: Free Press, 1995.

Rothel, David. *The Gene Autry Book.* Madison, NC: Empire Publishing, 1988.

———. *The Roy Rogers Book.* Madison, NC: Empire Publishing, 1996.

———. *The Singing Cowboys.* Cranbury, NJ: A.S. Barnes, 1978.

Seemann, Charlie. "Gene Autry." *The Journal of the American Academy for the Preservation of Old-Time Country Music*, no. 22 (August 1994): 9–11.

Smith, Jon Guyot. Liner notes, *Sing, Cowboy, Sing*, Rhino.

"S-Q Rodeo Act Proves Gene Autry's Gun-Grip on Kids Undimmed by Army," *Variety*, May 1, 1946, 56.

Tuska, Jon. *The Filming of the West.* New York: Doubleday, 1976.

———. *The Vanishing Legion: A History of Mascot Pictures, 1927–1935.* Jefferson, NC: McFarland, 1982.

Wakely, Linda Lee. *See Ya up There, Baby: The Jimmy Wakely Story.* Canoga Park, CA: Shasta Records, 1992.

Whitburn, Joel. *Top Country Singles 1944–1988.* Menomonee Falls, WI: Record Research, 1989.

———. *Top 40 Country Hits: 1944–Present.* New York: Billboard Books, 1996.

Wolfe, Charles K. "The Triumph of the Hills: Country Radio, 1920–1950." In *Country: The Music and the Musicians.* New York: Abbeville Press, 1988.

5

Peace in the Valley

The Development of John Lair's
Enterprises during WWII

Michael Ann Williams

Beginning the concluding chapter of *Renfro Valley Then and Now,* John Lair wrote, "Discharged from the service in 1918, I came back to Renfro Valley to find it greatly changed from the way I had known it in earlier days." While some young men left for the cities of the industrial north and infected others with "restless longings," Lair dreamed impossible dreams of taking Renfro back to the "old care-free days of the past."[1] The events that shaped Lair's creation of Renfro Valley may have been far more complex than attested to in his romanticized account, but John Lair did fulfill his dream of owning the valley and presenting his own version of its past. By the time the Renfro Valley complex took its full shape, two decades had passed and another great war gripped the world.

Lair contrasted his own nostalgia with the restlessness of other young men, but, in reality, he too possessed the yearnings of the generation who came of age during the First World War. Although he did not "see Paree"— he, in fact, never left the United States—Lair felt no more content to settle down on the farm after military service than his contemporaries.[2] By all accounts, Lair had a "good war." If service did not lead him off to cities any more exotic than Washington, D.C., and New York, it did allow him to hone skills that would serve him the rest of his life. Although quite possibly born with a theatrical temperament, during active military duty Lair developed an abiding passion for the limelight.

While stationed in Washington, Lair became involved in a theatrical

Fig. 1. John Lair, second from left, during service in World War I. (Courtesy of Southern Appalachian Archives, Berea College.)

show, *Atta Boy,* originally staged at Camp Meigs and later by the men of the Aberdeen (Maryland) Proving Grounds. The production eventually opened at the Lexington Theater in New York, receiving favorable notice from the *Times*: "The music of 'Atta Boy' is unusually tuneful, and no doubt Broadway will be whistling 'Strolling 'round the Camp with Mary,' which seemed particularly to please the good-sized first-night audience which greeted the soldier-actors."[3] The extent of Lair's participation in the production is unclear, but, by his own account, Lair wrote at least one of the sketches, guaranteeing himself a spot on stage when the Ziegfeld Follies incorporated the show into its production.[4] However, a program from the Camp

Fig. 2. Cover of *Lest We Forget,* written and illustrated by John Lair while serving in the army. (Courtesy of Southern Appalachian Archives, Berea College.)

Meigs production merely lists Lair as one of well over one hundred performing privates.[5] Whatever the truth, Lair's military experience allowed him to absorb the traditions of popular theater, especially vaudeville.

During his service, Lair also wrote and illustrated a small book, *Lest We Forget.* In the same vein as *Atta Boy,* the volume humorously depicts camp life, including shooting craps, courting good-looking dames, and KP duty. Far more irreverent than the verse Lair produced later in his career, the poems, all beginning "You won't forget," reflect the sensibilities of the serviceman rather than of those on the home front. Even the sentimental poems, such as the one commemorating wartime romance, are from the perspective of the soldier:

> You won't forget
> The little girl who lived near camp
>   Who was so sweet to you,
> Although her heart was far away
>   Where Norman lilies grew.

You knew that you'd be happy
  With the dear old girl back home;
She knew Her lad was sailing
  Back to her across the foam;
But the kiss, your words at parting,
  And the tear that dimmed her eye
In each heart will sweetly linger
  As the sands of time run by.

Only the final poem, dedicated to the soldiers who did not return from overseas, presents a more sobering vision of wartime.[6] Although, much to his regret, Lair never fully pursued his talents as a cartoonist and illustrator, his light verse reveals a talent that he later honed in his song lyrics and stage patter. The publication also gave him one more opportunity to stand in the spotlight. According, again, to his own account, prominent actress Helen Ware read one of the poems on stage at a theater in Washington and introduced Lair to the audience.[7]

All in all, Lair took such pleasure in his military service that, according to a family story, he later refused a bonus. Daughter Barbara Lair Smith recalled, "I remember Mother saying one time that after they were married, or around that time, that the government gave the veterans of World War I a bonus, a small bonus, and Daddy sent his back with a letter saying he had the best time he'd ever had in his life. . . . 'I should pay you,' you know, because he probably never would have gotten out of the county . . . without that experience."[8]

Although John Lair may have been saddened by the transformations he encountered upon returning to his home in rural Rockcastle County, Kentucky—a community called Renfro Valley did not yet exist—Lair's vision of his place in the world had changed. Lair did not find an immediate outlet for his theatrical longings, but he did escape rural life for a career in the big city. Working for the Mutual Insurance Company in Chicago during the 1920s, Lair discovered the barn dance broadcast over the airwaves of local station WLS. Here, at last, he found a way to unite his interests in the music and traditions of rural Kentucky with a passion for vaudeville-inspired theater. Lair missed the infancy years of the radio barn dance, but joined WLS just as the era of commercial sponsors and live audiences blossomed. During his early years at WLS, Lair kept his day job in insurance, until certain he could make a living at this new industry. Despite his part-time status, Lair proved his talents as an innovator, creating popular shows and acts for the station. While working at WLS, he also gradually introduced the radio audience to a place called Renfro Valley, at that time a mythical on-air community.[9]

The Depression helped fuel the surge in radio, and Lair rode the crest. By 1937 he itched to be his own boss. In September Lair decamped to Cincinnati, where he began the *Renfro Valley Barn Dance*. At the same time, with "more guts than sense" and a borrowed sum of $500, he struck out to build a business near the confluence of the Little Renfro and Big Renfro creeks in Rockcastle County, Kentucky, where he had spent his childhood.[10] Homesickness may have motivated Lair's return, but he also had his eye on the developing business of auto-tourism. The newly constructed Dixie Highway, which linked Michigan to Florida, bisected Rockcastle County, and Lair purchased land easily accessible to the highway. No longer content to construct an imaginary community on the air, Lair began to build tourist cabins and a "real barn" to stage shows. Meanwhile his newly created *Renfro Valley Barn Dance* began its life on Cincinnati's WLW, then the nation's most powerful radio station, broadcasting at an incredible five hundred kilowatts.[11] Lair staged his live shows in Cincinnati, then Dayton, and then, on November 4, 1939, broadcast his first show live from Renfro Valley, Kentucky.

While Renfro Valley soon became, in terms of live audiences, the most popular barn dance on radio, its success hardly came guaranteed. A number of Lair's most popular performers balked at the idea of moving to Kentucky from Chicago or Cincinnati, and Lair had to rebuild his acts. Furthermore, Lair's business sense must have failed him when he decided to relocate in November. Tourists were few during bad weather—fewer yet were those who wished to sit through a program in an unheated barn. Still Lair tried to maintain an optimistic outlook. Although tourists rolled in with the spring weather and Lair's shows proved popular, the financial success of the enterprise remained in doubt. Throughout the tenuous early years of Renfro Valley, John Lair hid from his performers the fact that his business partner, advertising executive Freeman Keyes, firmly controlled the financing of the operation.

A man of lesser vision than John Lair might have seen his dreams crumble when Japan attacked Pearl Harbor on December 7, 1941. Although Lair's programs and live shows had proven to be popular, the enterprise teetered on the edge of collapse. While the entry of the United States into war may have pushed less optimistic men over the edge, Lair explored the business opportunities, including the possibility of leasing Renfro to the government for use as a training base. In March of 1942 Keyes wrote Lair that their joint venture was in dire financial straits (although the money owed was to Keyes's own company). The only way the debt could be written off would be for Renfro Valley to go into bankruptcy, "which, of course, is impossible." Keyes, however, encouraged Lair's scheme to rent out Renfro Valley: "I am vitally interested in your plan to rent the entire Enterprise to the government for a training base. $2,000 a month on this basis, plus $2,000 a month from your tent show, with no expenses, would pull you out of the red in a hurry. If there is anything I can do—any strings we can pull—to help consummate this plan, let me know immediately."[12]

The following week Lair responded that his banker had received a letter from a Colonel Cassidy stating that the proposal to use the facilities at Renfro Valley for air corps training had been filed for future reference and that the army would contact them if they required the property. Lair added to Keyes, "In spite of this statement, however, I believe that you should make it a point to have a talk with the colonel, as soon as possible or at the time of your next visit to Washington." Lair's response also indicates that although America's participation in the war was only months old, he had already begun to think ahead to peacetime. While he pessimistically stated that he was "definitely certain that we should not attempt to go through another Winter here, especially in view of present day conditions," he clearly had his eye on the future: "Incidentally, if we could make the proper deal with the Government on this site we could afford to put up a large barracks room to be later converted into a horse barn or use to seat a larger audience than our present barn will accommodate and have it paid for by the time we are ready to use it again."[13]

The leasing deal with the government never materialized, and Renfro Valley continued as an entertainment venue. Remarkably, John Lair managed to continue to pursue his building plans for the valley throughout the war years. When Renfro Valley opened in fall of 1939, Lair had completed his barn for performances and the basic tourist facilities. The Lair family lived first in the upstairs of the new lodge and then in the tourist cabins, moving finally to an old house owned by Renfro Valley Enterprises. In early 1941 Lair wrote to Keyes that the house was "just too cramped for us and too danged hard to heat in the winter time." Lair hoped that Renfro Valley Enterprises would sell him a piece of land for a new home close to the other facilities, "as I don't want to get too far away from camp." Lair con-

Fig. 3. The John Lair Home, built during the Second World War. (Courtesy of Southern Appalachian Archives, Berea College.)

cluded, "My object is to convert some of my other real estate holding around here into enough money to build the kind of home I would like to settle down to bring the kids up in and of course I wouldn't want to do that unless I owned the property on which the house stood."[14]

Despite wartime restrictions, Lair accomplished this dream, completing his 3,500-square-foot home in 1944. Although Lair hired "neighbors" to work on it and the construction methods for the stone and log structure cited tradition, the architect-designed eleven-room dwelling was hardly traditional. Whatever financial straits Lair may have found himself in, the substantial house, with its cedar-lined closets, laundry chute, and tile bathroom, spoke of upward mobility. A year later Lair completed a massive limestone and vertical-board stable with six dormers, a cupola, and a gabled wing off the center. The twelve-stall stable housed horses and ponies ridden by three of his four daughters, as well as the horses he managed for Freeman Keyes.

With their close proximity to the Renfro Valley Barn, the house and stables made a public, as well as private, statement. Lair announced to the world that here lived a prosperous gentleman, firmly in control of his world. While the architectural statement may indeed have rankled some of the performers who had to listen to Lair's sad stories about why he could not pay them more, it did not intimidate visitors to the valley. Much to the chagrin of Lair's wife, Virginia, tourists treated it as a public building and dropped by at all hours to meet the genial man they felt they already intimately knew from his radio presence. As Lair's oldest daughter, Ann, recalled, "Mother always said everybody took him very literally when he said, 'You all come see us.' Because they did. They'd knock on the door, 'Here we are!' You know. So he always invited them in, and you know, glad to see whoever."[15]

The Second World War seems to have posed only minor obstacles to Lair's ambitious building of Renfro Valley. Building his cast proved to be another matter. Because of its relative isolation, prominent stars, such as Red Foley, showed reluctance to move to Renfro, while the up-and-comers, whom Lair had nurtured, often quickly moved on, for fear that they might, in the words of Jerry Byrd, "dry rot" if they stayed in Renfro too long.[16] The war also took its toll. The most popular act shaped by Lair after the move to Renfro belonged to Henry Haynes and Kenneth Burns. Lair cast "Homer and Jethro" as two rubes who "come frum the hills but refuse to sing hill country music."[17] This comedic framing allowed Lair to feature jazzy music on his program while upholding his own reputation as the defender of tradition. Before the predatory big radio stations could lure Homer and Jethro away with promises of larger incomes, Uncle Sam laid claim to Jethro Burns. After Burns's return to civilian life, Lair made the reunited duo an offer, but Homer and Jethro sought further fame and fortune elsewhere.[18]

During wartime, Lair did hold one ace up his sleeve when it came to attracting performers—his inexplicable ability to obtain rationed gas. Banjo player Emory Martin, who had previously booked through the Grand Ole Opry and had toured with Uncle Dave Macon, returned home to work for his father, a rock mason, during the war. Hearing from a friend that Lair still had touring shows, Martin auditioned, and Lair hired him for his big tent show. Martin felt lucky to get the work. As he recalled, "'Cause when I come here, I'd already checked around and there wasn't nothing going on in the way of bookings." Although Lair eventually hired him to be the driver for the musicians, Martin never knew how Lair acquired the gas rations.[19] A few months after hiring Martin, Lair sent a talented young musician named Linda Lou out on the tent show. Emory and Linda Lou Martin married in November of 1943, and they worked for Lair most of the rest of their professional lives.

During the early 1940s Lair sent out two tent shows. The local unit toured close enough that the performers could return to Renfro Valley on

Fig. 4. Lilly and Hank Holland with the Renfro Valley Tent Show, 1944. (Courtesy of Southern Appalachian Archives, Berea College.)

the weekends for the broadcast shows. The Martins toured with the "Big Show," managed by the Ketrows, a former circus family who took care of all the setting up. Emory Martin claimed that it was "one of the easiest jobs that I had in my life," and Linda added, "Now when we played the theaters and auditoriums in the winter, that was hard, that's where we had the long jumps and everything. But on the tent show, we would, maybe we could sleep till nine o'clock, or something like that, and get up and eat breakfast."[20] The "Big Show" toured the Deep South during the winter, working in the North for the summer.

Although Lair had one of the few shows touring at the time, his tent shows did not always break even. In November of 1943, Gene Cobb, manager and emcee of the "Big Show," wrote to Lair that if the grosses "don't start to climb soon I am afraid I will be ebbed so ebby that I will need hospitalization." Cobb speculated that the audiences in rural Georgia could either not afford the show or could not obtain gas rations to get into town, adding, "Maybe they are real patriotic and wont do any cheating along these lines." Cobb noted, however, that the audiences who did attend showed great enthusiasm: "The public's reaction on the show here is, that it's the best hillbilly show they ever saw, absolutely the best show that ever appeared in Newman [sic] . . . (NOT BARING [sic] ACUFF)."[21] A few days

Fig. 5. The cast of the "Big Show" in 1944, with Gene Cobb and Chess Davis at the microphone. Emory Martin holds the banjo, and his wife, Linda, stands behind. (Courtesy of Southern Appalachian Archives, Berea College.)

later, Cobb wrote Lair, "If these RED weeks doesn't cease soon, we had better Join The Russian REDS."[22]

Rationing may have affected the audience numbers, but Lair managed to keep his Renfro Valley folks touring. Some support possibly came from the Ballard & Ballard Flour Company, which began to sponsor a number of Lair's radio shows in 1943. Although the company did not officially sponsor the touring show, it provided free publicity and support through its network of agents, in exchange for the publicity the tours brought to the company's network radio shows. Perhaps the company also helped Lair obtain the needed gas, although no evidence of this exists in Lair's business records; Lair may have just been particularly adept at manipulating the local board that controlled wartime rationing.[23] Whatever difficulties Lair encountered, at least he recognized that the wartime restrictions also created problems for the competition. In October 1943 Ches Davis, Lair's advance man for the touring unit, reported to Lair from Atlanta that the *Renfro Valley Barn Dance*'s old WLW rival, the *Boone County Jamboree*, had just passed through town and he had had the chance to talk to two of its promoters. Davis wrote, "Bell is leaving this week to go in some other kind of business on the Coast. Bell told me that they felt the gas ration this year, but Bill McCluskey said they had a great season."[24] McCluskey, a former colleague of Lair's at both WLS and WLW, may have been reluctant to reveal to the competition the problems they had experienced.

Back home at Renfro Valley, John Lair continued to craft his programming, realizing that it, rather than the star power of his performers, brought listeners, and visitors, to the valley. In 1943 Lair debuted his most enduring radio show, the *Sunday Morning Gatherin'*.[25] While the *Renfro Valley Barn Dance* shared many similarities to all the other barn dances broadcast across the country, Lair made the *Gatherin'* uniquely his own. The show capitalized on Lair's storytelling abilities and, unlike the *Barn Dance,* moved at a slow, deliberate pace. Former performer Linda Martin noted another difference: "[Lair] never did rehearse that barn dance, it never was rehearsed. He didn't want it rehearsed. But he rehearsed the heck out of that Sunday morning program, he used to drive me nuts. I mean everything was just right down to the minute, boy, and timed."[26] According to Lair's daughter Barbara Smith, the *Gatherin'*, rather than the *Barn Dance*, held the place closest to Lair's heart. She recalled, "The *Sunday Morning Gatherin'* is probably what Daddy enjoyed the most, because that's where he wrote the entire script, and he wrote the songs that were sung. And if he didn't write the song, he wrote the introduction to the song which involved a story . . . of some kind."[27] The show also proved popular with sponsors, such as Ballard & Ballard Flour, its original sponsor, because it offered a novel format.

Not a church-going man himself, John Lair infused the *Gatherin'* with a religious ambience. According to Linda Martin, many listeners mistook Lair for a preacher. She recalled, "[H]e didn't do anything that would make them think like that, but there was a lot of hymns . . . and the church bell [actually a brake drum off a truck] at the end of the program."[28] Although the show contained many of the trappings of organized religion, it also embraced nostalgia and patriotism. Lair regarded the show as a technological expansion of the community get-together. On the opening broadcast, September 5, 1943, Lair expanded on this idea: "Anyway, we've kep up the custom of the Sunday mornin' getherin's because we've felt that it wuz things like this that helped make the America we love to remember an' will fight to preserve. Now, more than ever before, people need that old stick-together spirits of neighborliness, an' with that thought in mind Ballard an' Ballard thought it would be a might fine thing if we could jest enlarge the circle with radio an' make one big community getherin' for everybody that wanted to be with us, so here we are."[29]

Despite the corniness of Lair's delivery, the program struck a serious chord with listeners. Many wrote personal letters to Lair requesting that songs be played in memory of lost loved ones. Others wrote poems they had written in honor of a loved one or submitted poems sent to them by men in the service. A woman signing herself "Your Radio Pal and Listener/ Your unseen friend" wrote, "I'm going to enclose a poem that my other sister wrote about 2 weeks ago, she was inspired to write this poem when our brother didn't come home. You see, he was in the hospital and had just returned from the southwest Pacific where he had been serving in the army. He was overseas for 11 months and came back in a pretty bad condition. He was shell shocked and had malaria. But he is doing nicely now."[30] Although the nostalgia of the *Gatherin'* appealed especially to older listeners, not all of Lair's listeners were adults. Marjorie Bains wrote, "I am a little girl 10 years old. My mother uses Ballards Oblisk Flour and we think it's better than any made . . . [We] would like very much to have the Holden Brothers sing on your Sunday morning program, 'There's a Star Spangled Banner Waving Somewhere' in memory of my brother who was killed in action in North Africa on July 12, 1943."[31]

Since Lair's days at WLS, his programs elicited responses of a strongly personal nature from his radio audience. Those who listened to him on the radio felt they knew him and often poured out their life stories and problems.[32] The war intensified the loneliness, grief, and dislocation that many rural radio listeners felt, and they contrasted the changes they witnessed around them with Lair's "valley where time stands still." Lair and Ballard & Ballard encouraged listener response by offering five-dollar- and occasionally twenty-five-dollar prizes to listeners who had their letters or poems read on air. To win, the listeners had to include coupons from Ballard's flour, although the company exempted service people and "shut-ins" from this requirement. Perhaps to heighten their chance of being read, even many serious letters, such as the one written by little Marjorie Bains, included endorsements for Ballard's flour. Still this commercial aspect did not seem to detract from listeners' perceptions of Lair's sincerity. Eloise Gilchrist wrote that she heard "traces of tears" in Lair's voice when he read sad poems.[33]

The poetry and prose John Lair wrote during the Second World War differed significantly from the irreverent serviceman poetry he had written while a soldier himself. However, while primarily targeting the home folk, the sentiments of the *Gatherin'* also found an audience among young soldiers far from home. Private Jerry Barlow wrote from the Air Corps Technical School at Keesler Field, Mississippi:

> Sunday morning as I was turning the dial on my radio, I came across your program. I had never heard your program before, so I left it on, mostly to see what your program was about. Well, the part that I wanted to tell you is this. As your program went on, more boys came up around the radio, before long every soldier in our barracks was sitting around the radio. Some of the boys had tears in their eyes, others had very straight faces, yes they were thinking of home. As your program went on, you kept everyones attention, no other program can do that. Sir, you and the program sure did wonders for the soldiers here in our barracks, and I am sure that it did the same in other barracks, in camps all over the great U.S.[34]

Private Robert Williams wrote from the Regional Station Hospital in Coral Gables that he and about thirty other fellows in the same ward "listen to your program every morning, above all the one on Sunday." He added, "Thanks for a swell program. Keep the good work up. We will always be listening. We are always sitting by the radio waiting for your programs to come on the air."[35] Signing himself "The Tennesse [*sic*] Kid," Dallas Lee Hawkins wrote that "us bunch of sailors is here in Miami in the Brig we heard you people singing and wondered if you would play some songs for us and my people."[36] Some servicemen even got into the fun of promoting flour. Writing from southern France, Ralph Barlow requested that Lair play a number, any number, for his four children. He ended, "All are ardent listeners & can they—the boys—inhale Hot Biscuits Made from your flour? Yes sir—!"[37]

Servicewomen also responded to the show. Private Thelma Pitts, a WAC serving at Camp Campbell, Kentucky, wrote, "As I stood in the Laundry room at the ironing board this morning clearing some red mud from Ft. Oglethorpe from my rain coat and listened to your program I couldn't help but think 'Thank God for that Program.'"[38] Ruth Cronan, who wrote that she had joined the WAVES despite her mother's disapproval, sent a poem to be read for the Mother's Day show so her mother would know just how much she meant to her.[39] The exuberant Private Goldie Hayes, a Kentuckian stationed at Fort Oglethorpe, wrote to Lair several times and had one of her poems selected for the *Gatherin'*. Like many listeners, Hayes found comfort in Lair's voice.

> The Army is'nt so bad, in fact, I really like it, but there are moments one has awful feelings. It's people like you and your programs that make us stop and realize things. It brings home nearer—no matter how far away you are. I'd truly be willing to go any-wheres in this world to help those who fight—just to keep that sweet peace we use to know and enjoy. We're coming back someday soon too! My Daddy died Dec. 6th and home will never be the same but we still have a lot to live for. To hear you reminds me of my Dad.[40]

In 1944 John Lair launched yet another enterprise, a monthly newspaper. The *Renfro Valley Bugle* contained information about the performers and goings-on at Renfro, as well as brief historical stories and, of course, letters and poems submitted or requested by subscribers. In October 1944 the requested poem began:

> You were in the Army, Dad;
>   'twas not so long ago.
> You wore the uniform I wear
>   and knew the things I know,
> You fought for things that you
>   hold dear, just like I soon
>   will do . . .
> That sort of makes us buddies,
>   Dad—you wore the khaki
>   too.[41]

The cover of the same issue of the *Bugle* features a story on the *Renfro Valley Barn Dance* and mentions a number of "old, familiar faces" missed during the past year, including "Homer and Jethro, Shorty Hobbs, the Holden Brothers and the rest of our boys now in the service of our country," as well as "Judy Dell, Guy Blakeman, Roland Gaines—those of the folks who left the Valley for the defence factories."[42] An issue a few months earlier also noted "while many of the Talent have been called by Uncle Sam . . . their places have been promptly filled and the show goes on. The Sunday morning program is especially important during these war times."[43]

While Lair insisted on the importance of his shows to the war effort, he realized that he had to be sensitive to the fact that listeners might wonder why his male performers were not in uniform. His sponsor also applied pressure on this point. In April of 1944 Vic Engelhard wrote him suggesting that Ballard & Ballard and all its subsidiary companies and radio programs should make a statement that their employees who had been called were either in the service or "have been deferred for some good sound reason." He added, "I think instead of attempting to make an excuse because someone is 4F we should take the positive position and capitalize on the fact that we are doing our part."[44] A few weeks later, in the script for the *Gatherin'*, Lair mentioned that performer Jack Holden was serving at Camp Gordon and added, "And right at this point maybe it might be a good idea to tell the folks about some of our boys in service and just why the others are not in. I guess maybe folks listenin' to these programs have wondered why some of our boys here now are not in uniform, and they're intitled to know."[45]

At the same time, performers exempt from service hoped that the war might provide them with new opportunities. Female performers, of course, had always been central to Lair's shows.[46] During the war years, male performers seeking employment quickly pointed out their status. As early as June 1942, Bill Ballard from Detroit wrote seeking work for his three-piece unit, "all southern & army exempt for quite some time."[47] In May of the following year Bill Devore from Horse Cave, Kentucky, wrote, seeking a job from Lair, "I'm past the army age and play the five string banjo, have two daughters that play with me."[48] Some active servicemen also hoped to eventually find employment with Lair. In 1944 Sgt. Edwin Fulkerson wrote from Germany that he had "not been able to tune in W.H.A.S. & listen to your program lately." Despite the war, Fulkerson and his friends found a "silver lining" in the hillbilly group they had been able to form that "met with the approval of our fellow 'buddies' here." Fulkerson added, "We feel that if given a proper audition we can make some program on our return. Yours would be our choice."[49]

Although John Lair focused primarily on entertaining the home folks during the war, his shows could sometimes be heard overseas, broadcast over shortwave radio, and some servicemen also had copies of the *Bugle* sent to them by their families. In October of 1943 Charles E. Arnett of Renfro Valley Enterprises, Inc., sent letters to Keen Johnson, the governor of Kentucky, as well as Senator Alben Barkley, expressing Lair's interest in sending Renfro performers overseas: "Mr. John Lair, in the interest of the war program, would like to send a unit of not less than seven people to England, or elsewhere to entertain the soldier boys. Many of which come from the mountains of Kentucky, Tennessee, North Carolina, West Virginia, Maryland and other mountainous states, and who I'm sure are longing for some of their own kind of music." Earlier in the letter, noting the popularity of the Renfro programs broadcast on the CBS network, he commented, "We have heard from General McArthur [sic] regarding our programs."[50] A few weeks later, Arnett sent a similar letter to Eleanor Roosevelt, although her secretary quickly replied that the first lady had "nothing to say in regard to the entertainment sent to the boys overseas."[51]

Senator Barkley, a native of Kentucky and future vice president of the United States, did write back to say that he would be glad to bring Arnett's request to the attention of the USO. He added, "I was at the White House the night the Renfro Valley group entertained the King and Queen of England and enjoyed it very much."[52] A month later, Lou Wolfson of the Overseas Department of USO-Camp Shows, Inc., in New York wrote to Arnett, stating that they would be happy to consider a unit from Renfro. He added, "Of course, one thing must be understood; there can be no commercial tie-up for this unit, as the War Department does not allow any group sponsored by a commercial organization to go overseas." Wolfson noted that the FBI would have to clear each performer first, and he requested further information about the acts.[53] Arnett responded that the group they hoped to send included Molly O'Day, Lynn Davis, Slim Miller, and the Coon Creek Girls. Although he mentioned the Coon Creek's legendary performance before the king and queen at the White House in 1939, the lineup of the group he proposed to send overseas—Molly O'Day, Opal Amburgey, and the Travers Twins—included none of the performers who had sung in D.C. Arnett also mentioned that Slim Miller had served in the last war and the army had recently turned down Lynn Davis, "so I feel sure that we would have no trouble getting draft releases on these male members of the unit."[54]

John Lair never did send a performing troupe overseas, but Renfro Valley went beyond regular programming in doing its part for the war effort. In November of 1943 Vic Engelhard of Ballard & Ballard wrote to Charles Arnett encouraging him to schedule a visit to an army hospital in Louisville when one of the traveling shows passed through the area. He added, "While it is true that no publicity will be given to anyone in connection with this show, it seems to me that since these boys did enjoy the previous show that we should go out of our way to do a job for them when we are so close."[55] Indeed the month before, the chief recreation worker at the hospital had expressed enthusiasm for the program in a memo to a colleague: "The hillbilly show, given by the Renfro Valley Barn Dancers, and sponsored by Ballard & Ballard Flour Co., is the best show of the kind we have been able to secure at Nichols General Hospital. Their singing is good, their jokes funny without being vulgar, and their girls attractive-looking and entertaining. They are cooperative and a pleasant group with which to work. The patient reaction was splendid."[56] The following year, Ballard & Ballard, in conjunction with radio station WRVA, presented "Renfro Valley Folks Special War Bond Barn Dance" at the Mosque Theater in Richmond, Virginia. Rather than performers from the road-show units, this special performance featured Lair himself as emcee, as well as some of the Renfro stars, including Slim Miller and the Coon Creek Girls.[57]

As the war dragged into 1945, the letters to Lair became even more heartfelt. The majority of listeners found comfort in Lair's shows, particularly the *Sunday Morning Gatherin'*. However, although Lair had been largely successful at gauging the sentiments of his listeners, he received a strong rebuke from a woman writing from Danville, Kentucky: "How can you big strong men sit back and carry on all this non-sense when so many people are in such distress? There never was a time when so many are in trouble and times should be devoted to prayer and serious thinking for our boys who are going thru hell for you. There is no devotions or prayers over the radio for boys and their families who are suffering many deaths. No one who has their heart on this troubled world can sit back and act a fool."[58] Lair not only acknowledged her note on the *Gatherin'*, he also had Ballard award the author a twenty-five-dollar check. "I guess in broadcasts like this the usual procedure is to award the prize to those who brag on the program most and say nice things about us, but Mrs. H. Quinn, of Danville, Ky, didn't mince matters at all when she sailed into us for going along our way on our daily broadcasts with music and fun when there was so much pain and suffering in the world today," Lair announced. While suggesting that perhaps people needed a little laughter and music, Lair conceded that Quinn had a point:

> Where she hits us all is in her calling attention to the fact that of all the programs on the air, no one regularly devotes any part of its time to a prayer for our boys in the thick of battle. You know, that's a pretty terrible indictment of radio programs and we who make them up, we should have thought of it ourselves, but we just didn't do it. I guess a lot of folks have thought about it, but maybe lacked the courage of Mrs. Quinn to come out

with it. Well, you may be sure that at least one radio program is going to carry such a period from now on—starting right this morning and continuing as long as our listeners request it.[59]

A flood of letters ensued from listeners asking that loved ones in the service be placed on the "prayer list," a feature that Lair continued until the end of the war. In responding to Quinn, Lair turned a criticism into an asset. A few weeks after Lair began the new feature, Mrs. Harrison Gill wrote of the *Sunday Morning Gatherin'*, "I didn't think there could be any thing added. But since you added a special prayer for our boys, it is complete, it is perfect."[60]

Within a few months, Lair began to anticipate the coming peacetime. He spoke of the plans for building a new studio and museum and of his plans to help provide support for veterans. During the *Gatherin'* on July 7, 1945, Lair advised, "And, boys, when you come back frum over there I hope that many of you will be coming back to the farm you were raised on. You're needed there as much as anywhere else in the world."[61] When peace finally arrived in August, Lair celebrated the victory on air, and in the ensuing months helped distribute a book from Ballard & Ballard, *Welcome Home Civilian*, advising veterans of their new benefits. During the months following VJ Day, he read letters from mothers heartbroken that once their sons had returned home, they did not want to stay home, and he advised the young men to pursue their education.

Soon enough, however, John Lair and much of America eagerly sought to leave the war behind. Just two months after victory in Japan, Lair laid the cornerstone for his new building, a massive log and stone structure, which encompassed a museum of the past and a modern studio. The *Gatherin'* morphed back into a more secular show. When a listener in November 1945 wrote requesting that the show feature more nonreligious songs, Lair once again addressed the intent of the *Gatherin'*: "Our sincere and able ministers and our splendid churches are well able to take care of the religious phases of American life and our many beautiful hymns can bring the more sublime emotions to the soul. We'll be satisfied for our part if something you hear at the Renfro Valley Getherin' makes you a better neighbor, more considerate of the feelings of others, more appreciative of yore home and family."[62]

Two years after the end of the war, John Lair published a new *Renfro Valley Keepsake*. Barely this side of bankruptcy when the first *Keepsake* had been published in 1940, Lair in seven years had accumulated all the trappings of a country gentleman. The new publication included a photo of Lair's palatial new home, as well as pictures of Lair and his family with their favorite horses and ponies. Wartime had once again been good to John Lair. Lair had prospered with what country music historian Bill Malone has characterized as country music's "great wartime surge," but difficult changes lay on the horizon.[63]

In 1948 Ballard & Ballard withdrew its sponsorship of Lair's programs, the worst of a number of business setbacks Lair suffered during the late 1940s. While the next decade would bring a few notable achievements for Lair, including the lucrative General Foods sponsorship of the early 1950s and a brief television show sponsored by Pillsbury in the mid-50s, the tide began to turn against John Lair. Taste in country music moved away from the old-fashioned and traditional fare that Lair favored. Recording companies reassumed ascendancy in country music, and the double whammy of disc jockey radio and the birth of commercial television came close to polishing off the radio barn dance. Finally, Lair stood in no position to compete with the growing Nashville-based country music industry. Still, Lair was no quitter. He ran Renfro Valley until 1968, when he sold it to Nashville-based interests. In 1976, frustrated with the changes he saw taking place before his eyes, he bought it back. John Lair died in 1985, at the age of ninety-one, still the owner of Renfro Valley.

John Lair's active career spanned over a half century. If Lair discovered his talents as a soldier during the First World War, he fully realized his dreams during World War II. Despite all the challenges the war posed for the new financial enterprise, Renfro Valley hit its peak during wartime. A nation heartsick and homesick found solace in Lair's valley "where time stood still." Time unfortunately did not actually stand still at Renfro Valley, and eventually Lair would have to promote Renfro to older listeners nostalgic for the valley's glory days. However, during the 1940s, Lair accurately took the temperature of his audience and captivated the attention of both young and old alike, at home and in the service. In 1944, W.S. Frye, a World War I veteran, wrote to Lair of his family, expressing how a passion for the music promoted by Lair cut across the generations: "A lot has happened since I was in France 26 years ago and today I have a boy in France some where. He is just an old fashioned kind who likes the old songs and the old string music just like I always did and still do. His mother is an Army nurse. I met her in the last war and she too loves the old time songs."[64]

Acknowledgments

This article is largely based on materials in the John Lair Collection at Berea College, as well as oral history interviews, funded by a grant from the Kentucky Oral History Commission. Thanks, as always, to Harry Rice, for his help identifying relevant materials in the Lair Collection. Thanks also to my former graduate assistants, David Baxter, Larry Morrisey, and Brian Gregory, for their able work on the Lair project, as well as to my current assistant, Rachel Baum, for her always helpful editorial advice.

Notes

1. John Lair, *Renfro Valley Then and Now* (privately published, 1957), 31.

2. As Sam M. Lewis and Joe Young wrote in their famous postwar song of 1919: "How ya gonna keep 'em, down on the farm, After they've seen Paree? How ya gonna keep 'em away from Broadway; jazzin' aroun', And paintin' the town?"

3. "Frank Tinney Shines in 'Atta Boy,'" *New York Times,* December 24, 1918. Although in *Renfro Valley Then and Now,* Lair mentions returning from the army in 1918, army records indicate that his service was from September 20, 1917, to March 3, 1919.

4. John Lair, typed manuscript on microfiche, Country Music Foundation, Nashville, Tennessee.

5. Program, "Atta Boy. Camp Meigs Washington D.C.," (n.d.), box 1, John Lair Collection, Southern Appalachian Archives, Berea College (hereafter abbreviated as Lair Collection).

6. John L. Lair, Headquarters Co., A.R.D., *Lest We Forget,* n.d., box 1, Lair Collection.

7. John Lair, typed manuscript on microfiche, n.d., Country Music Foundation, Nashville, Tennessee.

8. Barbara Lair Smith, interview by Larry Morrisey, Hopkinsville, Kentucky, October 25, 1996, tape recording, author's collection.

9. Although the Little and Big Renfro creeks existed in Rockcastle County, a community called Renfro Valley did not exist until Lair invented it.

10. John Lair, interview by Loyal Jones, April 30, 1974, Renfro Valley, Kentucky, tape recording, Lair Collection.

11. In March 1939, more than six months before Lair left Cincinnati, WLW returned to a normal power of fifty kilowatts. After moving to Renfro Valley, Lair continued to use WLW to broadcast his shows until the spring of 1941, when he switched affiliation to WHAS in Louisville.

12. Freeman Keyes to John Lair, March 10, 1942, box 16, Lair Collection.

13. John Lair to Freeman Keyes, March 18, 1942, box 16, Lair Collection.

14. John Lair to Freeman Keyes, February 12, 1941, box 16, Lair Collection.

15. Ann Lair Henderson, interview by Larry Morrisey, Mt. Vernon, Kentucky, May 22, 1997, tape recording.

16. Jerry Byrd, telephone interview by Larry Morrisey, February 14, 1997, tape recording.

17. Scripts, "Monday Night Show," August 5, August 19, September 9, 1940, box 36, Lair Collection.

18. Homer and Jethro, "From Moonshine to Martinis," *Journal of Country Music* 16, no. 1 (1995): 4–5.

19. Emory and Linda Martin, interview by David Baxter, Mt. Vernon, Kentucky, May 16, 1995, tape recording.

20. Ibid.

21. Gene Cobb to John Lair, November 2, 1943, box 7, Lair Collection.

22. Gene Cobb to John Lair, November 8, 1943, box 7, Lair Collection. While "red weeks" may refer to rationing, it probably means the weeks when the show failed to make a profit and was "in the red."

23. Over 5,600 War Price and Rationing Boards, conceived of by the government as "committees of neighbors," existed to administer the rationing overseen by the Office of Price Administration. Gasoline, rationed from May 1942 to August 1945, was allocated according to differential coupon rationing, which provided shares of the commodity according to varying needs. See U.S. Office of Price Administration, *Rationing in World War II* (Washington, D.C.: GPO, 1946), 2–3.

24. Ches Davis to John Lair, October 17, 1943, box 7, Lair Collection.

25. The show is also referred to as the *Renfro Valley Gatherin'*. Lair also used the spelling "Getherin'," especially in the early years.

26. Linda and Emory Martin interview.

27. Barbara Lair Smith, interview by David Baxter, Hopkinsville, Kentucky, March 3, 1995, tape recording.

28. Linda and Emory Martin interview.

29. Script, *Sunday Morning Gatherin'*, September 5, 1943, box 48, Lair Collection. Lair typically used "eye dialect" in his scripts. I have retained his original spellings.

30. Virgie Grantham to John Lair, October 10, 1943, box 71, Lair Collection.

31. Marjorie Bains to John Lair, n.d., box 71, Lair Collection. Marjorie Bains's letter was read on the *Gatherin'* on November 4, 1943, for the show honoring the twenty-fifth anniversary of Armistice Day.

32. See Brian Gregory, "'I'm So Anxious to See Renfro Valley': Traditional Music, Modern Architecture, and the Semiotics of Attraction at an Early Site of Auto Tourism" (paper presented at annual meeting of the Southeast Chapter, Society of Architecture Historians, 1999); and Kristine M. McCusker, "'Dear Radio Friend': Listener Mail and the National Barn Dance, 1931–1941," *American Studies* 39, no. 2 (summer 1998): 173–95.

33. Eloise Gilchrist to John Lair, August 26, 1944, box 72, Lair Collection.

34. Pvt. Jerry P. Barlow to John Lair, October 10, 1943, box 71, Lair Collection.

35. Pvt. Robert Williams to John Lair, n.d., box 71, Lair Collection.

36. Dallas Lee Hawkins to John Lair, February 20, 1944, box 71, Lair Collection.

37. Ralph W. Barlow to John Lair, January 23, 1945, box 72, Lair Collection.

38. Pvt. Thelma L. Pitts to John Lair, September 19, 1943, box 71, Lair Collection.

39. Ruth M. Cronan to John Lair, April 6, 1944, box 72, Lair Collection.

40. Pvt. Goldie Hayes to John Lair, January 23, 1944, box 71, Lair Collection.

41. *Renfro Valley Bugle* 1, no. 9, October 15, 1944, 3.

42. Ibid., 1.

43. Ibid., no. 4, May 14, 1944, 3.

44. V.H. Engelhard to John Lair, April 13, 1944, box 16, Lair Collection.

45. Script, *Sunday Morning Gatherin'*, May 7, 1944, box 48, Lair Collection.

46. See Michael Ann Williams, "Home to Renfro Valley: John Lair and the Women of the Barn Dance," in *The Women of Country Music: A Reader*, ed. Charles K. Wolfe and James E. Akenson, 88–108 (Lexington: University Press of Kentucky, 2003).

47. Bill Ballard to John Lair, n.d. (answered by Lair, June 30, 1942), box 7, Lair Collection.

48. Bill Devore to John Lair, May 23, 1943, box 71, Lair Collection.

49. Sgt. Edwin P. Fulkerson to John Lair, September 28, 1944, box 71, Lair Collection.

50. Charles E. Arnett to Gov. Keen Johnson, October 27, 1943, box 7, General Business Correspondence 1943, Lair Collection. A handwritten note on the letter states that it was also sent to Senator Barkley.

51. Charles E. Arnett to Eleanor Roosevelt, November 7, 1943, and Malvina C. Thompson to John Lair, November 13, 1943, both in box 7, Lair Collection.

52. Sen. Alben W. Barkley to Charles E. Arnett, November 6, 1943, box 7, Lair Collection.

53. Lou Wolfson to Charles E. Arnett, December 6, 1943, box 7, Lair Collection.

54. Charles E. Arnett to Lou Wolfson, December 15, 1943, box 7, Lair Collection.

55. V.H. Engelhard to Charles Arnett, November 19, 1943, box 16, Lair Collection.

56. Memo, Mary Rehfuss to Pauline McCready, October 22, 1943, box 16, Lair Collection.

57. Program, Renfro Valley Folks Special War Bond Barn Dance, November 20, 1944, box 1, Lair Collection.

58. Postcard, Mrs. H. Quinn to John Lair, January 9, 1945, box 72, Lair Collection.

59. Script, *Sunday Morning Gatherin'*, January 21, 1945, box 49, Lair Collection.

60. Mrs. Harrison Gill to John Lair, February 11, 1945, box 72, Lair Collection.

61. Script, *Sunday Morning Gatherin'*, July 7, 1945, box 50, Lair Collection.

62. Script, *Sunday Morning Gatherin'*, November 25, 1945, box 50, Lair Collection.

63. Bill C. Malone, *Country Music, USA,* rev. ed. (Austin: University of Texas Press, 1985), 18. See chapter 6 for a complete account of the expansion of country music during the war.

64. W.S. Frye to John Lair, June 10, 1944, box 72, Lair Collection.

6

Hayloft Patriotism

The National Barn Dance *during World War II*

Wayne W. Daniel

World War II, beginning on September 1, 1939, and ending on September 2, 1945, has been ranked with the Civil War and the Great Depression as one of the three most traumatic epochs in American history.[1] As long as the fighting was limited to belligerent nations across the seas, most Americans thought of the war as being far removed from their daily lives and something over which they had no control. All that changed on December 7, 1941, when Japan bombed Pearl Harbor and the United States became directly involved in the hostilities. Overnight, the war became the dominant force in the lives of American citizens. Old and young, frail and strong, and rich and poor joined in the quest of one objective—winning the war. The opposing forces were well defined, and the news media bombarded the populace with constant reminders of which was our friend and which was our enemy, making it easy to identify targets for the venting of outrage and anger. From the American point of view, the Allies composed the virtuous friend: the United Kingdom, China, the Soviet Union, and other supportive countries; conversely, the Axis represented the evil enemy: Germany, Italy, Japan, and other countries that sided with them. There quickly developed among Americans a widespread sense of "We're all in this together" that inspired both an eagerness to pitch in and a willingness to make personal sacrifices to aid the Allies in achieving a speedy victory. Americans from all walks of life planted Victory Gardens in anticipation of food shortages; collected tons of scrap metals, rubber, and other materials to be con-

Fig. 1. Burridge D. Butler, from the
WLS Family Album 1945. (Author's
collection.)

verted into tanks, planes, and guns; bought government-backed war bonds
and stamps to help finance the war; and stoically endured the rationing of
sugar, shoes, gasoline, and other essential household goods. These civilian
efforts on the "home front" were considered essential to the success of military personnel serving on the front lines of battle across the seas.[2]

The home-front phenomenon was a ready-made vehicle for the expression of the populist and patriotic sentiments of Burridge D. Butler,
owner of Chicago's radio station WLS and its corporate parent, the *Prairie
Farmer*, an influential Midwestern agricultural newspaper. Butler realized
the value of radio in the mobilization of Americans for defense and used
the medium effectively throughout the war. He inspired the station's employees to participate in a phenomenal patriotic undertaking that included
all the elements of the home front: war bond sales, scrap material collecting, Victory Garden cultivation, and other activities designed to further the
war effort. Station personnel followed Butler's direction as a matter of course,
for their employer had a long history of community service. Since 1925 the
WLS Relief Fund had raised money to help victims of natural disasters. A
Neighbor's Club, organized in 1935, funneled listener donations into chari-

Fig. 2. The cast of the *National Barn Dance* in October 1944. (Author's collection.)

table channels at Christmas time. Other WLS-sponsored service activities included the operation of a community kitchen during the Depression, education and promotion in rural fire-prevention, home talent shows, and regular broadcasts of educational programs for classroom use in the Midwest's public schools.[3] Now that his country was at war, Butler, in an editorial statement, reminded WLS listeners, *Prairie Farmer* readers, and his employees that "There is work to do, early and late, the biggest job in all the history of mankind. We are charged with the tasks of the home front. Soldiers march, and so do we!"[4]

WLS, a 50,000-watt station since 1931, was famous for its agricultural news and service to Midwest farmers, as well as its generous array of entertainment geared to their tastes. For years the WLS daily schedule featured heavy doses of live hillbilly and western music. During the war, the station's broadcast day began with four or more acts performing on the *Smile-a-While* program from 5:00 to 6:00 AM. This program was followed by six quarter-hour programs featuring one or two individual acts. At least two acts were heard on the *Prairie Farmer Dinnerbell Time*, which aired from

Fig. 3. The cover of this *National Barn Dance* souvenir program bears the autographs of many of the show's artists. (Author's collection.)

12:00 to 12:30. Mid-afternoon listeners could tune in to another thirty-minute program given over entirely to cowboy and mountain music. The Saturday night offering, including the *National Barn Dance,* typically ran five hours, from 7:00 PM to midnight. Because of the large number of rural-oriented musicians heard on WLS and other Windy City stations, Chicago gained the nickname "Hillbilly Heaven."[5]

The *National Barn Dance* was the crème de la crème of WLS programs. It was one of the first and most influential of the numerous combination stage show and radio program productions that were broadcast by radio stations all across the country from the 1920s to 1960. The show, first heard on WLS on April 19, 1924, remained the station's most popular offering until WLS dropped it from its program lineup in April 1960. By the 1930s the *Barn Dance* aired from early Saturday evening to midnight. In 1933 an hour-long segment of the show began airing on the NBC radio network.[6] At the time of the outbreak of World War II the *National Barn Dance* was heard on sixty-seven NBC stations around the country and boasted a cast of more than one hundred performers, who were fondly referred to as the Hayloft Gang.[7]

Among the more popular *Barn Dance* artists during the war years were Louise Massey and the Westerners, a family act that featured vocalist Louise

Fig. 4. *National Barn Dance* performers Lulu Belle and Scotty. (Courtesy of Lulu Belle Wiseman Stamey.)

Massey's western songs and love ballads; the Hoosier Hot Shots, a four-man novelty act; Red Foley, a ballad singer who became a country music superstar after the war; Patsy Montana, a singer of western songs, whose recording of "I Wanna Be a Cowboy's Sweetheart" became country music's first million-seller by a female artist; the Prairie Ramblers, a four-man combo that played string band music with a western flair interspersed with selections from an eclectic vocal repertoire of solos, duets, trios, and quartets; Lulu Belle and Scotty, a husband-and-wife team whose musical offerings included novelty pieces, folk songs, and current country compositions sung to their own guitar and banjo accompaniment; and Luther Ossenbrink, known to radio listeners as Arkie the Arkansas Woodchopper, who played guitar, sang, and called the square dances on the *Barn Dance* shows.[8]

Fig. 5. The Prairie Ramblers, ca. 1943. Left to right: Jack
Taylor, Alan Crockett, Dale "Smokey" Lohman, Chick Hurt.
(Courtesy of Nancy Hurt Perrigo.)

Following the attack on Pearl Harbor, WLS officials wasted no time in
utilizing the station's lineup of *Barn Dance* talent in a demonstration of support for the war effort. Station management allotted the Chicago Defense
Committee five hundred seats in the twelve-hundred-seat Eighth Street Theater, home of the Saturday night *Barn Dance* since 1932. These seats were for
the use of soldiers and sailors wishing to attend the performances of the *Barn
Dance* on December 20 and 27. WLS's general manager announced that more
seats for service personnel would be made available upon request.[9]

Throughout the war years, the NBC segment of the *National Barn Dance*
was often organized around some patriotic theme featuring relevant dialogue and music. On the January 24, 1942, show, for example, the Hayloft

Gang presented a musical salute to the nations allied with the United States. The theme for the May 16, 1942, broadcast was a "Red, White and Blue" party in honor of "I Am an American Day." The December 5, 1942, program was devoted to recognition of the first anniversary of the Japanese attack on Pearl Harbor. All of the musical selections featured on this show were war related, including the square dance number "Soldier's Joy," a banjoist's rendition of "Stars and Stripes Forever," and "Soldier, Will You Marry Me?" sung by Lulu Belle and Scotty.[10]

National Barn Dance shows became staple attractions of the United Service Organizations for National Defense, Inc. Known as the USO, the organization was established on February 4, 1941, for the purpose of providing social, welfare, and recreational services for members of the United States Armed Forces and their families.[11] *National Barn Dance* entertainers chalked up an impressive record of personal appearances on behalf of the USO. By the end of October 1942, for example, one USO "Camp Show" unit consisting of *National Barn Dance* talent had given a show a day for 139 days.[12] The unit started out in Illinois the first of June and wound up the month at an army hospital in Massachusetts, after having played for troops quartered all over New England. At the end of the tour this *Barn Dance* contingent had covered ten thousand miles and performed in twenty-five states.[13] Other *Barn Dance* performances designed for the entertainment and aid of armed services personnel included a sold-out show before more than twelve thousand fans in Cleveland, Ohio, for the benefit of the local Stage Door Canteen, a gathering place for servicemen that provided free food and drink and a chance to dance with stars of stage and screen and chat with other entertainment personalities.[14] In January 1942 and again in February 1943, the *Barn Dance* gang journeyed to Buffalo, New York, to entertain for the benefit of the Smokes-for-Soldiers Fund. The 1942 Buffalo gig, a three-hour show that included the NBC broadcast, drew a crowd of more than twelve thousand fans.[15] In the fall of 1945 the Hoosier Hot Shots were part of a USO Camp Show that performed for troops in Europe. Theirs was the only *Barn Dance* act to participate in overseas entertainment on behalf of the war effort.[16]

World War II was financed in part through the sale of war bonds and war stamps. Stamps priced from ten cents to five dollars and bonds that could be bought for $18.75 (worth $25.00 at maturity) enabled children and low-income citizens to participate in this home-front effort. Between September 1942 and the end of the war in 1945, the United States con-

Fig. 6. Western singer Patsy Montana in 1945. (Courtesy of Patsy Montana.)

ducted seven nationwide war bond drives.[17] Along with Boy Scouts, Girl Scouts, movie stars, and other organizations, celebrities, and businesses, the *National Barn Dance* performers and their WLS colleagues could be counted on to publicize, promote, and participate in these bond drives. For example, admittance to some *Barn Dance* shows required the purchase of a war bond. To kick off the seventh war loan drive, the *Dinnerbell* program was broadcast direct from the Chicago Treasury Center.[18] Individual performers and small groups of *Barn Dance* acts sold war bonds at their personal appearances; for example, Patsy Montana sold $6,000 worth of war bonds at a 1943 one-day booking in Illinois.[19] Attending a *Barn Dance* show was not the only way that fans could participate in WLS's war bond initiative. On August 8, 1942, listeners were informed that "Last week WLS accepted the invitation of the United States Treasury Department, which authorizes WLS to sell War Bonds over the air directly." The announcement reminded listeners, "You farm folks won't have to take time away from the task at hand for a trip to the local War Bond headquarters to purchase your share." All they had to do was send their money by mail to WLS.[20]

WLS and the *Barn Dance* performers were duly rewarded for their efforts on behalf of the bond drives. In 1942 in recognition of the fact that all WLS–*Prairie Farmer* employees were buying U.S. war bonds on the payroll allotment plan, the U.S. Treasury presented Burridge D. Butler with a Minute Man flag that took its place below the American flag on the pole atop the WLS–*Prairie Farmer* headquarters building.[21] For their assistance with bond drives, more than fifty *Barn Dance* cast members were awarded individual citations by a Treasury Department representative onstage at the Eighth Street Theater on Saturday night, November 11, 1944.[22]

Over three years earlier, on the day before the Japanese bombed Pearl Harbor, the *Wall Street Journal* had stated in a front-page article that "the biggest single threat to the defense program is the shortage of steel and iron scrap." The article went on to report that steel executives were urging the government to take the lead in encouraging all citizens to participate in a campaign that would salvage scrap from "every backyard and corner lot."[23] Aluminum was also in short supply, and housewives were urged to turn in their old pots and pans.[24] Eventually a shortage of labor in the forestry industry, accompanied by massive wartime demands for lumber, brought on a severe shortage of wood pulp for the manufacture of paper products.[25] With most of the world's rubber trees in the hands of the Japanese, America's meager reserves of one of its most in-demand materials began to rapidly dwindle, and once again citizens were called upon to donate their old overshoes, floor mats, hot water bottles, and other rubber goods to the cause.[26] WLS and the *National Barn Dance* artists answered these calls for help with a vengeance. *Barn Dance* performers partnered with local patriotic organizations in promoting the effort and collecting scrap materials. Throughout the Midwest, WLS listeners, in lieu of money, exchanged scrap metal, paper, or rubber for tickets to see performances of their favorite *Barn Dance* stars.

The price of admittance to a *Barn Dance* show in the summer of 1942 in Normal, Illinois, for example, was 100 pounds or more of scrap metal or 50 pounds or more of scrap rubber. The 7,500 fans who attended donated 600,000 pounds of scrap metal and nearly 60,000 pounds of scrap rubber. Donations included cream separators, obsolete farm machinery, and a junked automobile. The fan who brought in the most scrap, 4,190 pounds, won an all-expense-paid trip to Chicago.[27] To see one of three *National Barn Dance* shows presented in Ottawa, Illinois, in the summer of 1944, fans were required to donate 50 pounds of wastepaper. By August 1944, the

Fig. 7. During the war, the cover of each annual *WLS Family Album* depicted a scene that reminded readers of the impact of the global conflict on American homes. Here, a mother is shown reading a letter from her soldier son, whose picture is prominently displayed on the family radio. (Author's collection.)

National Barn Dance had aided in the collection of more than 3 million pounds of scrap metal, rubber, and wastepaper.[28] WLS became the first and, at the time, only radio station to receive a U.S. War Production Board Citation for salvage collection.[29]

Probably the most popular of the war's home-front projects was the Victory Garden program. Americans were encouraged to raise part of their food on whatever amount of soil might be available, whether a large farm or an apartment window box. Fearing they might, at any moment, be faced

Fig. 8. The cover of the 1943 edition of the *WLS Family Album*. The flag with the blue star indicates that a member of the household is serving in some branch of the U.S. military. (Author's collection.)

with a food shortage, gardeners and would-be gardeners responded by the millions.[30] As early as 1942 *Barn Dance* artists were diligently participating in the Victory Garden program. In 1943 some forty-five WLS–*Prairie Farmer* employees operated a Victory Garden on Burridge D. Butler's five-acre Burr Ridge Farm in suburban Chicago. Among the *Barn Dance* artists who participated in the project were the Hoosier Hot Shots, Connie and Bonnie Linder, Grace Wilson, Doc Hopkins and his band, Red Foley and his family, the DeZurik Sisters, the Arkansas Woodchopper, and Ted Morse, who performed under the names Otto and Little Genevieve. Since most of the *Barn Dance* performers had grown up on farms, tending a Victory Garden was an activity at which they could excel. And they did. Produce from the

1943 employee Victory Garden was not only consumed fresh, but almost two thousand cans of it were preserved and divided among the participants.[31] The following year the *Barn Dance* gang started the gardening season off with their usual enthusiasm. The theme of the April 15, 1944, *National Barn Dance* program was "Victory Gardens." The cast, carrying hoes, rakes, shovels, and other such tools, assembled onstage dressed in overalls, straw hats, and sunbonnets. The Hayloft Gang, in songs like "Get Out and Dig, Dig, Dig" and "Plant a Little Garden in Your Own Backyard," implored listeners to get involved in the Victory Garden program, while emcee Joe Kelly emphasized that Victory Gardening was "serious business."[32] In 1944 the National Victory Garden Institute presented *Prairie Farmer*-WLS gardeners with a plaque commemorating their "outstanding work in the nation in growing a company Victory garden."[33]

With the coming of war, *Barn Dance* artists added patriotic and war-related songs and tunes, both old and new, to their repertoires. These numbers, intended to inspire, motivate, and console a nation at war, were sung on radio programs and stage shows. Those artists who held recording contracts also preserved the songs on 78 rpm records. One of the first World War II–inspired songs to appear on the scene was "I'll Be Back in a Year, Little Darling." The song expressed the expectations of the young men who had been drawn into the war by the Selective Service Act of 1940, which took effect on October 16 of that year and authorized the drafting of qualified male citizens to serve for one year in the peacetime army.[34] When the Prairie Ramblers recorded the song on January 22, 1941, they became the first *National Barn Dance* act to record a patriotic World War II piece. "I'll Be Back in a Year, Little Darling" is about a soon-to-be service member who promises to do his best each day for the "good old USA" so the loved one he's leaving behind will be proud of her "soldier boy."[35] Red Foley recorded his version of the song on March 25, 1941.[36] The topicality of "I'll Be Back in a Year, Little Darling" was short lived. In the summer of 1941 the government extended the commitment of draftees for another year,[37] a turn of events that inspired another of country music's ubiquitous "answer" songs. In short order an enterprising songwriter began pitching an "Answer to I'll Be Back in a Year, Little Darling." Louise Massey and the Westerners, featuring Louise on vocals, recorded the answer song on May 29, 1941.[38] In the song, the left-behind female, who could be the sweetheart, wife, or mother, vows to be "brave and true" and "help the USA the best [she] can" while waiting for her soldier boy's return. Under the title "I'll Be Waiting for

Fig. 9. The Hoosier Hot Shots, ca. 1943, as pictured in the *WLS Family Album 1944*. Left to right: Paul (Hezzie) Trietsch, Otto (Gabe) Ward, Ken Trietsch, Frank Kettering. (Author's collection.)

You, Darlin'," Patsy Montana recorded the song on April 24, 1941.[39] Some six weeks later, on June 10, the Prairie Ramblers engaged a female vocalist, identified on the record label as Gale Ryan, to do the singing chores on their recording of the song.[40]

Among *Barn Dance* artists, the Hoosier Hot Shots possessed one of the most extensive repertoires of topical war songs. As one would expect from a novelty act, the Hot Shots took a light-hearted approach to the subject. They succeeded in injecting comic relief into the canon of war songs that was heavily laden with flag-waving musical tributes to military accomplishments and sentimental ballads about far-away sweethearts. They vow in "If It's Gonna Win the War" to make any necessary sacrifices in the pursuit of victory. In the case of gasoline rationing, for example, they declare that they must do less driving—"and more parking," as one of them gleefully proposes in a double-entendre off-mike interjection. Accompanied by realistic sound effects, the Hot Shots sing jauntily of "Rosie the Riveter," the celebrated symbol of the female factory worker whom they credit with "making history working for victory" while everyone stops to admire the scene of Rosie working on a B-19. Their song "She's up to Her Heart in Victory" laments the absence of women from bars, cabarets, and matinees, but discovers that "them girlies" are hard at work in their Victory Gardens. Progressively, from verse to verse, it creates mental images of the ladies up to their ankles, knees, and waists in a variety of vegetables. They're "up at all hours looking at them cauliflowers," the song exclaims, and "they're saving their scallions for Hitler's battalions." The army recruit in their "K.P. Serenade" says that his uniform is an apron, that he's learning to cook and bake, and when he's discharged he'll make a wonderful wife. The Hot Shots' recording of "She's Got a Great Big Army of Friends" relates the predicament of a navy admiral whose command is located near the residence of an extremely popular young lady. The sailors spend so much time at the home of the winsome lass, the admiral in frustration concludes that "that gal better move, or I'll have to move the Navy." Bessie of "Bye Bye, Bessie, Bye Bye" is a cow, and in the song the Hot Shots describe the scene in which her farmer-boy master bids her farewell before going off to war. Although in this country blackouts never acquired the urgency they did in England, Americans were sufficiently aware of their use in the overall defense effort to appreciate the humor in the Hoosier Hot Shots' rendition of "She Was a Washout in the Blackout." The opportunist in the song thought that after the city lights were quenched he might be able to make progress in the romance department. But when he put his arm around his date to "steal a little kiss" she socked him "in the kisser, and boy she didn't miss." When all other amorous overtures were rebuffed, the hapless swain concluded that maybe he ought to join the army. The Hot Shots performed their war-inspired songs regularly on the *National Barn Dance* and other radio programs, as well as on commercial recordings.[41]

By far the most popular World War II song recorded by a *National Barn Dance* artist was Red Foley's "Smoke on the Water," a composition predicting that there would be "smoke on the water, on the land and the sea" when the Axis powers were defeated. Foley recorded the song for the Decca label on May 4, 1944. The record debuted on *Billboard*'s list of "Most Played Juke Box Folk Records" on August 26 and appeared there for a total of twenty-seven weeks, occupying the number 1 spot for thirteen consecutive weeks. Between September 30 and December 16, Foley's record appeared on *Billboard*'s pop music chart of "Most Played Juke Box Records" for eleven weeks, of which four were spent in the Top Ten.[42]

Other topical songs of the World War II era recorded by *National Barn*

Fig. 10. *National Barn Dance* artist
Red Foley. (Courtesy of Rusty Gill.)

Dance artists include Jenny Lou Carson's self-penned "Dear God, Watch
Over Joe," Patsy Montana's "Good Night, Soldier," a novelty song titled
"Sergeant, Can You Spare a Girl?" recorded by the Prairie Ramblers, and
two instrumentals, "Army Rookie Polka" and "Sailor Boy," from Louise
Massey and the Westerners' recording session of January 23, 1941.[43]

Besides the USO, whose stage shows introduced the *Barn Dance* performers to new audiences, two other war-inspired initiatives provided them
with additional exposure: the Armed Forces Radio Service (AFRS) and V-
Discs. In 1942 the AFRS, a War Department agency created to maintain
satisfactory morale among army personnel, began transcribing U.S. radio
network programs for rebroadcast to millions of service personnel and other
listeners all over the world. The *National Barn Dance*, one of the programs
included on the AFRS roster, was heard regularly on these overseas broadcasts from 1942 to 1948. Commercials were removed from network programs rebroadcast for AFRS, which consequently reduced the length of the
programs. To fill in the time, musical selections, usually by an artist or
group associated with a given program, were added. AFRS broadcasts of
the *National Barn Dance*, for example, frequently ended with performances
by Louise Massey and the Westerners in what the announcers called "a
special after-show treat."[44]

Fig. 11. Louise Massey and the Westerners. Left to right: Louise Massey Mabie, Allen Massey, Milt Mabie, Curt Massey, Larry Wellington. (Courtesy of Barbara Wellington.)

V-Disc was the name appearing on the individual labels of a series of 12-inch, 78 rpm phonograph records produced during the war by a military group in New York. V-Discs were for the use of military personnel only and, pursuant to negotiations with the American Federation of Musicians and other organizations protective of music industry interests, it was agreed that no commercial exploitation of the recordings would be made at any time. Over the program's lifetime an estimated eight-million-plus V-Discs were shipped overseas for use by U.S. servicemen and women. While the vast majority of musicians recording on V-Discs were mainstream pop artists, the talents of a few of the more popular country music performers of the day were recruited for the program. The *National Barn Dance* was represented by Louise Massey and the Westerners in a 1942 session and by the Hoosier Hot Shots in a February 1945 session.[45]

While the war had a considerable impact on the professional careers of *National Barn Dance* performers, it also affected their personal lives in ways familiar to all Americans who lived through the era. After the government's

Fig. 12. *National Barn Dance* performer George Goebel. (Courtesy of
Rusty Gill.)

January 31, 1942, ban on the production of civilian cars and trucks,[46] *Barn
Dance* performers and other WLS staff members began looking for ways to
reduce the wear and tear on the vehicles that they would have to rely upon
until the war's end. Bicycling became popular within the WLS community,
and at least two *Barn Dance* acts, the Prairie Ramblers and the WLS Rangers, began carpooling between their homes and the WLS studios for their
daily programs. "Using this plan," opined a *Prairie Farmer* columnist, "will
mean a great saving on their cars and tires."[47] Some *Barn Dance* artists took
jobs in war plants,[48] and several others, of course, were drafted or volun-
teered to serve in various branches of the armed services. The most highly
publicized departure of a *Barn Dance* artist for duty in military service was
that of George Goebel, who had joined the *Barn Dance* roster as a singer in
1932 when he was thirteen years old. Goebel was inducted into the U.S.
Army Air Corps in a ceremony that took place on stage during a broadcast
of the Saturday night *National Barn Dance*.[49] After the war Goebel became a
popular television comedian.

    By mid-1945, with the end of the war in sight, the emphasis in pro-
gramming at WLS, as at other stations around the country, began to shift
from war themes to postwar issues.[50] *Barn Dance* artists who had gone off

Fig. 13. This scene on the cover of the 1945 edition of the *WLS Family Album* is described in the volume's editorial as representing "a beautiful story that is being re-enacted in many communities. The soldier father, returned from distant shores, sees his child for the first time." (Author's collection.)

to war began returning home, and the Hayloft Gang settled into its peacetime routine of providing rural-oriented entertainment for their millions of fans. With the coming of peace, the *National Barn Dance* cast could look back at an impressive record of patriotic service to the country during an era of heightened interest in, and expanded exposure for, country and cowboy music. During the first year of the war, radio's listenership had increased by 20 percent, and it remained at a high level for the duration.[51] Although such statistics indicate that Americans were spending more time at home, WLS officials, more than a year into the war, reported that up to that time gasoline rationing had had little effect on attendance at the Saturday night *Barn Dance* shows. The cast regularly played to sold-out audiences twice on Saturday nights.[52] Despite long-standing wartime travel restrictions, *National Barn Dance* talent regularly entertained full-house crowds at personal appearances. During the first six months of 1945 alone, for example, 237,225 fans attended performances by *Barn Dance* talent.[53] Even a nationwide law that went into effect on Saturday, April 1, 1944, increasing the tax on tickets to the *Barn Dance* from 10 percent to 20 percent and thereby raising their prices to eighty-five cents for adults and forty-five cents for children, appears to have had no effect on attendance.[54] After all, the median family income of Americans had increased by 64 percent since the beginning of the war.[55]

When World War II started, the *National Barn Dance* had been a regular Saturday night radio show for seventeen years. It would be heard for fifteen more years after the war ended. The WLS *National Barn Dance* was broadcast for the last time on Saturday night, April 30, 1960, after having been on the air for thirty-six years.

Notes

1. Studs Terkel, introduction to *The Homefront: America during World War II,* by Mark Jonathan Harris, Franklin D. Mitchell, and Steven J. Schechter (New York: Putnam, 1984), 11.

2. Richard R. Lingeman, *Don't You Know There's a War On? The American Home Front, 1941–1945* (New York: Putnam, 1970).

3. Wayne W. Daniel, "Vintage WLS: 75th Anniversary of Chicago's 'Shirt-Sleeve' Radio Station," *Nostalgia Digest,* August/September 1999, 26–35.

4. *WLS Family Album 1943* (Chicago: Prairie Farmer Publishing Co., 1942), 2.

5. *Billboard,* August 21, 1943, 6.

6. Wayne W. Daniel, "The National Barn Dance on Network Radio: The 1930s," *Journal of Country Music* 9, no. 3 (1983): 47–62; Wayne W. Daniel, "WLS National Barn Dance: Uptown Downhome Music in the Old Hayloft," *Old Time Country* 8, no. 1 (spring 1992): 14–18.

7. *Variety,* December 3, 1941, 42; *Billboard,* June 27, 1942, 6.

8. Wayne W. Daniel, "The Ranch Romance of Louise Massey & the Westerners," *Journal of Country Music* 20, no. 3 (1999): 37–41; Wayne W. Daniel, "'Are You Ready, Hezzie?' and Other Harmonious High Jinks of Those Hilarious Hoosier Hot Shots," *Nostalgia Digest,* October-November 1996, 26–30; Ronnie Pugh, "Red Foley, the Old Master," *Country Sounds,* March 1987, 16; Wayne W. Daniel, "Patsy Mon-

tana: Everybody's Sweetheart," *Old Time Country* 8, no. 1 (spring 1992): 6–10; Wayne W. Daniel, "The Prairie Ramblers," *Discoveries*, February 1999, 34–43; Wayne W. Daniel, "Lulu Belle and Scotty: Have I Told You Lately That I Love You," *Bluegrass Unlimited*, March 1986, 70–76.

9. *Variety*, December 17, 1941, 39.

10. Information on the content of *National Barn Dance* programs from recordings of the show and previews in the *Atlanta Journal* on January 24, 1942, and May 16, 1942.

11. *Encyclopædia Britannica,* Encyclopædia Britannica Premium Service, http://www.britannica.com/eb/article?eu=76267, s.v. "United Service Organizations, Inc."

12. *Variety*, October 28, 1942, 34.

13. *Prairie Farmer*, June 27, 1942, 9, and November 14, 1942, 28.

14. *Variety*, May 23, 1945, 6.

15. Ibid., January 28, 1942, 3, and February 11, 1942, 25; *Billboard*, January 2, 1943, 141; *Variety*, January 20, 1943, 36.

16. *Prairie Farmer*, September 1, 1945, 7, and October 13, 1945, 34.

17. Ad Access On-Line Project, Ad #R0108, John W. Hartman Center for Sales, Advertising & Marketing History, Duke University Rare Book, Manuscript, and Special Collections Library, http://scriptorium.lib.duke.edu/adaccess/warbonds.html.

18. *Prairie Farmer*, November 25, 1944, 28, and June 9, 1945, 22.

19. Ibid., August 7, 1943, 25.

20. Ibid., August 8, 1942, 20.

21. Ibid., July 25, 1942, 12; *WLS Family Album 1943*, 33.

22. *Prairie Farmer*, November 25, 1944, 28.

23. *Wall Street Journal*, December 6, 1941.

24. William L. O'Neill, *A Democracy at War: America's Fight at Home and Abroad in World War II* (New York: Free Press, 1993), 131.

25. Lingeman, *Don't You Know There's a War On?* 261.

26. O'Neill, *Democracy at War*, 91–92.

27. *Prairie Farmer*, June 27, 1942, 10, and July 11, 1942, 16.

28. Ibid., August 5, 1944, 22.

29. *Variety*, August 30, 1944, 28.

30. Lingeman, *Don't You Know There's a War On?* 251.

31. *WLS Family Album 1944* (Chicago: Prairie Farmer Publishing Co., 1944) 8, 9; *Prairie Farmer*, October 2, 1943, 29.

32. *National Barn Dance*, April 15, 1944, tape recording, in author's collection.

33. *Prairie Farmer*, January 22, 1944, 21.

34. Geoffrey Perrett, *Days of Sadness, Years of Triumph: The American People 1939–1945* (New York: Coward, McCann & Geoghegan, 1973), 39–40.

35. William Agenant, *Columbia 78 RPM Record Listing 2001 thru 21571 plus Okeh Records 18001 thru 18059* (Zephryhills, FL: Joyce Record Club, 1996), 30.

36. Cary Ginell, *The Decca Hillbilly Discography, 1927–1945* (New York: Greenwood Press, 1989), 181.

37. Martin Folly, *The United States and World War II: The Awakening Giant* (Edinburgh: Edinburgh University Press, 2002), 21.

38. Ronnie Pugh, Country Music Foundation, personal communication, February 9, 1998.

39. Ginell, *Decca Hillbilly Discography*, 222.

40. Agenant, *Columbia 78 RPM Record Listing*, 30.

41. War-related songs by the Hoosier Hot Shots can be heard on several extant tapes of *National Barn Dance* programs, as well as on CD compilations of their original 78 rpm recordings available at sagamorerecords.com. An extensive Hoosier Hot Shots discography can be viewed at hoosierhotshots.com.

42. "Most Played Juke Box Folk Records" and "Most Played Juke Box Records," *Billboard,* individual issues between September 30, 1944, and January 6, 1945.

43. Information on songs recorded by artists from, respectively, Ginell, *Decca Hillbilly Discography*, 153; ibid., 223; Cary Ginell and Kevin Coffey, *Discography of Western Swing and Hot String Bands, 1928–1942* (Westport, CT: Greenwood Press, 2001), 126; and Ronnie Pugh, Country Music Foundation, personal communication, February 9, 1998.

44. Harry Mackenzie, *The Directory of the Armed Forces Radio Service Series* (Westport, CT: Greenwood Press, 1999).

45. Richard S. Sears, *V-Discs: A History and Discography* (Westport, CT, Greenwood Press, 1980).

46. Folly, *United States and World War II,* 38.

47. *Prairie Farmer*, April 4, 1942, 28, and May 16, 1942, 16.

48. *WLS Family Album 1944*, 16.

49. *Prairie Farmer*, October 17, 1942, 30.

50. *Billboard*, June 23, 1945, 4.

51. Lingeman, *Don't You Know There's a War On?* 272.

52. *Variety*, January 20, 1943, 36.

53. Ibid., July 25, 1945, 30.

54. Ibid., April 5, 1944, 11; *Prairie Farmer*, April 15, 1944, 23.

55. U.S. Bureau of the Census, *Historical Statistics of the United States, Colonial Times to 1970*, Bicentennial edition, vol. 2 (Washington, D.C.: GPO, 1975), 301.

7

"Jesus Hits Like an Atom Bomb"

Nuclear Warfare in Country Music 1944–56

Charles K. Wolfe

Technology has always been a pervasive, if minor, theme in folk and country music. By the early nineteenth century many segments of rural America had already felt industrialization's impact, and the folk song archives are full of songs referring to the threat new machines posed to the agrarian lifestyle and value system. A song called "Peg and Awl," which contains references to "the year of eighteen and one," is the lament of a shoemaker who has lost his job to technology: the new machine can make "a hundred pairs to my one." "A Factory Girl," a widespread folk song detailing life in a textile mill, dates from Massachusetts of the 1830s. Most people have heard at least one version of "John Henry," with its affirmation of man over machine.

Many more songs emerged in the late nineteenth and early twentieth centuries to chronicle the industrialization of the South.[1] When commercial phonograph companies came into the region to record in the 1920s, they preserved and disseminated many of these songs. Traditional music became commercial country music, and singers found that middle-aged and younger generations of southern workers who were leaving the land for factories, railroads, or mines responded to songs about these new jobs. Many of the early important country singers, in fact, worked in some form of industry at one time or another in their careers. Kelly Harrell, John Carson (widely credited with making the first country record), Henry Whitter (the first country vocal specialist), Clayton McMichen (prime mover of the Skillet Lickers), Frank Hutchison, and blue yodeler Jimmie Rodgers all spent time as factory workers, miners, or railroad men.

Yet many of these songs of industrialism primarily describe the new working conditions southerners found themselves facing, and only tangentially address technology itself. The related themes of industrialism and technology do overlap at some points, but they should not be considered synonymous. "Technology" in one sense is broader than "industrialism," for it includes all responses to machinery by a variety of people, regardless of whether they encounter the technology in a factory job or simply experience a change in lifestyle because of new inventions. If we define industrialism only as a manifestation of technology in the labor market, then we are still left with a great many rural Americans in the 1920s who, though not factory workers, miners, or railroad men, still encountered technology directly in their lives through such devices as the radio, the telephone, the railroad, the automobile, the phonograph record, and various electric- and gasoline-powered appliances and tools.

Most southerners, beholden to an acute reverence for the past and tradition, were hesitant to accept the separate products of technology until they could figure out ways to assimilate them into their own lives.[2] One of the most common methods of assimilation was the song. In early pre-1935 country music, most technological references are to trains and automobiles; songs with such references by far surpass, both in number and popularity, songs about factory or mining life, or those about the radio, telephone, or other inventions. While this is not the time or place for a full survey of train and automobile songs, a brief discussion of them reveals how many such songs use similar patterns to make technological subjects more acceptable to the rural audience.

One of the first best-selling country records (at least one million copies) was "The Wreck of the Old 97," a chronicle of a 1903 train wreck near Danville, Virginia. The song, which celebrates a brave engineer who dies trying to master his machine, set the tone for many subsequent songs about brave engineers. In many of these songs the engineers provide an entree for rural society into the technological world of the railroad; they are human, flesh-and-blood heroes who control, or seek to control, these mechanical monsters. In other cases, such as "The Lightning Express," railroad men affirm sentiment and traditional humanist values in the cold, efficient world of railroad business management. Still other songs focus on the awesome effects of a railroad accident. As trains increasingly became part of the everyday lives of rural Americans, they also became appropriate metaphors for writers of gospel songs. Trains were viewed as inexorable forces carrying one to heaven ("Life's Railway to Heaven") or to hell ("That Hell-Bound Train"). Such metaphors allowed machines to represent traditional values, and thus to be integrated into the belief structure of the society.

Automobile songs provide an even better barometer of the fledgling commercial country industry's response to a technological change, because the automobile industry's full development did not occur until after the phonograph record industry had matured. From early pop songs like "Get Out and Get Under," which pokes fun at cars, the country music industry was, by 1926, producing hits like Uncle Dave Macon's "On the Dixie Bee Line," which praises the virtues of the "Henry Ford car." The mass-produced cars of the early 1920s quickly endeared themselves to the people of the South, who found these machines to be not at all intimidating; they could be endlessly repaired, tinkered with, and modified. The car was much less of a mystery than the railroad engine, the telephone, or even the phonograph record, and the late 1920s were awash in songs praising Fords, Chevrolets, and even Terraplanes. Today these songs sound like blatant commercials, but they were genuine expressions of the way people felt about the cars. A full list of these songs would be lengthy, but it would have to include "Over the Road I'm Bound to Go" (Uncle Dave Macon), "Riding in a Chevrolet Six" (Oscar Ford), "Chevrolet Car" (Sam McGee), and "An Automobile Trip through Alabama" (Red Henderson). This last piece is especially significant, for it is little more than a retelling of the well-known folk tale "The Incredible Hunt," with a surrealistically animated car playing a leading role. This particular performance is the most dramatic example of the way the automobile technology was integrated into the folk culture of the time.

In fact, a superficial examination of early folk and country songs about technology suggests that they embody a fairly distinct pattern of response. The technological advance usually appeared first as simply the subject of a song. Then, if the piece of technology affected the lives of a substantial number of people, it became a metaphor. Almost always the metaphor was molded into a traditional value system, and the new machine thus became a part of the culture spoken to by the music. This pattern can be seen in the gradual acceptance of the train, the quicker acceptance of the automobile, and the more diffuse acceptance of the telephone. A fuller and more complete study of these specific technological themes in country music is still necessary, and probably has not yet been undertaken because of the difficulty in establishing parameters for such a study.[3] These themes are extremely broad and reflected in a very wide spectrum of music, and are by no means extinct in modern country music. Indeed, new forms of technology continue to enter the lower-middle-class culture and find reflection in country music: airplanes, trucks, and CB radios represent only three very recent examples.

One technological theme, however, did enjoy a limited, intense, well-defined period of popularity in country music, and thus offers an inviting microcosm for one wishing to explore the interface between technology and tradition. The theme—the atomic bomb and atomic warfare—first emerged in the music in 1946, and by 1952 it had run its course; in between, it surfaced in some of the most interesting, and some of the most bizarre, country songs ever written. These songs not only offer us a model case study for the way in which country music, with its alleged conservatism and rural values, dealt with technology, but they also offer us insight into how the popular culture of the time responded to the most shattering technological advance in the twentieth century.

Country Music in Transition

Before we examine the specific products of country music's encounter with atomic energy, a note is in order about the musical era that produced these songs: the late 1940s. The interim between the end of World War I and the advent of Hank Williams has been shamefully neglected by historians of the music. The period does not seem quaint enough, or pure enough, to interest the devotees of old-time or hillbilly music, nor is it modern enough to interest the students of Hank Williams, Johnny Cash, or Sun Records. The major singers of this period—artists like Red Foley, Jimmy Wakely, and Tex Williams—have received less critical attention than third- or fourth-rate performers of the 1920s and 1930s. A few historians have recognized the significance of this era as a vital transitional era; Bill Malone has heralded the 1940s production of King records as a crucial watershed in the music's development, Doug Green and Ken Griffis have begun to document the western music of this period, and Ivan Tribe's inquiries into early bluegrass have made inroads into the era.[4] But, in general, we know far too little about the 1940s, the era when country music first began reaching a truly national audience.[5]

We do know that the postwar period was a boom time for country music. Dozens of independent record companies sprang up after the war, and everyone seemed to have money to buy records. The jukebox, having fully emerged as a major outlet for the music, made such an impact on country music that *Billboard* reported the top jukebox hits instead of over-the-counter sales. Radio, invigorated by the new transcription technology, provided a decent living for thousands of musicians. The concept of the album in record sales was not really yet a factor in country music—though the first country LPs were produced during this time—and the single was still the major medium for the music. With so many new record labels vying for songs and artists, competition was fiercer than at any time in music history. Many artists from the music's "golden age" (1925–35) were still active musical influences, and much of the 1940s' sound still retained some of the simplicity of the prewar music; yet the newer sounds, featuring the electric guitar, the steel guitar, and even an occasional horn, were also in evidence. On one hand was a demand for modernism in the music; on the other, a desire to return to the "normalcy" of prewar music. Country music was able to balance these two contradictory impulses much better than were other popular forms; jazz, for instance, quickly made its peace with the fact that postwar jazz was not to be a function of the big bands, but rather the small group bop of Parker and Gillespie. Country, for a while, had it both ways, and the songs in this study make evident this ambivalence.

Nuclear Country

The song that really started the fad for atomic bomb songs was Fred Kirby's "Atomic Power" (1946). "Atomic Power," for all practical purposes the first song to come to grips with the unique aspects of the unleashing of nuclear power, was by far the most commercially successful of all the atomic songs.[6] The song's commercial success and cogent statement of its theme made it the model for many of the songs that immediately followed. Consequently, looking more closely at the song's composer, history, and its introduction to the American public is warranted.

When he wrote "Atomic Power," Fred Kirby was a well-established singing star who had for years been a fixture in and around the Charlotte, North Carolina, area.[7] In the mid-1940s he was featured on the CBS network program "Carolina Calling," as well as a number of other shows originating at station WBT, Charlotte. Under circumstances that will be explained later, Kirby wrote the song the morning after the blasting of Hiroshima in August of 1945. For the next several months, Kirby would perform the song routinely on his local radio shows, including a disc jockey show he hosted called "Hillbilly Star Time," which broadcast at night. Kirby thinks that someone from the New York publishing firm of Leeds Music Corporation heard him sing the song live on one of these night programs. The firm at once flew a representative to Charlotte to secure publication rights, which pleased Kirby, to be sure, but he also wanted a chance to record the song.

Leeds apparently showed the song to Bob Miller, then working as a producer for RCA Victor Records. Miller offered Kirby "two sides" for Victor if he wanted to record it himself, but Kirby refused. "I didn't think it was worthwhile to go all the way to New York to tape two sides. In the meantime, the Sonora Record Company came down here to Charlotte and offered me a $2,000 bonus if I would record with them, and they would give me eight sides." Kirby signed with Sonora and soon went to New York to record a session for them, a session that included "Atomic Power." Miller, meanwhile, arranged to have the song recorded on Victor by the Buchanan Brothers, a north Georgia singing duo that was then riding the crest of newfound popularity resulting from several successful singles and a string of personal appearances.

Thus it came to be that on May 1, 1946, *Billboard* announced the release of two versions of "Atomic Power," Kirby's (Sonora H-7008) and the Buchanan Brothers' (Victor 20-1850). The limited resources of a fledgling independent label like Sonora were no match for the promotional and distribution system of an established company like Victor, and it was the latter's version that *Billboard* previewed in its influential "Reviews of New Records" section:

> BUCHANAN BROTHERS
> (Victor 20-1850)
> Atomic Power—FT; V. [vocal]
> Singing an Old Hymn—FT; V.
>
> During the three verses of "Atomic Power," the Buchanan Brothers (Chester and Lester) trace the history of the atomic bomb and issue a warning that all of us will be blown to Kingdom Come if the power is misused. It's a fast hymn-like tune and it keeps you listening. . . .
> The Buchanan Brothers are popular enough to make both sides pay off.[8]

The song caught on immediately in the country music record industry, which, in 1946, was burgeoning with dozens of new independent record companies, each hoping to get a piece of the lucrative jukebox trade and over-the-counter sales. The competition among record companies was probably more intense than at any time in history. Consequently, within three weeks of the first two versions' release, no fewer than three other cover versions of "Atomic Power" hit the market, with four more in production. These included versions by artists like cowboy singers Riley Shepard, Rex Allen, and Red River Dave, and country singers Rufe Davis and Red Foley, certainly the most popular country singer of the late 1940s. An advertisement taken out by Leeds in the May 25, 1946, issue of *Billboard* is headlined "The whole world is talking about ATOMIC POWER, the Greatest Folk Song in Twenty Years." Later, weekly ads ran under the headline "Atomic Power News" to keep readers abreast of the song's runaway success. One such ad, for June 8, 1946, announced that "Riley Shepherd [*sic*], the cowboy philosopher, is now rounding up 'buffaloes' for Juke Box Operators with that atomic song hit, 'Atomic Power.'" Shepard's cover version, incidentally, was the only cover to really achieve much success; it was the only other one previewed by *Billboard* (June 20, 1946). The trade described it as a "Western favorite with hymnal qualities," and predicted that the record "may show phono strength on the song popularity of 'Atomic Power.'"

To some extent all of this promotion paid off. The Buchanan Brothers' version of the record climbed onto the list of "Most-Played Juke Box Folk Records" on June 29, 1946, as one of the top six in the country.[9] It stayed on the list, hovering around the number 6 slot, for about a month, then quietly dropped off. Little was heard of the other versions, and Kirby himself recalls that he received most of his composer royalties from the Buchanan Brothers' version. Like many of the event songs of the 1920s, "Atomic Power" enjoyed an intense popularity for a few years; numerous well-established singers recorded it. Kirby himself became so identified with the song that it threatened to eclipse his other impressive achievements. He recalls hearing from numerous returning servicemen that they had heard the song translated into Japanese and German. Perhaps the most colorful illustration of the song's popularity came when Kirby was asked to ride in the inaugural parade for Harry Truman in January 1949. Kirby remembers: "I was passing by the reviewing stand, the stand with Truman and [Vice President Alben] Barkley, and our chief of police from Charlotte was just beyond that place and he could not resist—well, he did it before he even thought of it—he yelled 'Atomic Power!' just as I had bowed to the President and Barkley and the people in the stand. It scared me to death. And he said later that he would have given a million dollars for a hole to crawl in. But there were no holes." In fact, for years afterward, Kirby reports, "everywhere I'd go, instead of calling me Fred Kirby, they would say 'Atomic Power' and get my attention that way." Kirby still occasionally performed into the 1990s and had a regular children's television program over WBT, Charlotte, where he continued to get requests for "Atomic Power." Because he felt that the original song was somewhat dated, Kirby revised the song to bring it up to date in today's post-atomic world.

While it is always important to remember that the popularity of a song may result from a number of factors other than its content, the message of "Atomic Power" did reach a large part of its audience, as made evident by the other atomic-motif songs that appeared in its wake. Because of the influential nature of the song's content, it is appropriate to look closely at exactly what Kirby was saying in the song, and at the song's reflection of the broader attitude regarding the atomic era. The text of "Atomic Power," as sung by the Buchanan Brothers, is as follows:

Atomic Power
(Fred Kirby)

Oh this world is at a tremble with its strength and mighty power,
They're sending up to Heaven to get the brimstone fire,
Take warning my dear brothers, be careful how you plan,
You're working with the power of God's own holy hand.

Refrain   Atomic power, atomic power,
           Was given by the mighty hand of God,
           Atomic power, atomic power,
           It was given by the mighty hand of God.

You remember two great cities in a distant foreign land,
When scorched from the face of earth, the power of Japan,
Be careful my dear brothers, don't take away the joy,
But keep it for the good of man, and never to destroy.

Refrain

Hiroshima, Nagasaki, paid a big price for their sins,

Scorched from the face of the earth, their battles could not win,
But on that day of judgment, when comes a greater power,
We will not know the minute, and will not know the hour.

Refrain

© Copyright 1946 by MCA Music, a division of MCA Inc.
Used by permission. All rights reserved.

Three major motifs emerge from the song: a warning about the possible consequences of fooling with such awesome power, a noticeable lack of revenge sentiment in the references to Japan, and, finally, an association of atomic power with God. The warning, as expressed in stanza 1, was part of the common popular reaction to the news of the atomic bomb: a tendency to worry about how anyone was going to control the use of the new force. Scholars of science fiction have noted that the belief that "there are things man was not meant to know" has been quite common in twentieth-century popular culture; the actual phrase was apparently popularized in the original *Frankenstein* film of 1933,[10] but the sentiment—a general suspicion toward the dramatic advances of modern science—gained new credence in the atomic era. As the *Billboard* review made clear when it noted that "all of us will be blown to Kingdom Come if the power is misused," few people missed the warning Kirby was offering. Kirby, for his part, was working in a songwriting tradition that was conventionally moralistic and cautionary; even in the nineteenth century, Americans often changed the Old World form of folk ballads by adding a moral to them, and the event songs of the 1920s—chronicles of disasters, murders, outlaws, and tragedies—were seldom subtle in stating the lesson that listeners were to learn from the event at hand.

The references to Japan are remarkably magnanimous, considering that Kirby wrote the song while songs like "Smoke on the Water" were still popular. Kirby says that we are not to take satisfaction from the destruction of Hiroshima and Nagasaki; on the contrary, we are to be unsettled by it. Not that there is any hint of whose responsibility the bombing was: the cities simply paid a price for their "sins."

Pulling God into the song, giving it a "hymn-like" quality, is perhaps the most significant aspect of "Atomic Power." The country music audience—still heavily rural in 1946, still lower and middle class, still the product of southern Protestant values—must have seen in the atomic bomb a phenomenon for which no superlative in their vocabulary, no metaphor in their folk speech, was adequate. The power of the Hiroshima blast was widely reported as being the equivalent of twenty thousand tons of TNT, but how many people had ever witnessed the detonation of twenty thousand tons of TNT? Unlike the earlier manifestations of technology, the bomb offered no easy way for the people to integrate it into their lives. Their natural response was to turn to the most effective superlative they knew: religion.

Fred Kirby confirmed that he wrote the song from religious impulses. "I wrote it the morning after the blasting of Hiroshima. It was just such a shock. I know I heard about it that night and I couldn't hardly sleep. And the next morning I yelled 'Atomic Power' and I just felt spiritually toward writing the song. This was an idea that should not be used to destroy mankind, but to benefit mankind, who had such energy. It was a kind of spiritual feeling that came over me and that's why I wrote it." Did Kirby classify the song as a hymn or sacred song? "I would say as a . . . spiritual type, because it's fast moving, as they sing the old time religion, you know, with a beat to it." After the song became popular, Kirby sang it often, though not exclusively, in churches.

When he wrote and recorded "Atomic Power," Fred Kirby had a secure reputation as a songwriter and singer, but not especially as a gospel singer or writer. A native of Florence, South Carolina, Fred was playing and singing on Charlotte radio station WBT by the time he was eighteen. Like most singers of the time, he started out doing numbers in the style of Jimmie Rodgers, and his first recordings, made for Victor (Bluebird) in Charlotte in 1936, were songs in this vein. Most of Kirby's recorded repertoire, in fact, comprised cowboy songs and blues like "Columbus Stockade Blues." During World War II he traveled to a number of stations as "The Victory Cowboy" and was awarded a special citation by Secretary of the Treasury Henry Morgenthau for his work in selling war bonds, raising money for the Red Cross and March of Dimes, and entertaining in service hospitals. He made a film, *Kentucky Jubilee,* in 1945, and by the time he returned to WBT in late 1945, he had a secure reputation as a cowboy hero, a singer of patriotic country songs such as "The Hand Is Writing on the Wall," and a prolific composer of hundreds of songs. In short, Fred was well fixed in the pop-country-cowboy tradition, and could by no stretch of the imagination be called a "folk composer"; he was a thoroughgoing professional, and his monster hit "Atomic Power" emerged less from any gospel or semi-gospel tradition than it did from a strong topical tradition Kirby had embraced during the war.

Nor was the success of "Atomic Power" due solely to Kirby's skill as a songwriter, or to the message of the song. In order to fully understand the impact it made, we must look at both the A & R (artists and repertoire) man responsible for producing the song and the singing group that recorded the best-selling version of the song.

The A & R man responsible for taking the song from the Leeds publishing company and fitting it to an appropriate recording group was Bob Miller. Miller's role in the song's history is highly significant, for he was one of the major supporters of the topic-song genre in country music.[11] Miller, whose role in country music's development has been shamefully neglected, was born in Memphis in 1895 and received formal training in several respectable music conservatories before he began composing and writing country songs in the late 1920s. The event song, or topical song, was the first type of country song to be fully developed via the phonograph record, and writers like the Reverend Andrew Jenkins and Carson J. Robison sold hundreds of thousands of records in the 1920s with songs like "The Death of Floyd Collins" and "The Mississippi Flood." It goes without saying that such topical songs, usually written, recorded, and released within days after a disaster or tragedy occurred, were modern analogues to the eighteenth-century British broadside ballads. Miller, though, saw them only as a successful commodity, and by 1930 he had inherited the mantle, slightly frayed through overuse, of Jenkins and Robison. He produced a number of interesting Depression-era songs like "Eleven Cent Cotton and Forty Cent Meat," "Dry Voters and Wet Drinkers," "Pretty Boy Floyd," "Outlaw John Dillinger," "The Death of Jack 'Legs' Diamond," and "The Death of Jimmie Rodgers"; Miller continued the tradition during World War II by contributing "We're Gonna Have to Slap the Dirty Little Jap" and contributing to "There's a Star Spangled Banner Waving Somewhere," the latter a best-seller that netted Elton Britt country music's first gold record. By the early 1930s Miller was also doing extensive A & R work for companies like Columbia, RCA, and Crown, and often worked to move the country music he produced in the direction of pop.

Certainly this was the case in Miller's relationship with the Buchanan Brothers. When he discovered them in 1941, he was managing several different country acts in and around New York City. The Buchanans, Chester and Lester, had come to New York from rural north Georgia to get work at the Bethlehem Steel shipyards in Brooklyn.[12] Miller apparently saw in them good raw material—authentic voices and accents—that could be used to promote Miller's own country songs. For a time the arrangement was successful; from 1944 to 1946 the Buchanans were immensely popular, recording for Victor, appearing widely on the Northeast circuit, and even appearing on radio's famous *Gangbusters*. They recorded with Gene Autry's studio band, and also recorded a number of Miller's topical songs, such as "Colin Kelly, Will You Tell the Boys up Yonder?" and "(You Got to Pray to the Lord) When You See Those Flying Saucers."

But by the time the Buchanans recorded "Atomic Power" in 1946, things were coming to a head with Miller. He was pushing them too far toward pop; one of the Buchanans later recalled that "'Atomic Power' . . . stunk. He shoved all his stuff down our throat." Both brothers objected not only to some of the songs themselves, but also to some of the arrangements. Both, for instance, complained about the oboe in "Atomic Power." Although "Atomic Power" went on to be influential in its own right, the Victor recording arose from an unstable synthesis of slicked-up New York country and traditional backwoods north Georgia country.

For whatever reasons, "Atomic Power" defined the theme of country music's most common topical-song type in the immediate postwar years. The song also attached a religious connotation to the atomic power idea, a connotation that was, remarkably, unique to country music. The pop music world in general was, in 1946, filled with all manner of references to the new adjective "atomic." Jazz musicians especially latched onto the reference, and 1946 saw such jazz-tinged records as "Atom Buster" (Barney Kessel), "Atomic Boogie" (Pete Johnson), "Atomic Cocktail" ("Slim" Galliard), and "Atomic Did It" (Maylon Clark); there was even an "Atomic Polka" (Brunon Kryger) and a West Coast jazz record label called Atomic, whose label featured a picture of a mushroom cloud. Yet none of these popular connotations of the word "atomic" suggested any of the reverence or awe found in the country uses of the word.[13] For the next several years, a number of country songs emerged that developed the themes presented in Kirby's song: sheer awe at the power of the atom, an association of this power with religion, and a warning not to misuse this power. These songs included "There Is a Power Greater than Atomic" (Whitey and Hogan, 1946), "Old Man Atom" (Sons of the Pioneers, 1946), "Jesus Hits Like an Atom Bomb" (Lowell Blanchard, 1949), "Great Atomic Power" (Louvin Brothers, 1951), "Brush the Dust from the Old Bible" (Bradley Kincaid, 1950), and "When

They Found the Atomic Power" (Hawkshaw Hawkins, 1946). There are also probably scores of other similar songs registered in copyright offices, recorded by lesser-known singers, or circulated in oral tradition; the ones listed here are merely some of the major songs recorded on major labels by recognized country singers.

The immediate successor of "Atomic Power" was a deliberate sequel titled "There Is a Power Greater than Atomic." Produced about three months after "Atomic Power" peaked in popularity, the song was written by two close friends and coworkers of Fred Kirby's, Arval Hogan and Roy Grant. Hogan and Grant, known professionally as Whitey and Hogan, were a couple of North Carolina boys who teamed up and began singing duet-style proto-bluegrass music in 1935.[14] Unlike Kirby, they had always had a healthy dose of gospel music in their repertory; they recorded one of the very first versions of Albert Brumley's classic "Turn Your Radio On" for Decca in 1939. By 1946 the team was playing regularly with the Briarhoppers over WBT, Charlotte, and touring with Fred Kirby. They watched with interest and envy as "Atomic Power" began to climb onto the charts in the summer of 1946, and often found themselves singing Kirby's song.

Then, in July 1946, the government began the first series of peacetime atomic weapons tests off Bikini Atoll in the Pacific. Dubbed "Operation Crossroads," the test involved exploding an atomic bomb in the air over a series of target ships; only five of the ninety target ships were sunk, a fact that surprised many Americans who had been thinking of the bomb as the ultimate weapon. A second test, on July 25, yielded similar results. Two Americans especially impressed with the ships' survival were Whitey and Hogan.

Hogan recalled in a 1977 interview, "We just got to thinking about it when they had that big test out in the Pacific; those ships still standing after the blast, that's what gave us the idea." Whitey Grant added:

> Just prior to that Fred Kirby had written his song, "Atomic Power," so Hogan and myself, both being children of devoted Christians, the idea came to us one night going to a personal appearance. And I said, "Well, gee whiz, somewhere in the world there ought to be a power greater than atomic," and we put two and two together and starting writing words that night and in a short while the song was completed. We didn't do anything with it until Fred's song started dying down. Then we turned ours over to our publisher, Hill and Range, and we recorded it. We recorded our version in the WBT studios in Charlotte, for the DeLuxe label. The Buchanan Brothers in New

York also recorded it on the RCA Victor label, and since Victor had better coverage and better distribution, it did pretty good for us.

Whitey and Hogan, like Kirby, had been active in singing war songs, especially enjoying success with one called "We Didn't Invite Them Over, but We're Gonna Return the Call." After the war, they continued to transcribe *Carolina Calling* for broadcast overseas, and it was on this show, they believe, that they first sang "There Is a Power Greater than Atomic."

A look at the original text of "There Is a Power Greater than Atomic" reveals some interesting changes to the premises of Kirby's song.

There Is a Power Greater than Atomic
(Whitey and Hogan)

When they talk about his power, of his strength in every way,
How he can take the lives of those and rule them all some day,
There is one thing he's forgetting in the great plan he doth make
That God gave to him everything, and everything can take.

Refrain   There is a power greater than atomic,
    It's the power of one that sits on high,
    When He strikes us with His mighty power
    Not just some, but everyone, must die.

When this power that I tell you falls upon this sinful land,
Every rock within the mountain will melt at his command,
So when you're planning power that will melt away the sod,
Don't forget there is no power to equal that of God.

Refrain

To the island of Bikini great men came and plans were made,
To prove to all the people, what a power he had made,
But after it was over, even through the blinding steam,
The targets left should prove to us that God is still supreme.

Refrain

Whitey Grant recalled that this song drew "quite a few comments from gospel groups, and a lot of ministers requested it, wanted us to come to their church and sing it." After a closer look at the song, it is not hard to see

why. Whereas in "Atomic Power," religion is a means to an end—a metaphor invoked to explain the awesome new forces—here religion is an end
in itself. The song uses atomic power as a metaphor to illustrate God's
power. Leaving theological implications of this shift aside, it does seem
significant that, within a matter of months, country music was able to assimilate the atomic metaphor into the values of traditional gospel music.

In the same year that saw the development of the atomic-religious theme,
other country artists were commenting on the phenomenon of atomic power
in more secular ways. Hawkshaw Hawkins's "When They Found the Atomic
Power" (King 611) chronicles the actual development of the bomb by
American scientists, who worked long hours at Alamogordo, Los Alamos,
Oak Ridge, and El Paso "in the downpour of rain" to produce "the thing
that had never been before." Hawkins's song admits that the power was
acquired only "when the Lord held out His mighty hand," but emphasizes
the work of the scientists and the fact that "this world, it must be free."
When he recorded the song, Hawkins was performing on the WWVA *Jamboree* in Wheeling, West Virginia, and he had not yet established the reputation he was later to have as a major country honky-tonk singer.

An even more secular, but in some ways much more effective, anti-
atomic song was "Old Man Atom," written in 1946 by West Coast newspa-
perman Vern Partlow. This song, which is often referred to as "Talking Atom,"
is in the form of the talking blues, a style invented by North Carolinian
Chris Bouchillon in the 1920s and popularized by protest singer Woody
Guthrie in the 1940s. The song is an explicit warning about the misuse of
atomic power: "you know, Einstein said he was scared, and if he's scared,
brother, I'm scared." Partlow attacks both the scientists who developed the
power—there is no hint here of the Lord sanctioning the work at Alamogordo
—and the diplomats who suggest that we "atomize world peace" by extinguishing "every damn atom that can't speak English." In 1946, one must
remember, only the United States, Britain, and Canada had developed atomic
fission, and at its first session the United Nations formed an atomic energy
commission, but failed in its attempt to curtail immediately the development of atomic weapons. Partlow makes a caustic reference in his song to
the "UNO," as the UN was then called, and concludes by saying that the
people of the world "must decide their fate"; "all men / could be cremated
equal."

"Old Man Atom" seems much more politically sophisticated than many country songs, and probably for this reason it was revised when the Sons of the Pioneers recorded it a year later for RCA Victor (Vi 21-0368). The stanza criticizing the UNO and containing the reference to extinguishing "every damn atom that can't speak English" was omitted, and a couple of new stanzas were added to emphasize the need for the people of the world to get together and stop the threat. Anything that the Sons of the Pioneers recorded in the 1940s—their heyday—was bound to circulate widely and receive heavy airplay, but there's no indication that "Old Man Atom" reached anything like hit status for them. The song, however, made a comeback in the folk revival of the 1960s and was performed by numerous urban folksingers. It attained even wider circulation when Tom Glazer included it in his collection *Songs of Peace, Freedom, and Protest* in 1970.

In the fall of 1949, Russia exploded its first nuclear device, and the prospect of an atomic war became more than just a vague fear. Cold war tensions were beginning to mount, as reflected in the 1948 Berlin Airlift and the 1949 founding of NATO, and American popular culture reacted accordingly. Philip Wylie's best-selling novel *Tomorrow* gave America a detailed picture of what a nuclear war could be like, and the effects of radiation were widely discussed in popular magazines. In country music, a new generation of atomic songs emerged that preached one message loud and clear: the only real solution for cold war tensions was Jesus Christ.

Perhaps the most colorful of these new songs was "Jesus Hits Like an Atom Bomb" (1949). The song laments that while everybody is worried about the atomic bomb, "nobody's worried about the day my Lord will come," but when he does come, he will "hit, Great God Almighty, like an atom bomb." Though the song admits that every country "across the line" now has the bomb, one need not worry—instead just seek "King Jesus." There seems to be no available information about this song's composer, Lee V. McCullom, but the song seems to have originated around the Knoxville, Tennessee, area. People associated with the Knoxville country music scene at WNOX made recordings of it: Lowell Blanchard and Johnnie and Jack (Johnny Wright and Jack Anglin). The former, for Mercury, is done in the style of gospel quartets, while the latter, for Victor, is done in the classic country duet style.

More popular was the Louvin Brothers' "Great Atomic Power" (1951), recorded by them on both MGM and Capitol. The Louvins, by far the most popular gospel duet of the early 1950s, wrote most of their successful gospel songs, including "Great Atomic Power." The imagery in "Great Atomic Power" is so successfully merged with traditional gospel imagery that the entire text of the song needs to be quoted in order to fully appreciate it.

Great Atomic Power
(C. Louvin, I. Louvin, B. Bain)

Refrain   Are you ready (are you ready) for the great atomic power?
              Will you rise and meet your savior in the air?
              Will you shout or will you cry, when the fire it comes on high?
              Are you ready for the great atomic power?

Do you fear this man's invention that they call atomic power?
Are we all in great confusion, do we know the time or hour?
When a terrible explosion may rain down upon our land?
Creating horrible destruction, blotting out the works of man.

Refrain

There is one way to escape it, be prepared to meet the Lord,
Give your heart and soul to Jesus, he will be your shielding sword,
He will surely stay beside you, you will never taste of death,
Your soul will fly to safety and eternal peace and rest.

Refrain

There's an army who can conquer all the enemy's great men
A regiment of Christians guided by the Savior's hand.
When the mushroom of destruction falls in all its fury great,
God will surely save his children from that awful, awful fate.

Refrain

© Copyright 1952 by Acuff-Rose Publications, Inc.
Used by permission of the publisher. All rights reserved.

In this song, atomic power has become so integrated into the popular religious vocabulary that the doomsday vision can be equaled with the Day of Judgment. American folk hymnody is full of attempts to describe the apocalypse; "When the Stars Begin to Fall" and "Sinner Man" are but two well-known examples. Notable country treatments of the theme must include Roy Acuff's "This World Can't Stand Long," "Brother Take Warning," and "Pale Horse and His Rider"; the Bailes Brothers' "He'll Strike You Down," "Avenue of Prayer," and "There's a Hand Writing on the Wall"; and other pieces like "He Will Set Your Fields on Fire." The classic *Broadman Hymnal*, used for decades by hundreds of southern churches, has an entire section of "Warning" songs that focus on the Day of Judgment theme. The Louvins, all too familiar with such a gospel tradition, found in the vision of atomic war a ready-made metaphor for the apocalypse. The vision of atomic holocaust was current, on the minds of all Americans, and very relevant; it was an extremely effective way of visualizing the Day of Judgment. Furthermore, the military overtones of atomic war are complemented by the traditional references to Christian militancy in the last stanza. "Great Atomic Power" represents perhaps the fullest integration of the atomic imagery into gospel music; it is, in fact, one of the few successful blends of themes of science and religion in pop music.

A similar use of atomic holocaust as Day of Judgment is found in Bradley Kincaid's "Brush the Dust from That Old Bible" (Capitol, 1950). Kincaid interprets the biblical prophecy that the world will be destroyed a second time by fire as a foreshadowing of atomic destruction. "You'd better seek the solace of your Savior / When that atom bomb's placed on the firing line." There is little here of the argument that irresponsible scientists or muddling statesmen have used atomic power carelessly; here the atomic holocaust is caused simply by too much sinning. Like the Day of Judgment, it is an inevitable, almost natural occurrence. In spite of his reputation as one of country music's most respected traditional singers, Kincaid did not enjoy much popular success with the song; he recalled, "I thought that would be a big hit, but it refers to the bombs, and, I don't know, people might have been afraid of it."[15]

By 1951 the atomic metaphor had become so closely associated with country song tradition that a song like "The Atomic Telephone" could be written. Recorded as a gospel song on King Records by the Harlan County Four, a group that reportedly included the Delmore Brothers, the number's key phrase is "I have talked to Jesus on the atomic telephone." No other mention is made of "atomic" in the song: there is no hint of atomic bombs or atomic holocaust. "Atomic" functions solely as a religious adjective, and the song seems modeled on earlier telephone-to-God songs like F.H. Lehman's well-known "The Royal Telephone," Wade Mainer's "God's Radio Phone," and even the Victorian vaudeville song "Hello, Central, Give Me Heaven."

By 1950, then, the atomic metaphor had become fairly routine in country music, and as the Korean conflict, which began in June 1950, escalated into a full-blown war, country songwriters found themselves with a new topical, patriotic subject for songs. During World War II the music had produced a plethora of patriotic war songs, ranging from rather simple jingles like Carson Robison's "1942 Turkey in the Straw" to sophisticated low-key pieces like Floyd Tillman's "Each Night at Nine." One of the most effective formats, though, especially as the war neared its end, was Zeke Clements's "Smoke on the Water," a song that foretold the fall of Japan and Germany in violent, apocalyptic imagery. The Korean War did not produce the number of topical songs that World War II did, but some of the best took this "Smoke on the Water" approach, directed it toward Russia, and merged it with the atomic holocaust motif. Three such songs were Fred Kirby's "When the Hell Bomb Falls" (Columbia, 1949), Jackie Doll's recording of "When They Drop the Atomic Bomb" (Mercury, 1950), and Roy Acuff's "Advice to Joe" (Columbia, 1951).

Fred Kirby doesn't remember much about his second atomic song, "When the Hell Bomb Falls," but the author of "Atomic Power" does recall that the song was the B-side of one of his biggest hits, "The Old Country Preacher." Therefore, it circulated fairly widely. "When the Hell Bomb Falls" begins with the conventional warning of sinners in the face of the atomic "weapon of destruction"; in the second and third verses, though, Kirby explicitly mentions the fighting in Korea, and asks the Lord to lend "a helping hand" to preserve freedom. The song stops short of advocating our use of the atomic bomb in Korea, but the implication is certainly there. However, there is nothing implicit in Jackie Doll's "When They Drop the Atomic Bomb." This song, which was actually written by someone with the last name of Howard, specifically advocates letting General MacArthur drop the bomb in Korea. Much of the imagery of the song's refrain seems to echo "Smoke on the Water": there will be fire, dust, and metal "lying around"; the "Radioactivity will burn them to the ground"; and if there are "any Commies left," they'll be on the run. Just "leave it to the General," for he "really has the nerve" to give the Communists their just deserts. The specific historical context of the song was probably MacArthur's plan to bomb Communist bases in Manchuria, one of the factors that led to his conflict with Truman.

At one point in the song, Doll mentions "old hard-headed Joe"—Stalin, of course; Roy Acuff's "Advice to Joe" brings Stalin even more into the picture. The peaceful nations of the world will unite to oppose Communist ambition; Stalin will see "lightning flashing" and hear "atomic thunder" and Moscow will lie in ashes. "When the atomic bombs start falling, do you have a place to hide?" the singer asks Stalin. "Smoke on the Water" pervades this song, too, and Acuff manages to associate Stalin with Satan and the atomic war with the wrath of God. Acuff never specifically mentions Korea; however, the song presumably functioned primarily as a cold war song. The atomic bomb, though, is clearly a tool that the righteous can use as a last resort against the wicked.

Advice to Joe
(Roy Acuff-Roy Nunn)

There's a Communist ambition now to rule or wreck us all,
With atomic ammunition they would like to see us fall,
Peaceful men of every nation would become as common slaves,
We'll prevent that situation, better we shall fill our graves.

Refrain   You will see the lightning flashing, hear atomic thunder roll,
When Moscow lies in ashes, God have mercy on your soul,
There's a question, Mr. Stalin, and it's you who must decide,
When the atomic bombs start falling, do you have a place to hide?

Uncle Sam will still be living when the smoke of battle's o'er,
He will make a noose to fit you, but will close up Heaven's door,
You'll come face to face with Satan, see the loved ones who have died.
So be sure when bombs start falling that you have a place to hide.

Refrain

Just remember Mr. Stalin how we both fought side by side,
When Hitler and Mussolini had you whipped and how you cried,
Uncle Sam, he came to help you, gave you strength, we gave you all,
And now your great ambition is to see our nation fall.

Refrain

© Copyright 1951 by Acuff-Rose Publications, Inc.
Used by permission. All rights reserved.

Thus, in the space of five years the image of the atomic bomb in country music shifted from that of an awesome, barely controllable force ("Atomic Power") to a well-defined but deadly tool ("Advice to Joe," "When They Drop the Atomic Bomb"). Although the very first atomic song, Karl Davis and Harty Taylor's "When the Atomic Bomb Fell," defines the bomb in political terms, most early songs define it in religious terms; by the end of the 1940s the pendulum had swung back to political terms ("Advice to Joe," "Old Man Atom," "When They Drop the Atomic Bomb"). It is in these two areas that the bomb gradually became integrated into the segment of popular culture represented by country music. Like most metaphors, the atomic reference was originally unique and exciting; after a period of over-use, though, the atomic metaphor, again, like most metaphors, became just another conventional image. Whereas songwriters in 1946 focused on the novelty of the atomic metaphor, by 1948 they were using it rather routinely as a conventional metaphor for God's power, for religious apocalypse, or for military might.

Unlike most technological metaphors appropriated by country music, the atomic metaphor was a victim of planned obsolescence. As new and more powerful weapons systems were developed in the 1950s—weapons like the hydrogen bomb—the word "atomic" began to lose its connotation of ultimacy. It began to appear less and less in country or pop songs.[16] The assimilation pattern was, in one sense, regrettably complete. The unique and awesome aspects of atomic power had become all too commonplace, foreshadowing the days to come when people of the South would be willing to accept things like a nuclear power station on the banks of A.P. Carter's Clinch River, or at Alton Delmore's Brown's Ferry. By 1990, the question raised by the Louvin Brothers—Are you ready for the great atomic power?—had become a moot point.[17]

Notes

1. See, for instance, Archie Green's notes to Mike Seeger's album *Tipple, Loom, and Rail*, Folkways 5273, 1966, and Archie Green, *Only a Miner* (Urbana: University of Illinois Press, 1972).

2. The ideological background for technology's penetration into rural America would have to include W.J. Cash, *The Mind of the South* (New York: Knopf, 1941); Leo Marx, *The Machine in the Garden: Technology and the Pastoral Ideal in America* (New York: Oxford University Press, 1964); and Peter J. Schmitt, *Back to Nature: The Arcadian Myth in Urban America* (New York: Oxford University Press, 1969).

3. One theme that has been written about more than any other is the railroad. Notable studies include Archie Green, notes to *Railroad Songs and Ballads* (Washington, D.C.: Library of Congress, 1969); Norm Cohen, "Railroad Folksongs on Record—A Survey," *New York Folklore Quarterly* (June 1970), 91–113; and Norm Cohen, *Long Street Rail* (Urbana: University of Illinois Press, 1978).

4. Bill Malone, presentation at National Popular Culture Association annual meeting, St. Louis, Missouri, 1975. Green and Griffis have published numerous articles, both serious and popular, on the musicians of the 1940s. Their most substantial works are Green, *Country Roots* (New York: Hawthorn, 1976) and Griffis, *"Hear My Song": The Story of the Sons of the Pioneers* (Los Angeles: John Edwards Memorial Foundation, 1975). Tribe's articles, far too numerous to mention here, often appear in *Bluegrass Unlimited*; especially significant are his studies of the Bailes Brothers and Molly O'Day, the latter published (with John Morris) as *Molly O'Day, Lynn Davis, and the Cumberland Mountain Folks: A Bio-Discography* (Los Angeles: John Edwards Memorial Foundation, 1975).

5. This expansion of the country music audience raises some interesting questions as to how "southern" or regional the audience was that responded to the atomic bomb songs of the 1940s. For the sake of this paper, and to put the 1940s into perspective, I am assuming a certain amount of continuity between the audience of the 1940s and the traditional country audience of the 1920s and 1930s. Although the country music audience had expanded, it did not appreciably shift, and the music retained most of its original audience while adding new elements. Future research may undermine this assumption.

6. Technically speaking, the very first atomic bomb song I can find recorded in country music is Karl Davis and Harty Taylor's "When the Atomic Bomb Fell" (Columbia 36982), which was released in April 1946, three months before "Atomic Power." In spite of the title, the song does not concentrate on the atomic bomb itself, but deals mainly with the bomb as a means to end the war. The bomb is "the answer to our fighting boys' prayer," and after an initial description of the bombing of Japan, the song focuses on the relief soldiers felt at the war's end. In fact, the song has more in common with conventional patriotic songs of World War II than the newly born atomic age.

7. Fred Kirby, interview by author, September 14, 1977, and Kirby, letter to author, September 20, 1977. All subsequent quotations are taken from these sources.

8. "Reviews of New Records," *Billboard*, May 1, 1946, 33.

9. *Billboard* during this time did not have a listing for country record sales price; the only popularity indexes they published for "race" and "folk" records were keyed to the jukebox popularity.

10. There is some question as to exactly how this cliché entered American popular culture. See James Gunn, ed., *The Road to Science Fiction: From Gilgamesh to Wells* (New York: New American Library, 1977), 163–64.

11. There is no extensive biographical account of Miller's career; the best available reference is Linnell Gentry, *A History and Encyclopedia of Country, Western, and Gospel Music* (Nashville: Clairmont Corp., 1969).

12. Howard Wight Marshall, "'We Was Just Kids out of the Hill Country': The Case of the Buchanan Brothers," *Journal of Country Music* 5 (1975): 83–88.

13. The only country song I have found that uses connotations of "atomic" similar to those in jazz and blues (i.e., suggesting exciting, sexy, or mind-blowing) is Ann Jones's song "Atom Bomb Baby," Victor 20-1985, 1947, by Dude Martin and His Round-up Gang.

14. Roy Grant and Arval Hogan, interview by author, September 1, 1977, and September 9, 1977, Charlotte, North Carolina.

15. Loyal Jones, "A Checklist of Bradley Kincaid's Songs," *JEMF Quarterly*, no. 44 (1976): 213.

16. However, the atomic bomb motif emerged again in the folk revival of the 1960s in such songs as Bob Dylan's "A Hard Rain's A-Gonna Fall" and Judy Collins's "Hiroshima Lullaby." Little ideology connects these "protest" songs of the 1960s and the country songs of the 1940s, and I have not included the former in this study. The atomic motif of the 1960s, however, is a topic that needs further exploration. Also, a few fascinating instances of the atomic motif show up in today's traditional music. One especially interesting example is folk composer Jimmy Womack's "Atomic Energy," recorded in the field (Houston) by Mack McCormick in 1959. See *A Treasury of Field Recordings,* vol. 2, *Regional and Personalized Song,* 77 LA 12/3, 1960.

17. For some years now, I have been known among record collectors as "the nut who collects atomic bomb songs," and I am grateful to the various collectors who humored me. I am especially thankful to friends and colleagues who made suggestions or additions to the project, including Bob Pinson, of the Country Music Foundation; Ivan Tribe; Doug Green, of the Country Music Foundation; Vernon Bogle; Stephen Davis; and my research assistant, Mrs. Betty Dalton, who transcribed many of the original songs. Part of the research for this project was made possible by a grant from the Graduate Committee of Middle Tennessee State University.

Atomic Bomb Songs in Country Music

"When the Atomic Bomb Fell" (Davis-Taylor). Karl and Harty. Columbia 36982. Circa Apr. 1946.

"Atomic Power" (Kirby). Buchanan Brothers. Victor 20-1850. July 1946.

———. Fred Kirby. Sonora H-7008. July 1946.

———. Red River Dave. Continental C-5061. July 1946.

———. Rex Allen and the Prairie Ramblers. Mercury 6008. July 1946.

———. Riley Shepard. Musicraft 1-5070. July 1946.

————. Rufe Davis. Mastertone 75-7. Fall 1946.

————. Red Foley. Decca 46-14. Fall 1946.

"There Is a Power Greater than Atomic" (Whitey-Hogan). Whitey and Hogan. DeLuxe 5038. Fall 1946.

————. Buchanan Brothers. Victor 20-2533. Fall 1946.

"When They Found the Atomic Power." Hawkshaw Hawkins. King 611. Fall 1946.

"Old Man Atom" (Vern Patlow-Irving Bibo). Sons of the Pioneers. Victor 21-0368. 1946.

"Atom Bomb Baby" (Ann Jones). Dude Martin and His Round-up Gang. Victor 20-1985. 1947.

"Jesus Hits Like an Atom Bomb" (Lee V. McCullom). Lowell Blanchard with the Valley Trio. Mercury 6260. Circa 1949.

————. Johnnie and Jack. Victor 20-0314. 1949.

"When They Drop the Atomic Bomb" (Howard). Jackie Doll and His Pickled Peppers. Mercury 6322. 1950.

"When the Hell Bomb Falls" (Kirby). Fred Kirby. Columbia 20740. 1950.

"Brush the Dust from That Old Bible" (Kincaid). Bradley Kincaid. Capitol 1276. 1950.

"Advice to Joe" (Acuff-Nunn). Roy Acuff and His Smoky Mountain Boys. Columbia 20858. Jan. 1951.

"Atomic Telephone" (Smith-Glover-Mann). Harlan County Four. King 1016. Oct. 1951.

"Great Atomic Power" (I. Louvin-C. Louvin-B. Bain). Louvin Brothers. MGM 11277. July 1952.

————. Louvin Brothers. Capitol 4686. 1961.

"Hydrogen Bomb" (Street-MacDonald). Al Rogers and His Rocky Mountain Boys. X 4X-0029. 1955.

"Atomic Energy" (Womack). Jimmy Womack. 77-LA 12/3, vol. 2. 1960.

8

Purple Hearts, Heartbreak Ridge, and Korean Mud

Pain, Patriotism, and Faith in the 1950–53 "Police Action"

Ivan M. Tribe

What one might term the "golden years" of pre–rock and roll hillbilly music coincided with the Korean War. Hank Williams, Hank Snow, and Lefty Frizzell were all at the peak of their popularity and influence. Kitty Wells emerged as a major solo female voice, distinct from the support role generally played by women singers as part of a duet or family act. Fiddles and steels dominated the instrumentation, and bluegrass music remained within the mainstream. Elvis Presley was still an obscure teenager in Memphis. American patriotism was also at a peak, and many feared that an all-out conflict with Soviet and/or Chinese Communism might be in the near future. The conflict in Korea tended to be viewed by many—if not most—Americans as a "hot" phase of the larger ideological struggle known as the cold war. Although cold war songs are treated elsewhere in this volume, the two cannot be totally separated from each other as they are indeed interrelated. Only a few songs touching on the conflict became major hits, but many of them were indeed quite popular, and attentive ears listened as lyrics expressed the mixed emotions felt by country folk about a war that ultimately took nearly 37,000 American lives.[1]

Songs with cold war themes were released as early as 1947, when the York Brothers' song "Let's Not Sleep Again" rejected the isolationist past and pointed toward internationalism. About that time, Lonnie Glosson's "Talk of Peace" expressed the belief that true peace would come only after Christianity had enveloped the world. This trend of merging cold war songs with Christianity continued with such songs as "The Bible on the Table and the Flag upon the Wall" and "The Red We Want Is the Red We've Got in the Old Red, White and Blue." After June 1950, Arthur "Guitar Boogie" Smith's "Mr. Stalin, You're Eatin' Too High on the Hog," Hank Williams's "No, No Joe," and Roy Acuff's "Advice to Joe" pointed to the Soviet dictator as the chief villain. The recitation "Let's Keep the Communists Out," by Terry Preston (Ferlin Husky), the widely recorded "They Locked God Outside the Iron Curtain," and the somewhat humorous "I'm No Communist" focused attention on the evils of Marxist doctrine. As late as 1966, Doc Williams's tale of the "Freedom Monkey" took a negative view of Communism.[2]

Bernard Baruch first used the phrase "cold war" in a congressional debate in 1947. One year later, in May 1948, South Korea was granted independence. Over the next several months, the American occupation forces, which had been in the country since the end of World War II, were sharply reduced. On June 26, 1950, the military forces of Communist-controlled North Korea launched a full-scale invasion across the thirty-eighth parallel. Within days of the surprise attack, the military situation grew steadily worse. The UN Security Council approved military action (Russian delegates were absent), with Gen. Douglas MacArthur as commander. The South Korean capital of Seoul fell to Communist forces in early July, and the outnumbered American and Korean forces retreated steadily until August, when they came within a few miles of the South Korean port city of Pusan on the southeastern tip of the peninsula and Gen. Walton Walker, who commanded the soldiers on the ground, gave his famous "Stand or die" order. Pusan held, and General MacArthur initiated the Inchon landing behind enemy lines in mid-September. The situation quickly reversed, and the North Koreans retreated within their own borders. The UN (i.e., mostly American) forces crossed into the north, but as the troops neared the Yalu River on the North Korea-China boundary, thousands of Chinese "volunteers" counterattacked; the Americans were driven southward again. Truman dismissed MacArthur in April 1951 and replaced him with Gen. Matthew Ridgway, who had earlier replaced Walker after his death in a jeep accident on December 23, 1950.

Truce talks began on July 10, 1951, but made little headway, particularly on the issue of return and repatriation of prisoners. Meanwhile, fighting continued, with bitter combat taking place in several locales just north of the thirty-eighth parallel. Some battles became known by local place names such as Kaesong, while others became known by American terms, typified by Old Baldy, Pork Chop Hill, and, most notably, Heartbreak Ridge. American troops captured this latter strategic position on October 7, 1951, after a bitter fight that lasted for thirty-seven days. The Truman administration gave way to that of Eisenhower in January 1953. On July 26, 1953, the negotiations at Panmunjom finally resulted in a cease-fire agreement. Prisoner exchanges took place over the next several months, and a sometimes uneasy armistice has held for half a century.[3]

Pain and patriotism, with religious feeling frequently strong in both, constitute the two dominant themes in songs about the Korean War. Although pain is probably manifested somewhat more often, the patriotic angle appeared first. Jimmie Osborne, a native of Winchester, Kentucky, who holds the distinction of being the first with a notable song focusing on the war, would ultimately record six songs touching on the subject, only one of which was a cover of someone else's hit. Osborne, born on April 8, 1923, sang on nearby Lexington radio in about 1939 and worked in a defense plant during World War II. Launching a musical career after the war, he worked for a time with the Bailes Brothers at KWKH in Shreveport, Louisiana. By 1947 he had signed with King Records of Cincinnati and had his first minor success with a Homer Bailes song titled "My Heart Echoes." Returning to Kentucky and billing himself as "The Kentucky Folk Singer," he scored a major hit in 1949 with "The Death of Little Kathy Fiscus," a topical ballad about a girl tragically trapped in a well in San Marino, California. In addition to the typical country fare dealing with broken romance, his other songs could be described as numbers with messages. He lamented fatal highway accidents in "A Million People Have Died" and the accidental shooting deaths of children in "My Saddest Mistake."

Osborne's success with message-oriented songs perhaps prompted him to record "God, Please Protect America" on July 26, 1950. Combining patriotism with prayer, the lyrics plead for the Almighty to "Give us victory in Korea," in order to "save our boys so fine" and "protect America in this troubled time." First appearing on the *Billboard* charts on October 7, 1950, and then peaking at number 9, the song had a fairly significant impact: schoolchildren in Ohio sang parts of it as they marched and pretended to be soldiers during recess. In 1964 Charlie Moore and Bill Napier altered the lyrics to make it a Vietnam War song and re-recorded the number.

Jimmie Osborne's follow-up song, "Thank God for Victory in Korea," contains lyrics that might be described as being somewhat premature. Recorded on October 2, 1950—after the Inchon landings of September 1950 and several ensuing weeks of spectacular successes by U.S. forces—the song assumes that an American triumph has ended the war: "Thank you dear God for victory in Korea, we're grateful that the battle's won / We give you the praise for victory in Korea, we thank you dear God for what you've done." However, on November 29, 1950, some 200,000 Chinese volunteers entered the fray, and the American forces suffered a series of reversals.

Osborne's third song, "The Voice of Free America," makes few specific references to the Korean War; rather, it focuses most of its praise on American democracy and the Voice of America radio network. Extolling in general the virtues of the American way of life, the lyrics mention the Iranian oil crisis, note that "on the other side Korea is a sea of blood today," and urge listeners to "get on their knees and pray." Shortly after the cease-fire of July 27, 1953, Jimmie Osborne rendered a less jingoistic and more somber account of the conflict. "The Korean Story," recorded on August 3, addresses his earlier false assumption of an American triumph: "China entered in, MacArthur was dismissed, there was no chance to win. . . ." Finally, the song thanks God that the conflict has apparently ended.

A final Jimmie Osborne lyric on the Korean conflict deals with a subject not mentioned in any other song. During the prisoner exchanges, twenty-three Americans chose to remain with the Communists, and many in this country found themselves asking why. "Come Back to Your Loved Ones (My Prodigal Son)," recorded on November 10, 1953, singles out an unnamed soldier who wants to stay behind the bamboo curtain as being "Alone in Korea confused and heartsick, / his mind all upset by a Communist trick." Urging them to come home and reminding them that they have done their duty as soldiers, the song suggests that the men are free to return and that they will be forgiven. The Kentucky Folk Singer continued to record for King until 1955, and he remained active on the country music scene in the Louisville area, primarily as a deejay; but his career stalled, and he took his own life on December 26, 1957.[4]

"Korea, Here We Come," by Harry Choates, presents another patriotic view of the Korean conflict. A Cajun fiddler and vocalist with tremendous talent, Choates made numerous recordings in both French and English for such regional labels as Gold Star, Humming Bird, and Macy's. Unfortunately, he was also a chronic alcoholic, and his career ended in his tragic death in an Austin, Texas, jail on July 17, 1951.[5] A few months before his death Choates recorded "Korea, Here We Come" on the Macy's label. His lyric contains only short verses (sung twice on the record):

Our dear old mother's heads are hanging low,
Got our orders to Korea we must go,
So mothers don't be sad,
They've done made us mad,
Korea, Korea, Korea, here we come!

We hoped and prayed this day would never come,
But for freedom we would never never run,
We'll fight until we die,
That's the American cry,
Korea, Korea, Korea, here we come!

Perhaps the most militant pro-war song of the era is Jackie Doll and his Pickled Peppers' "When They Drop the Atomic Bomb," which stops just short of advocating the destructive weapon's use. Little is known of Doll or his musical career, except that he had two Mercury sessions in 1951 several months apart, with a total of six released sides, and that the composer for the song in question is credited on the record as "Howard."[6] The lyrics undoubtedly date from after China's intervention, but before MacArthur's dismissal. Although the word "if" prefaces many of its lines, the song clearly suggests that the nuclear option would produce a quick and satisfactory victory:

And the radioactivity will burn their playhouse down;
If there's any commies left they'll be all on the run,
If General MacArthur drops the atomic bomb.

The subsequent removal of Gen. Douglas MacArthur by President Truman on April 11, 1951, led to an outpouring of sympathy and tribute to one of the nation's most admired military heros (in the short run much of the public supported MacArthur, somewhat oblivious to the fact that the real question dealt with subordination of the military to the civilian commander in chief). The most notable tribute, "Old Soldiers Never Die," was based on MacArthur's comment "Old soldiers never die, they just fade away," which he made in an address to a joint session of Congress on April 19. The following day Gene Autry recorded the song for Columbia Records, and it made the country charts on June 9, 1951. A popular version by Vaughn Monroe and His Orchestra ranked even higher on the *Billboard* popular lists, and Jimmy Wakely covered it on Capitol. To be sure, the lyrics pay more tribute to MacArthur's achievements in World War II, but the timing of the song's release reinforced his position on Korea. Roy Acuff's recording of Earl Nunn's "Doug MacArthur" is even more pointed in its support for the "Far East" general's views on contemporary events:

> Though he did the best he could,
> There were some who thought he should,
> Let the Communists take over all creation.

Other patriotic songs addressing the Korean War convey a more subdued form of support for the cause. For instance, "Wrap My Body in Old Glory," credited to Arthur Q. Smith (James Pritchett) and initially recorded by Carl Sauceman and the Green Valley Boys for Capitol, describes the final moments of an American soldier known simply as "GI Joe." As his buddies gather around him, Joe reminds them that "Old Glory" is "the flag of the country I love so" and admonishes them "not to falter." Finally he instructs them to tell his parents that he has sacrificed his life "for precious liberty that we all cherish so." At a later Sauceman session, sideman Don McHan wrote and sang "A White Cross Marks the Grave," which salutes the fallen soldiers as having "done their best with hearts so true and brave." Manson Smith, a singer from nearby Man, West Virginia, recorded "Johnny Sleeps in Korea." It memorializes Johnny, a dead soldier who "died not in vain for the red, white and blue" and has gone to a better world to be "a soldier for God." Don Reno and Red Smiley's tribute to the fallen, "Forgotten Men," reminds us that "The flag still waves so proud and free, across our land today / Let's not forget the boys who died across the watery spray." (Reno, the song's composer, was a World War II veteran of the China-Burma-India Theater.)

Canadian country and western vocalist Wilf Carter contributed an upbeat view in "Goodbye Maria (I'm Off to Korea)." His soldier is an Iowa corn farmer who has an Italian war bride. Recalled to service, he either voluntarily reenlists or is conscripted. On departure he tells Maria as he promises to be home soon, "It's the same old story and it's up to Old Glory to win another fight for liberty."

Somewhere between patriotism and pain are the songs that deal with battle fatigue and exhaustion. The most notable of these, "Rotation Blues," was composed by a soldier named Stewart Powell. It was initially recorded by Elton Britt on RCA Victor, but was then covered by Bill Monroe on Decca, Ken Marvin on Mercury, and Terry Preston (Ferlin Husky) on Four Star.[7] The lyrics concern the military practice of rotating soldiers on the front line. The narrator, "a lonely soldier, sittin' in Korea," longs for his tenure at the battlefront to end, and for rotation to "set him free," expressing his belief that "the F.E.C. [Far East Command] is too far East for me." He knows that he has been in the combat zone too long, because "the honey pots in Korea started smelling good to me." "Heartbreak Ridge," which takes the form of a soldier's letter to his mother, was released by Alabama's Delmore Brothers—twenty-year veterans of the recording studios—at the twilight of their careers. Recorded at approximately the time that American forces secured the ridge's high ground in mid-October 1951, the song has a narrator who views the war as a clear struggle between good and evil; he describes a bloody battle where "we fight the Reds trying to win to rid this world of hatred and sin." Various lines define the North Koreans as "an enemy that can't see the light," recall fondly the narrator's buddy from "down the street" who died "a hero, an honorable man," and pray that the opposition "will heed freedom's call." The narrator concludes by surveying the battle scene "on Heartbreak Ridge [where] I stand tonight with nothing but wounded and dying in sight."

Another Elton Britt song, "Korean Mud," calls for another type of patriotism in urging civilians to donate blood "to protect the dying soldier boys." The piece begins with a dramatic scene:

> An American soldier lay dying out in the Korean mud
> And all that was needed to save him was a pint of somebody's blood;
> And now as I think about it a tear comes to my eye
> For there was no blood to save him and this poor boy had to die.

The strong message could well have been a public service commercial for blood banks. Britt had gained considerable fame for his 1942 recording of "There's a Star Spangled Banner Waving Somewhere," which ranked as the most popular country song of World War II. Although his Korean War efforts never achieved the same success, in terms of quantity they came in second only to those of Jimmie Osborne. On the flip side of Britt's plea for blood was another powerful but more generic message song narrated by and titled "The Unknown Soldier," which closes with the line "Unknown I'll remain in God's Hall of Fame till there's peace in the world again."

Although the other songs with a Korean War setting do not lack patriotic sentiment, they primarily emphasize pain, such as that felt by a father, mother, friend, or lover upon the loss of a loved one. The pain may also be that felt by the soldier after a broken romance.

A father's loss is perhaps best expressed in the Paul Roberts composition and Lone Pine (Harold Breau) recording of "Fuzzy Wuzzy Teddy Bear." Roberts had earlier gained a degree of immortality as coauthor of the World War II classic "There's a Star Spangled Banner Waving Somewhere."[8] In this sentimental ballad, the father of a son lost "somewhere in Korea 'cross the sea" finds the teddy bear that had been his child's favorite toy. He recalls the many hours expended in youthful play in which his son would "have to kiss old Fuzzy Wuzzy too" at bedtime, but now, "in Korea is his grave." He continues:

> "Somewhere in Korea" that's the way the message read,
> Blinding tears were falling from my eyes;
> They were sorry but they had to tell me that my boy was dead,
> And so far away from home tonight he lies.

The distraught parent is "proud he died a hero, but no joy prevails tonight." He sadly concludes that "old fuzzy wuzzy teddy bear sits all alone . . . and seems to face the bitter truth so brave."

A mother's loss of a son has long been a subject of country music; the tradition dates back to such lyrics as "Darling Little Joe" and "Put My Little Shoes Away" and includes the World War II classic "Soldier's Last Letter." The Korean conflict produced its share of such songs, beginning with "Robe of White" by the Louvin Brothers. According to Louvin biographer Charles Wolfe, the song had originally been written for World War II, but after that conflict concluded, the brothers updated the song for Korea and recorded it for MGM on August 5, 1951.[9] The lyrics describe a postman delivering a letter to an anxious mother. Realizing that all is not well when the mailman tells her that she must sign for a registered letter, she knows that "her darling son was dead" when she sees "his Captain's name was written" on the return address, instead of "Jimmie's name and number." She concludes with a prayer that a "blooming rose" be placed "upon his grave" because her "soldier boy has won his robe of white." The next year the Louvins came back with a similar message. In "From Mother's Arms to Korea," the mother receives "an unfinished diary that she once gave her darling son" when he left for military service. The final entry, penned as the soldier enters combat and sung as the song's chorus, reads " 'From mother's arms to Korea, and tomorrow I'll face the front line' / But the next line was wrote by his buddy, 'From a foxhole to a mansion on high.'"

Other songs in the same vein include "Purple Heart," written by bluegrass sideman Curly Seckler and recorded by Jim and Jesse (McReynolds) and the Virginia Boys (including Seckler) on Capitol in mid-1952. In this lyric, "they sent him to Korea," where the soldier is killed. The grieving mother, who receives a "Purple Heart in memory of her son," consoles herself with the comforting feeling that her son is in heaven:

> I know that he is happy now away up in the sky,
> He'll never have to fight no more, nor see his buddies die;
> Jesus now has called, him to reign with him on high,
> Although I can't say goodbye to him, I'll meet him again sometime.

Yet another such song, "The Battle in Korea," does not specify the survivor's relationship with "my loved one." Ralph Pennington's composition was recorded by L.W. (Lambert) and Harold (Tomlin) and the Carolina Neighbors, a local bluegrass band, on the small North Wilkesboro, North Carolina, Blue Ridge label. Composer Pennington contributed the tenor vocal. Like the mother in "Purple Heart," surviving family members hope for a joyous reunion "in heaven some day": "He has lost his wife and children since the day he had to go away, / But I know they'll meet him when the angels carry him away."

Soldiers whose precombat romances came to a sad end also had their pain memorialized in song. Doubt clouds the mind of "A Heartsick Soldier on Heartbreak Ridge," as interpreted on disc by Ernest Tubb, Gene Autry, and Wesley Tuttle, among others. The lonely, homesick GI longs for the girl left behind, from whom he has received no letters. While continuing to wonder about the fate of his romance, he seems almost oblivious to the raging battle: "I'm a heartsick soldier on heartbreak ridge, across from the River of Sighs / Where the shells burst around me and cover the sound of a poor lonely heart when it cries."

No such doubt exists in the mind of the soldier in the Arthur Q. Smith composition "Missing in Action." Jim Eanes made the initial recording for the Blue Ridge label in early 1951. The Enoch Arden–like song had some impact in the Knoxville area before being covered by major country star Ernest Tubb, whose Decca recording gave it hit status and spawned additional cover versions by Ken Marvin, Jimmie Osborne, and Hollywood singing cowboy Jimmy Wakely.[10] In this sad lament the soldier, who escapes captivity after having been wounded, returns home only to find that his wife, who received a letter that he was "Missing in Action" and thus believed him to be dead, has remarried. Thinking that his wife will be better off with her new husband, he broken-heartedly "kissed her picture and whispered goodbye," determined to live out his life as a "vagabond dreamer . . . missing in action forever I'll be."

The song's lyrics, which dispel the notion that listeners always want happy endings, inspired an answer song, presumably by the same writer. Only Jim Eanes recorded "Returned from Missing in Action," also for Blue Ridge. In this seldom-heard number, the wife, still pining for her missing first husband, looks out the window and sees him walk onto the sidewalk and then down the street. Realizing that he has read the "missing in action" letter and seen her wedding picture, she runs out, catches up with him, and explains that he remains her only true love. Together, they go to the new husband and tell their story. Understanding the situation, he dutifully gives up his new bride to the soldier, and the original lovers presumably live happily ever after.

Eanes's recordings of the two Smith songs never had the same impact on the country market as Ernest Tubb's version of "Missing in Action," but they did help Smilin' Jim Eanes land a contract with Decca. In this capacity Eanes covered "They Locked God Outside the Iron Curtain" and "I'm No Communist," as well as the hitherto unrecorded "A Prisoner of War," a lyric somewhat akin to "Heartsick Soldier on Heartbreak Ridge." The essential difference between the latter two songs is that the prisoner of the first song is writing a letter to his sweetheart back in the United States. He describes his miserable surroundings—"where there's no table, no place to write"—and pledges his undying love:

> Here in this stockade with guards all around,
> Shackled with irons deep into the ground,
> Darling I'm weary and heartsick and sore,
> Bound in this prison, a prisoner of war.
> If by good fortune this letter gets through,
> Darling you know that my thoughts are of you,
> With love and kisses forever I'm yours,
> Heartbroken soldier, a prisoner of war.

Ironically, the biggest hit that came out of the Korean War appeared almost at the end of the conflict. Jean Shepard and Ferlin Husky recorded "A Dear John Letter" on May 3, 1953. It hit the *Billboard* country charts the week of July 25, an excellent if coincidental piece of timing on the part of Capitol executives, considering that the truce was signed at Panmunjom on July 27. One line, giving the impression of an American victory, reads, "For the fighting was all over and the battle had been won." The song consists of a letter from a girl whose "love . . . had died away like grass upon the lawn, and tonight I wed another dear John." In this case John is jilted by the girl to "wed your brother Don." The song, owned by Lewis Talley and Fuzzy Owen, was written by an aspiring musician and songwriter named Johnny Grimes, who was also known as Billy Barton. The latter "sold" his rights to the two Bakersfield club musicians, who brought it to the attention of Ferlin Husky. Husky then persuaded Capitol executive Ken Nelson to let him record the piece with Shepard.[11] In a sense the song elevated both the teenager Shepard and the somewhat more established Husky—who had only recently begun using his real name on disc, previously being known as "Terry Preston"—to a star status that they enjoyed for decades. "A Dear John Letter" remained on the charts for twenty-three weeks and held the number 1 position in country for six weeks; it even reached the fourth spot on the pop charts. The song also inspired two sequels, each written and recorded independently of the other after the truce had already been signed.

The first sequel to appear was "Dear Joan," by Jack Cardwell, an Alabama deejay who enjoyed an earlier hit that year with his topical ballad "The Death of Hank Williams." John replies that "ever since I'd been gone, I had prayed you'd find someone, for I also love another." John explains that even though he has broken up with his old flame, Joan's sister Sue, he still loves her; thus, Joan's marriage to Don provides a graceful way out for all the concerned parties. The song peaked at the seventh spot on October 1, 1953. The other sequel, titled "Forgive Me John," was penned by Talley and Owen and again featured Shepard and Husky on vocals. The girl (never named in their version) begs John's forgiveness and decides that she still loves him rather than his brother. John, however, rejects any idea of a reconciliation and closes with the line "There's nothing for me to come home to now, so I'll re-enlist and lead my lonely soldier's life."

The Korean War did not result in the type of antiwar songs that characterized much of the urban folk scene during the later 1960s and the Vietnam War. However, some hint of dissatisfaction is manifested in Louise Osborne's composition "A Brother in Korea." Bobby Osborne of the Osborne Brothers had been drafted into the marines in November 1951. Several months later, younger brother Roland (Sonny) Osborne recorded his sister's song on Carl Burkhardt's Gateway label. Louise's patriotism can hardly be questioned, as she had previously composed and recorded "New Freedom Bell," a tribute to the re-creation of the Liberty Bell that had been placed in West Berlin as a symbol of that city's tough stance against the Soviets. However, she was clearly upset by Bobby's conscription and fearful for his safety, although a closer examination suggests that perceived "inequities of the draft system" may have been more the source of her discontent.[12] For example, she wrote, "You can wander around in the bar room and find drunkards loafing around, / But never do they have to answer a call to serve Uncle Sam."

The themes of patriotism and pain found in many of the era's songs are often accompanied by a secondary theme: the reaffirmation of religious faith. Such faith appears as the predominant theme in a few instances, beginning with Shorty Long's "No Wars in Heaven," recorded for King on September 19, 1950. Long, who spent much of his career in Pennsylvania, often appeared with a band called the Santa Fe Rangers. A recitation midway through the song begins "Thousands killed last month the radios and papers say, / and hundreds more are called up and dying every day," and ends "But one thing we've forgotten, death just opens up the door, / to that place where there'll be no wars, anymore." Somewhat later Preston Ward reassured his listeners, "we'll keep our priceless freedom won by boys who fought and died / as long as God is on our side."

Probably the most successful country music message of faith to emerge during the Korean War was "The Weapon of Prayer" (1951), written and recorded by the Louvin Brothers, first on MGM and then on Capitol. In 1966 the song appeared on a sacred album by the bluegrass duo of Jim and Jesse. Perhaps the most inspiring aspect of the song arose from the fact that one could contribute to the war effort without being in the midst of battle:

> You don't have to be a soldier in a uniform to be of service over there,
> While the boys so bravely stand with the weapons made by hand,
> Let us trust and use the weapon of prayer.

Other songs of faith plead for salvation and support of the troops through the power of prayer. "The Great Atomic Power," a 1951 Louvins offering, uses the threat of nuclear holocaust to urge people to prepare their souls for salvation, asking, "Will you shout or will you cry when the fire rains from on high, / Are you ready for the great atomic power?" "Pray for the Boys," penned by gospel songwriter Videt Polk and recorded by Lester Flatt and Earl Scruggs in November 1952, admonishes listeners:

> Don't forget to often pray for the boys so far away,
> They have gone to take your place out there;
> They are on the battle lines in defense of yours and mine,
> Hold them up to God in humble prayer.

The song (ironically not released until 1955) struck a sufficient chord with bluegrass fans that it was revived by Ralph Stanley for the 1991 Persian Gulf War. "God's Secret Weapon," also recorded in 1952 by Carl Sauceman and the Green Valley Boys, holds that "the army of the Lord would never fail."

Two final songs with religious messages followed the truce of July 1953. "The Red Deck of Cards," as rendered by singing cowboys Tex Ritter and Jimmy Wakely, revamps the World War II classic by T. Texas Tyler into a narration. The newly exchanged prisoner of war tells his listeners that the North Korean Communist guards had used playing cards to denigrate both the United States and Christianity: the ace stood for the one true God, "the State"; the deuce for "Lenin and Stalin"; the trey for the three foolish religions that would be destroyed—"Protestant, Catholic and Jewish"; and so on up through the spade, with which they "would dig our own graves." Tearing up the cards after coming through the "Freedom Gate," the soldiers of the song enter a humble nearby "chapel in Korea." Finally, although "There's Peace in Korea" is thankful that the fighting has ended, Henry Ford's song retains a pessimistic tone and closes with a rhetorical question:

> There's happiness today singing in the air,
> We hope it might be in answer to our prayers
> Can we build a lasting peace that will help us to atone,
> For all the soldier boys that won't be coming home?

Today, after a fifty-year period in which the United States was involved in three more wars, one might say that the question has yet to be answered. During the early cold war years, songwriters and singers expressed, albeit with occasional ambivalence, many of the same attitudes held by the broad spectrum of Americans. Country songs of this typically approach the Korean "police action" in terms of patriotism, pain, and the reaffirmation of faith, but none really glorify war. Most such songs hope for victory, but many decry the loss of life and desire a lasting peace. Finally, a few express some hint of dissatisfaction or bewilderment, but not the type of outright opposition that would ultimately surface during the Vietnam War.

Notes

1. The best survey of country music in this era is chapter 7 of Bill C. Malone, *Country Music, USA,* 2nd rev. ed. (Austin: University of Texas Press, 2002), 199–243.

2. All cold war songs referred to and/or quoted in this text are listed in the discography, which includes the relevant artists, record label, original release, catalog number, and approximate or actual date recorded. Many of the songs have been reissued on either vinyl album or compact disc.

3. Standard accounts of the Korean War include Joseph C. Gouldon, *Korea: The Untold Story of the War* (New York: New York Times Books, 1982); Matthew B. Ridgway, *The Korean War* (Garden City, NY: Doubleday, 1967). The time line in Ridgway, 253–58, is especially useful for correlating events in the war with specific recordings.

4. Osborne's life and career merit further study, but a brief sketch may be found in Ivan M. Tribe, "Jimmie Osborne," in *Definitive Country: The Ultimate Encyclopedia of Country Music and Its Performers,* ed. Barry McCloud, 604–5 (New York: Perigee Books, 1995).

5. An early sketch of the short life of Harry Choates is Mike Ledbitter, "Harry Choates: Cajun Fiddle Ace," *Old Time Music* 6 (spring 1972): 20–22, which has recently been supplanted by the booklet by Andrew Brown, *Harry Choates: Devil in the Bayou* (Hamburg, Germany: Bear Family Records, 2002).

6. For songs dealing with the atomic bomb, see Charles K. Wolfe, "Nuclear Country: The Atomic Bomb in Country Music," *Journal of Country Music* 6, no. 4 (January 1978): 4–21, as well as his essay in this volume.

7. For background on "Rotation Blues," see Louis M. "Grandpa" Jones, *Everybody's Grandpa: Fifty Years Behind the Mike* (Knoxville: University of Tennessee Press, 1984), 127–28.

8. W.K. McNeil and Louis Hatchett, liner notes for *Elton Britt: The RCA Years* (Collector's Choice CCM 031-2, 1997). McNeil and Hatchett provide a short biography of Dorchester, Massachusetts, native Paul Roberts, whose full name was Paul Roberts Metivier. See also their essay in this volume.

9. Charles Wolfe, *In Close Harmony: The Story of the Louvin Brothers* (Jackson: University Press of Mississippi, 1996), 47–48.

10. Pete Kuykendall, "Smilin' Jim Eanes," *Bluegrass Unlimited* 7, no. 8 (February 1973): 9–10.

11. Chris Skinker, *The Melody Ranch Girl: Jean Shepard* (Hamburg, Germany: Bear Family Records, 1998), 10–11.

12. Neil Rosenberg, "The Osborne Brothers," *Bluegrass Unlimited* 6, no. 3 (September 1971): 7–8.

Selected Discography

Song Title	Artist(s)	Original Release and Date
Advice to Joe	Roy Acuff	Columbia 20858, 1/51
As Long As God Is on Our Side	Preston Ward	Hit Parade 7064
The Battle in Korea	L.W. & Harold & the Carolina Neighbors	Blue Ridge 204, 1952
The Bible on the Table and the Flag upon the Wall	Georgia Crackers	RCA Victor 21-0016, 1/18/49
A Brother in Korea	Sonny Osborne	Gateway 3005, 2/53
Come Back to Your Loved Ones (My Prodigal Son)	Jimmie Osborne	King 1295, 11/10/53
Daddy's Last Letter (from Korea)	Tex Ritter	Capitol 1267, 9/20/50
Dear Daddy Uncle Sam	Georgia Crackers	RCA Victor 21-0016, 1/18/49
Dear Joan	Jack Cardwell	King 1269, 8/3/53
A Dear John Letter	Jean Shepard-Ferlin Husky	Capitol 2502, 5/19/53
Doug MacArthur	Roy Acuff	Columbia 20828, 5/51
Forgive Me John	Jean Shepard-Ferlin Husky	Capitol 2583, 8/20/53
Forgotten Men	Don Reno & Red Smiley	King 5024, 8/27/56
Freedom Monkey	Doc Williams	Wheeling 1037, 10/19/66
From Mother's Arms to Korea	Louvin Brothers	Capitol 2510, 3/23/53 Capitol LP 1721, 7/25/61
Fuzzy Wuzzy Teddy Bear	Lone Pine (Harold Breau)	RCA Victor 20-4482, ca. 1952
God, Please Protect America	Jimmie Osborne	King 893, 7/26/53
God's Secret Weapon	Carl Sauceman	Capitol 2060, 1952
Goodbye Maria (I'm Off to Korea)	Wilf Carter (Montana Slim)	RCA Victor 47-4523, 1/24/52
The Great Atomic Power	Louvin Brothers	MGM 11277, 5/20/52 Capitol LP 1721, 7/25/61
Heartbreak Ridge	Delmore Brothers	King 1005, ca. 1951
Heartsick Soldier on Heartbreak Ridge	Ernest Tubb	Decca 46389, 11/13/51
	Wesley Tuttle	Capitol 1992, 11/30/51
	Ken Marvin	Mercury 6373
	Gene Autry	Columbia 20899, 12/27/51
I'm No Communist	Lulu Belle & Scotty	Mercury 6400
	Grandpa Jones	RCA Victor 47-4771, 5/20/52
	Jim Eanes	Decca [BCD 1594], 6/19/52
Johnny Sleeps in Korea	Manson Smith	Cozy 378
Korea, Here We Come	Harry Choates	Macy's 141, 1950/51

Selected Discography (cont'd)

Song Title	Artist(s)	Original Release and Date
Korean Mud	Elton Britt	RCA Victor 20-5140, 1952
The Korean Story	Jimmie Osborne	King 1268, 8/3/53
Let's Keep the Communists Out	Terry Preston [Ferlin Husky]	Four Star 1518
Let's Not Sleep Again	York Brothers	King 669, 1947
	Blue Sky Boys	Starday LP 205, ca. 1950
Missing in Action	Jim Eanes	Blue Ridge 601, 1951
	Ernest Tubb	Decca 46389, 11/30/51
	Jimmie Osborne	King 1038, 12/51
	Jimmy Wakely	Capitol 1936
	Ken Marvin	Mercury 6373
Mr. Stalin, You're Eatin' Too High on the Hog	Arthur Smith	MGM 10829, 1950
New Freedom Bell	Louise & Sonny Osborne	Kitty 502, 1951
	Country Gentlemen	Starday 455, 6/59
No, No Joe	Hank Williams (as Luke the Drifter)	MGM 10806, 8/5/50
	Ernie Lee	Mercury 6289, 1950
No Wars in Heaven	Shorty Long	King 906, 9/19/50
Old Soldiers Never Die	Gene Autry	Columbia 39405, 4/20/51
	Vaughn Monroe	RCA Victor
	Jimmy Wakely	Capitol 1534
Our United Nations Flag	Charlie Arnett	Cozy 255
Our U.S. Volunteers	Charlie Arnett	Cozy 254
Pray for the Boys	Lester Flatt-Earl Scruggs	Okeh 18004, 11/9/52
A Prisoner of War	Jim Eanes	Decca 28387, 6/19/52
Purple Heart	Jim & Jesse & the Virginia Boys	Capitol 2365, 6/13/52
The Red Deck of Cards	Jimmy Wakely	Coral 61112, 1953
	Tex Ritter	Capitol 2686, 12/3/53
The Red We Want Is the Red We've Got in the Old Red, White and Blue	Elton Britt	RCA Victor 48-381, 1950
Returned from Missing in Action	Jim Eanes	Blue Ridge 201, 1951
Robe of White	Louvin Brothers	MGM 11065, 8/5/51
		Capitol LP 1721, 7/27/61
Rotation Blues	Elton Britt	RCA Victor 48-0494, ca. 1951
	Bill Monroe	Decca 46344, 4/1/51
	Terry Preston [Ferlin Husky]	Four Star 1573
	Ken Marvin	Mercury 6353

Selected Discography (cont'd)

Song Title	Artist(s)	Original Release and Date
Shoot That Bear	Bobby Gregory	Hillbilly 71003
Stalin Kicked the Bucket	Ray Anderson	Kentucky 573, 4/53
Talk of Peace	Lonnie Glosson	Mercury 6074, 11/47
Thank God for Victory in Korea	Jimmie Osborne	King 908, 10/2/50
There's a Star Spangled Rainbow	Wesley Tuttle	Capitol 40073, 11/20/47
There's Peace in Korea	Henry Ford?	Delta 417
They Locked God Outside the Iron Curtain	Little Jimmy Dickens	Columbia 20905, 1/25/52
	Wesley Tuttle	Capitol 1992, 1/30/52
	Boots Woodall	Mercury 6380
	Jim Eanes	Decca 46403, 1/21/52
	Bobby Grove	Grove 19578
This Old Cold War	Bill Clifton	Starday LP 213, 9/62
Unknown Soldier	Elton Britt	RCA Victor 20-5140, ca. 1952
The Voice of Free America	Jimmie Osborne	King 988, 10/11/51
The Weapon of Prayer	Louvin Brothers	MGM 10968, 2/20/51
		Capitol LP 1721, 7/27/61
	Jim & Jesse	Epic LP 26204, 3/31/66
When That Hell Bomb Falls	Fred Kirby	Columbia 20740, 8/4/50
When They Drop the Atomic Bomb	Jackie Doll	Mercury 6322, ca. 3/51
A White Cross Marks the Grave	Carl Sauceman	Republic 7047, 1953/54
	Bill Clifton	Starday LP 213, 9/62
Wrap My Body in Old Glory	Carl Sauceman	Capitol 2060, 1952
	Rual Yarbrough & Dixiemen	Old Homestead, ca. 1974
	Osborne Brothers	Pinecastle PRC 1100, ca. 2000

"Dear Ivan"

Country Music Perspectives on the Soviet Union and the Cold War

Kevin S. Fontenot

Between the end of the Second World War and 1989, the United States waged a cold war with the Soviet Union. The results of that conflict reached deeply into every aspect of American life—from taxes to fund an expanding military to science fiction movies like *Invasion of the Body Snatchers,* which subtly exposed fears of the "enemy within." American popular music largely ignored the conflict until the Vietnam War, preferring to wallow in sentimentality and escapism. One form of American music, however, did not ignore the cold war and America's Soviet opponent. Country music presented the American case with forceful, corny, and sometimes deeply perceptive defenses of the American way of life and attacks on the glaring deficiencies of Communism. In the process, country musicians reinforced "plain folk" ideology and criticized their own government and fellow citizens whom they felt were guilty of treason.

Communism violated the basic tenets of the ideology embraced by the fans and practitioners of country music. "Plain Folk Americanism," as the ideology has been named by historian James N. Gregory, rooted itself in individualism, hard work, suspicion of outsider involvement and big government, Protestant Christianity, and a deep patriotism. The voice of the plain folk could best be heard in country music. "Where religion divided, country music . . . appealed across the moral-religious boundaries to illuminate the common denominators of their subculture, the essential values and symbols that over the years" identified the plain folk identity. Communism and its major defender, the Soviet Union, stood in direct opposition to these "common denominators."[1]

Although some of the plain folk had toyed with Socialism in the wake of the defeat of Populism at the turn of the century and during the Depression, most rejected Communism as fundamentally incompatible with plain folk values.[2] "What's good over in Russia," remarked Bill Hammett, "don't mean it's good for us." James Durham, a north Louisiana minister and cousin of Governor Jimmie Davis, located the failure of farmers' movements at the turn of the century in their attachment to "Carl [sic] Marx" and in their speaking "disparagingly of the church."[3] Davis, the most political of the country musicians, blasted the Soviets and Communism in a 1962 speech before the Grand Lodge of Louisiana, a speech overflowing with plain folkism. Khrushchev, Davis announced, promised beef and freedom, but delivered horsemeat and oppression. America could defeat the Russians, but not with political, economic, or military strength. America possessed all these, but still failed to prevent the expansion of Communism in Europe, Cuba, and Vietnam. For Davis, victory must be preceded by a cleansing of America and a return to national morality—in other words the national embrace of patriotism, Christianity, and hard work.[4] His words were well known to the plain folk. Country music had proclaimed this plan since the mid-1940s.[5]

Russia occupied a unique position in plain folk religion long before the USSR became a direct threat to America. Dispensational theology (which became increasingly popular during the twentieth century) identified Russia with the nations of Gog and Magog from the thirty-ninth chapter of Ezekiel. These nations led the assault on Israel in the final battle near the end of the world. This identification permeated the South through the Schofield edition of the Bible, which incorporated dispensational theology into the marginalia of the text. Rev. Alfred G. Karnes, an early hillbilly singer, distributed copies of a sermon that clearly proclaims the USSR to be Gog: "We know that Russia's plan is to swallow up the world in atheistic Communism . . God is against Magog, the land of Gog. So Russia fits exactly, characteristically, geographically, and prophetically (the land of Magog) . . . Russia will not be conquered until the Saved are gone with Christ."[6] The war against Communism and the Soviet Union was a holy war, a war winnable only by God, perhaps using the United States as his instrument.

The official Russian stance of atheism deeply troubled the plain folk, and atheism emerged as the major flaw in both Communism and the Soviet Union for most country musicians. Nowhere is this more obvious than in Little Jimmy Dickens's minor 1952 hit, "They Locked God Outside the Iron Curtain" (Columbia 20905). Dickens describes a land where "little children can not play" and the leaders have tried to chop down the old rugged cross and have placed on Satan's head a "kingly crown." For this, Dickens forcefully announces, obviously drawing on the Gog and Magog prophecy, God will destroy the Soviet Union and lock the sinners outside a heavenly curtain.

More disturbing is Red River Dave's "The Red Deck of Cards" (Decca 29002), a tale of attempted brainwashing of Korean War prisoners by the Communists. "The Red Deck of Cards" is a reworking of T. Texas Tyler's 1948 hit, "The Deck of Cards" (Four Star 1228), which tells the story of a young World War II GI who uses his card deck as a reminder of theological lessons.[7] In the 1953 version, the Communists pervert the innocent theology to teach the lessons of Marx, Lenin, Stalin, and atheism. "Deck of Cards" had been wildly popular, and the reaction to the rewriting certainly served to underscore both the deviance of Communism and the difference between the political systems. In the final lines of the recitation, the soldiers destroy the playing card representations of Communist doctrine and walk off to a small chapel.

Russia also violated the basic plain folk principles of individualism and private ownership of both land and tools to work the land. Exactly how much the southern yeomanry knew about Stalin's brutal repression of the kulaks is difficult to determine, but the folk were well aware of the abolishment of private property. Scotty and Lulu Belle Wiseman sang the joys of private ownership in "I'm No Communist" (Mercury 6400), a song aimed as much at internal traitors as it is at Russia. Again, the symbols of the old agrarian lifestyle and independence predominate—"I believe a man should own his own land and plow"—as does praise of small, Jeffersonian-style government, a dream most plain folk saw slowly evaporating by the 1950s.

Whatever the strengths and perversions of Russia and Communism as viewed by the plain folk, most had no question that both would be defeated. How that defeat would be achieved was something of a conundrum for the folk. Early after the Second World War, the United States was viewed as the obvious instrument of defeat. And the United States possessed a literal instrument of defeat—the atomic bomb. Country artists embraced the bomb as a symbol of American vigor and ingenuity; the bomb was a gift from God, the "brimstone from Heaven," according to the Buchanan Brothers, who recorded two songs celebrating the weapon. The Almighty entrusted "Atomic Power" to the United States to use wisely for the protection of freedom.[8] And if Russia pressed her agenda too far, destruction must obviously follow. America would not hesitate to use the bomb, Roy Acuff reminded Stalin in "Advice to Joe" (Columbia 20858), an apocalyptic warning of terror raining from the skies to prostrate the USSR. Acuff manipulated imagery from the Book of Revelation, equating the "Communist ambition now to rule or wreck us all" with demonic expansionism by Satan. The fact that America had the bomb indicated that the nation was God's chosen instrument of destruction.[9]

Hank Williams Sr. also expressed his confidence in America's ability to defeat Russia. Unlike Acuff, though, Williams gently poked fun at Stalin in "No, No Joe" (MGM 10806).[10] He warned Stalin not to puff himself up until the buttons popped off his vest and not to take confidence in a "system we know ain't sound." If all else failed, a "mess of Yanks" could handle any "fair sized tanks" Stalin might throw at the United States.

Others were not as sure as Acuff and Williams. God, not America, Little Jimmy Dickens sang, would tear the iron curtain down. If the United States proved to be the instrument of victory over the Soviet Union, its use was incidental to God's plan. Jimmie Davis added that at its greatest moment of strength, America exhibited strong weaknesses—those of pride, increasing softness, and abandoned vigilance. Even worse, some Americans had turned their backs on the Republic and engaged in espionage for the Communists. The American government itself gravitated toward Communist-type interference with high taxes, lazy employees, and increasing involvement in what the plain folk saw as clearly local matters, primarily race relations and education. The threat of Communism and Russia came not from the outside but from within.[11]

Lulu Belle and Scotty's "I'm No Communist" reflects the growing fear of infiltration by Russian agents. The song celebrates private ownership and independence and promises that if the narrators are brought before the "committee" (the House Committee on Un-American Activities) they will shout their loyalty so Stalin will hear it in Russia. But the true theme of the song lies in the criticism of the American government's increasing expansion of power, a clear violation of the old Jeffersonian principle that the government that governs best governs least. The Wisemans' song essentially identifies government—American or Russian—as the problem.

The plain folk regarded patriotism as a central tenet in their ideology.

Throughout the Second World War, patriotic anthems flowed from the pens of hillbilly songwriters such as Denver Darling. "There's a Star Spangled Banner Waving Somewhere," recorded by Elton Britt, dominated the country and western chart. The patriotic fervor easily transferred into the cold war era, with songs like Jimmie Osborne's "The Voice of Free America" and the somewhat premature "Thank God for Victory in Korea." To this category belongs Jack Boles's "The Red We Want Is the Red We Got in the Old Red, White, and Blue," which oozes patriotism and faith in the U.S. government and anticipates Merle Haggard's "The Fighting Side of Me." But that optimism faded with the Russian acquisition of the bomb, the fall of China, and the setbacks of the 1960s. The folk never lost faith in America, but were confused by what they saw as a perversion of the basic American beliefs and power.

This growing frustration with the American government over segregation and the expansion of federal power coincided with the Cuban missile crisis and fears of a strengthening Russia. The situation produced a unique view of U.S.-USSR relations in Jimmy Dean's recitation "Dear Ivan."[12] For all its sentimentality and, at times, corniness, "Dear Ivan" marks a decided break in views of Russia. Dean addresses his "letter" to an average Russian and goes on to play on Jeffersonian ideals of agrarianism, family, individualism, independence, religion, and the virtues of small government. If only the plain folk of both nations could meet and, under God's guidance, discuss matters, all of the troubles could evaporate. Government was not the answer, government was the problem, the divisive factor in world affairs. Realistically, Dean's vision could not be realized, but it expressed how deeply plain folk values still resonated with southerners, how disturbing the cold war had become for them, and how they retained their ability to empathize with the Russian people.

Following the early 1960s, country music grew silent on the subject of the Soviet Union. The musicians become increasingly occupied with the issue of division at home. Songs such as Sara and Maybelle Carter's "I Told Them What You're Fighting For" and Merle Haggard's slightly comical anthem "Okie from Muskogee" and his more strident "The Fighting Side of Me" detailed plain folk frustration with those they deemed unpatriotic and treasonous. Southernism as the best form of Americanism gained in popularity among younger plain folk, who embraced southern rock, an offspring of country music that tackled both the unpatriotic and the government with a force equaled only in the wrestling ring (where the common enemy was often a Russian, such as Nikolai Volkoff). Lynyrd Skynyrd delivered "Sweet Home Alabama," and the Charlie Daniels Band reintroduced Russia into the country dialogue with "In America." Coming shortly before the ascension of Ronald Reagan and in the midst of the humiliating final year of Jimmy Carter's administration, Daniels declared that the divisions in America were only illusions and that America could and would fight to defend her institutions. She had "put her feet back on the paths of righteousness," and if the "Russians don't believe that, they can all go straight to hell." Daniels combined the religious indignation of Dickens and Acuff with the combativeness of Haggard to produce a confident vision in which no deals would be struck with the devil. Reagan carried the plain folk vote in the South and in the pockets of the southern diaspora in California and the Midwest. Echoing Reagan's aggressive stance, Ronald Roberts released "Dear Mr. Andropov," which revives the letter format to point out that the Soviet Union's defeat—a defeat rooted in Russia's economic failure—is now inevitable. Danny Day expressed moderation with his "Open Letter to President Reagan and Prime Minister Andropov," which reflects the influence of the television movie *The Day After*.[13] The plain folk, like most Americans, were clearly disturbed by tensions in the early 1980s, but they did not abandon their belief that the Soviet Union was fundamentally "evil." Within ten years, due to a wide range of factors, the Soviet threat collapsed. At least partly to credit was the aggressive stance of the plain folk, who embraced Reagan's hard-line position.

Then a curious thing happened. Evil old Russia, Gog the Terrible, morphed once again into an American ally. Carson Robison had celebrated the Russian ally during World War II with his "1942 Turkey in the Straw," but nothing positive had been heard since then.[14] In 1990 Hank Williams Jr. revived the old letter format, which had been used by his father, Roy Acuff, and Jimmy Dean, to record "Don't Give Us a Reason," a strutting warning to Saddam Hussein that America was finished being weak and that the "desert ain't Vietnam." Amid all the bluster, almost unnoticed, is one line that indicates just how much things had changed: "the eagle and the bear make a mighty tough pair." For Hank Jr., a weakened Russia could now be safely added to the list of American allies.

The country music dialogue on the Soviet Union and Communism followed closely the southern philosophy of Plain Folk Americanism, contrasting the folk values of patriotism, hard work, individualism, and religion with a Russia seen as atheistic, class oriented, and fundamentally evil.

But it also used the anti-Russia argument to criticize the American government and fellow citizens who the folk deemed "un-American." The real question pulsing just below the text is, what disturbed the folk more—the Russian threat or their own government, which they felt was growing increasingly intrusive and Socialistic?

Notes

The author wishes to thank Bill C. Malone for much direction and continued interest, Nolan Porterfield for dubbing rare recordings from his extensive collection of 78s, and Ronnie Pugh of the Country Music Foundation.

1. James N. Gregory, *American Exodus: The Dust Bowl Migration and Okie Culture in California* (New York: Oxford University Press, 1989), 223. Gregory provides a detailed discussion of this philosophy, particularly on pages 139–248. The term "plain folk" is used to mean the southern yeomanry and working class and their descendants, including those of the white southern diaspora in areas of California and the Midwest. See also, for example, Frank Owsley, *Plain Folk of the Old South* (1949; repr., Baton Rouge: Louisiana State University Press, 1982), and Jack Temple Kirby, *Rural Worlds Lost: The American South 1920–1960* (Baton Rouge: Louisiana State University Press, 1987), for additional examinations of the plain folk. The best, and classic, study of country music is Bill C. Malone, *Country Music, USA*, rev. ed. (Austin: University of Texas Press, 1985).

2. For an examination of the plain folk experimentation with Socialism see James R. Green, *Grass-Roots Socialism: Radical Movements in the Southwest 1895–1943* (Baton Rouge: Louisiana State University Press, 1978). Some singers of plain folk origin gravitated toward radical politics and Socialism, the best known of these being Woody Guthrie and Aunt Molly Jackson. However, upon examination of their individual stories and their eventual association with New York left-wing radicals, they may be best understood as exceptions. See Joe Klein, *Woody Guthrie: A Life* (New York: Ballantine Books, 1980); Robert Santelli and Emily Davidson, eds., *Hard Travelin': The Life and Legacy of Woody Guthrie* (Hanover, NH: Wesleyan University Press; University Press of New England, 1999); and Shelly Romalis, *Pistol Packin' Mama: Aunt Molly Jackson and the Politics of Folksong* (Urbana: University of Illinois Press, 1999). Guthrie's Socialism seems to have arisen, like Eugene Debs's version, out of his personal experience with America. Jackson, who appears to have been opportunistic, violated just about every aspect of the plain folk code by the end of her life.

3. Hammett quote from Gregory, *American Exodus,* 154. Durham quote from John P. Durham, *Biography of James Lucius Durham* (Shreveport, LA: Journal Printing, 1961), 40. James Durham was the nephew of Davis's grandfather, Henry Davis.

4. Jimmie Davis, "Address before the Grand Lodge of the State of Louisiana," in *Sesquicentennial Celebration of the Grand Lodge of the State of Louisiana Free and Accepted Masons* (n.p., 1962), 71–76. Davis, strongly anti-Communist, cites the close ties between Henry Wallace and the American left as one of his reasons for supporting Harry Truman as vice president in 1944. This may be a later addition to his reasoning, as his main attraction to Truman seemed to be their common interest in music. Davis later played at the White House, possibly the first country music concert held in the presidential residence. See Jimmie Davis, conversation with Kevin S. Fontenot, Baton Rouge, LA, December 22, 1999, notes in author's collection.

5. Davis's comments on the Soviet Union's inability to provide necessities for its people are echoed in comedy routines by Whitey "The Duke of Paducah" Ford (early 1960s) and Lewis Grizzard (1980s). See Duke of Paducah, "Kruschev," on *Louisiana Hayride: Classic Comedy Radio* (Music Mill Entertainment MME-70021-2), and Lewis Grizzard, "There Ain't No Toilet Paper in Russia," *Live: The Goodwill Tour from Moreland to Moscow* (Southern Tracks STD 007). Ford's routine also notes Soviet atheism.

6. Rev. A.G. Karnes, "Prophecy against Gog," undated sermon flyer (probably early 1950s), copy in author's collection. Karnes was a "jake leg" Baptist preacher with an amazing guitar performance style. His complete recordings are available on *Kentucky Gospel* (Document Records DOCD 8013). For Russia's identification with Gog and Magog, see Paul Boyer, *When Time Shall Be No More: Prophecy Belief in Modern American Culture* (Cambridge, MA: Harvard University Press, 1992).

7. Tyler's hit version reached the number 2 position on the country and western charts and remained on the charts for thirteen weeks, easily making it the most popular recording discussed in this paper. All chart information is from Joel Whitburn, *Top 40 Country Hits* (New York: Billboard Books, 1996).

8. On the bomb's impact on American culture see Paul Boyer, *By the Bomb's Early Light: American Thought and Culture at the Dawn of the Atomic Age* (Chapel Hill: University of North Carolina Press, 1985). Boyer includes a discussion of several atomic bomb songs. Shortly after the Roswell incident the Buchanan Brothers also recorded a song about UFOs that views them as indicators of the end of time.

9. The imagery of "Advice to Joe" is similar to that of the World War II song "Smoke on the Water," which promises (surprisingly prophetic) destruction from the skies on Japan. All of this was made much more disturbing when the violent lyrics to "Smoke on the Water" were put to a western swing dance beat by Bob Wills and His Texas Playboys. The result is an image of cowboys two-stepping across the devastated Japanese landscape. This was fairly typical of wartime demonization of the enemy, particularly the Japanese, during World War II. See Jennie A. Chinn, "There's A Star Spangled Banner Waving Somewhere: Country-Western Songs of World War II," *JEMQ* 16 (summer 1980): 74–80, and (author not known), "Denver Darling: Illinois Cowboy," *Old Time Country* 7 (fall 1991):

4–11. Darling was the author of numerous anti-Axis titles, including "We're Gonna Have to Slap the Dirty Little Jap" and "Cowards over Pearl Harbor." Instructive to understanding the demonization of Japan in these songs is John W. Dower, *War without Mercy: Race and Power in the Pacific War* (New York: Pantheon Books, 1986). Dower's comments can also be profitably used to understand attitudes toward the USSR.

10. Williams used his pseudonym, "Luke the Drifter," on this and other recitations, which often reveal a deep social consciousness. His work remains at the core of the country music tradition. Williams's total record output is available on *The Complete Hank Williams,* Mercury 314-536-077-2.

11. For an examination of cold war culture see Stephen J. Whitfield, *The Culture of the Cold War* (Baltimore: Johns Hopkins University Press, 1996), and Richard M. Fried, *The Russians Are Coming! The Russians Are Coming!: Pageantry and Patriotism in Cold War America* (New York: Oxford University Press, 1998). In light of recent evidence, the history of espionage during the cold war is being rewritten with chilling effect on old views that mitigated the extent of Soviet infiltration of the United States. See Allen Weinstein and Alexander Vassiliev, *The Haunted Wood: Soviet Espionage in America, the Stalin Era* (New York: Random House, 1999), and Arthur Herman, *Joseph McCarthy: Reexamining the Life and Legacy of America's Most Hated Senator* (New York: Free Press, 2000).

12. Jimmy Dean, "Dear Ivan" (Columbia 42259). Dean's song, peaking at number 9 and remaining on the charts for ten weeks, was the follow-up hit to his wildly popular "Big Bad John."

13. Ronald C. Roberts,"Dear Mr. Andropov," Dee-Lark DL-10183; and Danny Day, "Open Letter to President Reagan and Prime Minister Andropov," Sundial SR 1001. Both records were released in 1983.

14. Many of the folk were uncomfortable with the idea of Russia as an ally. The blues singer Peter "Doctor" Clayton placed Stalin in the same group as Hitler and Mussolini, wishing leprosy on the Russian dictator and saying that Mussolini would have "heart failure" when he received the news that Stalin was dead. See Clayton's "41 Blues" on *Doctor Clayton: Complete Pre War Recordings in Chronological Order (1935–1942)* (Document DOCD 5179). The text of the song is reproduced in Guido van Rijn, *Roosevelt's Blues: African American Blues and Gospel Songs on FDR* (Jackson: University Press of Mississippi, 1997).

10

"True Patriot"

Brian Letton Goes to War

Rae Wear

Well known for his repertoire of patriotic songs, Brian Letton is one of the most overtly political of Australian country singers. His populist message evokes nostalgia for a golden age of innocence when life was better, fairer, and grounded upon traditional values. Fitting under this populist umbrella are his war-related songs, which present two main themes: The first suggests that military service is part of a citizen's duty to the state, in return for which the state is expected to guarantee certain rights. In a number of songs, Letton describes a situation where Australian citizens have fulfilled their obligation to fight for their country, but the state has failed to reciprocate by protecting their social rights. His second major theme is the need to defend the nation against military, financial, and cultural threats, each of which may destroy time-honored ways and values. His intensely nationalistic songs identify an imagined heartland that is constructed largely by looking inward and backward.[1] This heartland is populated by "true-blue" Australians who battle the elements, financial institutions, politicians, and a range of other forces, both internal and external, that threaten to destroy it.

To fully understand Letton's positions on both military service and defense of the heartland, one must appreciate the impact, especially on social rights, of relatively recent changes in Australia. Some of the most profound of these changes, which have strongly affected rural and regional areas, can be attributed to globalization, which, generally speaking, refers to "the increasing integration and global connectedness of trade, markets, products, resources and culture. It is enabled by technological innovations and underpinned by shifting power relations that sees finance capital as relatively dominant and transnational corporations as very powerful *vis-a-vis* the nation-state."[2]

One of the consequences of globalization has been the replacement of the interventionist policies of the welfare state by the laissez-faire stance of neoliberalism. Governments around the world have reduced expenditures, with consequent negative impacts on social rights, which T.H. Marshall identified as essential for complete participation in community life and for the full exercise of political and civil rights.[3] Social rights require state intervention to guarantee an adequate standard of living through transfer payments and benefits, usually delivered by an extensive bureaucracy and government-funded workforce.[4] Marshall believed that state intervention to moderate the effects of the market by providing social services, education, and a welfare net was essential if citizens were to have the material foundations and skills necessary to fully exercise their civil and political rights. For example, material inequality can mean that in practice all are not fully equal before the law, and inadequate levels of education can make informed voting impossible. In return for the state guarantee of rights, including social rights, citizens are expected to fulfill certain obligations, such as respecting the law and defending the state when called upon.

Citizens' Rights and Obligations in Brian Letton's War Songs

The winding back of social rights associated with globalization provides the context for many of Letton's songs, especially those focusing on the grievances of country people. War service is most often dealt with in passing, as a duty willingly fulfilled by citizens who then find themselves neglected by the state. Letton's underlying assumption is shared by those social scientists who argue that warfare contributed to the expansion of social rights in the twentieth century through the operation of a trade-off: mobilization of citizens by the state in return for redistribution of resources as compensation for involvement in war.[5] His songs, make clear, however, that the Australian state has not kept its side of the bargain, especially with regard to rural Australians. As veteran country music star Slim Dusty suggests in a song of the same name, "Things are not the same on the land."[6]

"Happy Anniversary," a song written by Stan Coster and featured on

Letton's *Footprints* album, is worth quoting at length because it incorpo-
rates both of his war themes: the state's failure to reciprocate to citizens
who have fulfilled their duties, and the need to defend a threatened Australian heartland. The first part of the song tells of a surprise visit to his parents for their golden wedding anniversary:

> I just stood by the doorway and watched them
> And the bitterness clawed at my heart
> As I thought how they had battled their whole lives
> And was this the reward for their part?
>
> This woman gave birth to eight children
> And she slaved like a man all her life
> And seldom complained of the hardships.
> Of the poverty, the sickness and the strife.
>
> This man was a soldier in two wars
> His sons, well we all fought in Korea,
> Now the old couple's work years are over
> And the future looks empty and drear.
>
> Oh is this what the old couple fought for
> Is this the reward for their sons and their daughters
> That they raised for Australia
> Is this the reward now they're done[?]
>
> Their reward that they exist on a pension
> Cold winters, ill-nourished poor health
> Aah! they'd battle to exist on a pension
> In this young country renowned for its wealth.
> . . . .
> The time's coming near when Australia
> Must fight a grim war all alone
> And if our young folks see nothing to fight for
> Then we stand to lose all that we own.

Letton makes clear in the first part of the song that he sees a strong
relationship between the fulfillment of citizenship duties and the social
rights the state is expected to guarantee. In this song, the old couple have
fulfilled their obligations to the nation through the raising of a family and
the completion of military service. In both undertakings, the sacrifices have

been extreme: eight children have been raised, and two generations have fought in three different wars. Letton's underlying assumption is that if the dangers of war are to be shared, so too should a country's resources. Clearly, this expectation has not been met, as the old couple tries to make ends meet on a government pension that is both inadequate for their needs and less than is their due. Although they have discharged their duties as citizens, they have been denied their entitlement to a reasonable standard of living.[7] If the next generation is to be willing to fight for their country, they must see that "old workers and soldiers reap peace and reward for their stands."[8]

The state's failure to secure social rights is underscored by Letton's reference to Australia's wealth: not everyone shares the parlous circumstances of Letton's old couple. The impact of globalization in Australia, as elsewhere, has been uneven, with many cosmopolitan elites benefiting from the opportunities offered. Some people with the necessary skills have profited from the new global economy, but in much of rural and regional Australia, the withdrawal of state support for family farm–based agriculture has been devastating, leading to the formation of a rural underclass that is socially, culturally, and politically isolated from the rest of the nation.[9] Although freer global trade may have meant net income gains, the uneven distribution of this income has resulted in greater inequality.[10] There is growing spatial differentiation within cities and, of particular relevance to country music, between city and country. Some commentators have gone so far as to suggest that Australia is at risk of becoming two nations, one urban and rich and the other rural and poor, where citizens feel alienated and undervalued for their contributions to community life.[11] Globalization has been a double-edged sword, causing both the eviction of farmers from their land and a reduction in financial support to them when they most need it. As economies fragment, and the relatively unfettered operation of the market creates economic winners and losers, citizens are no longer in the same boat together.[12] This explains the undertow of resentment in many of Letton's songs, as well as "the politics of grievance" that infuse contemporary Australian populism.[13]

Letton is very skilled at mobilizing listeners' resentment by painting a picture of hard-working folk who have fulfilled their obligations to the state and who find themselves, through no fault of their own, among society's losers, abandoned by the state whose duty it is to protect them. The theme of "Happy Anniversary" is repeated in "This Is It," which tells of a farmer forced by bank foreclosure to leave the land that three generations have farmed. His parents had worked hard, and his father had been killed in war, but these sacrifices count for nothing on the scales of injustice. The same theme reappears in "40,000 Reasons," which also deals with the forced sale of a family farm. This farmer also reminisces about his father, missing in action on the Kokoda Trail in Papua New Guinea, the site of a bloody World War II campaign against Japanese forces. The injustice of forced sales is not an isolated theme. Other country singers such as Raebekah Roycroft and Graeme Connors also deal with the topic and, like Letton, marshal listeners' anger against politicians and financial institutions blamed for throwing farmers from their land.[14] Understandably, circumstances like those described by country artists have led to growing anxiety, uncertainty, and insecurity in contemporary Australia, which in turn fosters nostalgia for the idealized heartland of the past.

Defense of the Heartland

The need to defend traditional Australia is a major theme running through numerous of Letton's songs. Through them he demonstrates the intense nationalistic pride that has cemented his reputation as a "true patriot" and "fiercely proud Australian who cares very much for the future of this great land."[15] His passionate nationalism is arguably connected with unease and anxiety associated with the changes brought about by globalization. For many populists the Australian heartland has been endangered not only by financial deprivation, but also by changes to the nation wrought by immigration. Whereas once non-Aboriginal Australians were primarily of Anglo-Celtic origin, now almost a quarter of Australia's population includes first- and second-generation citizens from non-English-speaking backgrounds.[16] Many of the losers from globalization have perceived their traditional identity as being threatened by official policies supporting multiculturalism and recognizing the rights of Aboriginal Australians and acknowledging their dispossession as a result of European settlement.[17] Anxiety about identity and fear of rootlessness drive much of populism's nostalgia for an idealized community located in the past. Letton's lyrics show that he shares these sentiments: he longs to return to the heartland that is central to his conception of Australian identity.

Most of his albums include songs of reminiscence, recalling an age of innocence, which, according to his rose-tinted recollections, was immune from problems such as drug and alcohol abuse.[18] His songs leave no doubt in his listeners' minds that, like the two old men in "When We Were Just Kids" (*My Australia*), he would like to return to the old days when the pleasures of childhood were simple and homemade. His protagonists in "Who's to Blame" (*Land of Waltzing Matilda*) dream of the past and hope to recreate it. In "Where Have the Old Ways Gone?" (*Footprints*) he wonders why anyone was ever tempted by new ways that take Australians away from the values of their forebears. He makes it clear that the changes wrought by government policies in response to new technologies, globalization, and the postwar waves of immigration from non-English-speaking areas have been detrimental to "his Australia," a place that bears little relation to the contemporary urban nation in which most of his fellow Australians live. The communities he describes and the imagery he uses are almost entirely rural, despite the fact that Australia is a highly urbanized nation, with most people living on the coastal fringes: the most densely populated 1 percent of the continent holds 84 percent of the population.[19] His characters are the traditional ones of settler, soldier, bushman, and farmer, who no longer exist as he describes them, and who fail to reflect the diversity of contemporary Australia.[20] Like many populists, he pines for the comfort and security of the old-fashioned rural society he describes, with its archetypal inhabitants who inevitably lived in harmony because of their shared language, ethnicity, and culture.[21] The more anxious and threatening the times, the more appealing is the prospect of returning to the comforting homogeneous cocoon of country life.

Notes published by his record producer about his *My Australia* album demonstrate the close connection between patriotism and feelings of insecurity: "In these uncertain times, there are a lot of Australians unhappy about recent events and the select few who call Australia home but seem to have forgotten what being Australian has always stood for—the love of country, freedom and to always help a mate. The old diggers [Australian soldiers] certainly had it right."[22] This statement emphasizes the point made plain by his songs: a number of Australians like him are unhappy about people who fail to appreciate being Australian in the same way he does. His songs also make clear that Australian soldiers were the ones who fought and died to secure the old Australia of his imagination, where agrarian mythology and Australian soldiers' exploits in battle, especially World War I, are linked.[23] Australian identity has habitually been described as having been shaped both by the pioneers' struggle with the land and soldiers' heroism on the battlefield. Both were nation-building exercises that demanded similar qualities of "comradeship and loyalty, resourcefulness and adaptability."[24] Soldiering and farming are activities to be proud of. "You'll Do Me, Mate" (*My Australia*) describes a father responding with pride to his son's khaki uniform. Letton's most conventional war song, "The Wells of Beersheba" (*Footprints*), pays tribute to the qualities demonstrated by the Australian lighthorsemen in the 1917 battle of Beersheba in the northern Sinai Desert. "I'm in Australia Blue," written by Bob Hirst and performed by Letton on *My Australia,* pays homage to the ANZACs (Australian and New Zealand Army Corps members) and their exploits in two world wars.

Letton intimates, however, that the troops may have fought in vain because "the country they fought for's surely changing." In "Where Have the Old Ways Gone?" (*Footprints*) he wonders how long Australia will remain free. The last part of "Happy Anniversary" demonstrates his feeling that old Australia faces a precarious future, with its warning that "the times are coming near when Australia / Must fight a grim war all alone." It is not clear from the lyrics what potential war Letton is referring to or who the freedom-robbing enemy is, although some Australian populists have long feared an invasion from Australia's northern neighbors. More often, however, he seems to feel that the enemy is winning the battle for Australia by economic means. In "Will We Still Really Be Australian?" (*For the Farming Families*) he suggests that the Japanese who were defeated by Australian troops in the Kokoda Trail campaign are buying what they could not take through war.

The rhetoric of economic nationalism has been adopted by right-wing populist parties around the world as they attempt to grapple with the implications of the movement of global capital and the activities of transnational corporations.[25] It appears to many, Letton among them, that profit, rather than heritage, is all that matters.[26] Country artists like Letton and Slim Dusty question the sense of casually selling off Australian land, and the former blames "foreign enterprises with wealth and might" for forcing small farmers from their land.[27] Even old allies must be guarded against, because they too threaten heartland traditions. Letton asks why Australians feel compelled to follow American trends, because Americanization, symbolized by kids riding skateboards in baggy shorts, sneakers, and caps turned backward, is pulling Australia away from its traditional roots.[28] Letton is not a lone voice. In "The Great Australian Dream" (*The Here and Now*), Graeme Connors makes a similar point by juxtaposing a series of iconic rural landmarks against a tour bus full of city kids with "their baseball caps

Fig. 1. Pauline Hanson, former leader of Australia's One Nation Party. (Courtesy of Queensland Newspapers.)

on backwards," their "Coca Cola, Nike shoes and Oakley shades." Ultimately, these country artists present an isolationist vision of an ideal Australia. The heartland community they wish to preserve is static and unchanging, and repels outside influences that threaten its integrity.

According to populist ideology, threats to the nation come not only from outside the country but also from groups living inside its borders. The enemy within is often perceived as even more dangerous than the enemy outside. Political populism in Australia, as elsewhere, has been marked by racism toward groups within the country who challenge traditional, monocultural ideas of what it means to be Australian. Pauline Hanson, former leader of the populist One Nation Party, which flourished briefly in the late 1990s, first came to prominence because of her attacks on indigenous rights and Asian immigration. She portrayed government support for these groups and multicultural policies that broadened the idea of citizenship as divisive and destructive of the national community. Early in 2003 she announced that she would be joining Letton in the studio to record a duet. In making the announcement, Hanson said of country music: "if you listen to the words, it's what I've been trying to say in my speeches."[29] That Letton shares her concerns about ethnic difference and the threats it poses to his idea of Australia is obvious in "Will We Still Really Be Australian?" which tells of visiting the city only to find that there are a "thousand different faces from a hundred different creeds" and that "all around me there's a language foreign to my beloved homeland tongue." This urban tower of Babel causes him to ask, "am I really in Australia or somewhere overseas?"

For Letton, the country he identifies with is not the urban melting pot that is contemporary Australia, but a rural, Anglo-Celtic heartland that has long since disappeared, and may never have existed in the idealized form he sings about. Like many populists, Letton, in his loyalty to this vision of Australia, denies the right to belong to those who fail to conform. Despite the fact that he describes Australian soldiers as having died for freedom, he is critical of those citizens who exercise that freedom by becoming pacifists or critics of the Australian way of life. He even goes so far as to suggest that those who do not love the country should leave.[30] From his perspective it is inconceivable that pacifists or critics might also love their country. He seems to feel, as many custodians of Australian identity do, that difference is threatening and that those who contest the old, monocultural vision of Australia are unpatriotic, do not belong, and are not entitled to citizenship rights.[31] This contrasts strongly with more recent ideas of citizenship that accept that Australia is a multicultural society composed of people of diverse cultures, ethnicities, and faiths, united by tolerance of each other and respect for the law, but lacking in shared experience.[32]

As many populists do, Letton longs for the security of a community whose members believe in and value the same things as a matter of course. When they exercise the freedom that the nation's soldiers fought and died for, they will reach identical conclusions because they are similar people, shaped by a shared past and desiring the same future. The exercise of the right to freedom will lead to consensus.[33] When it does not, the solution is to expel those who differ because they threaten the idealized community. As he puts it in "Sing Australia" (*The Land of Waltzing Matilda*), "if we stand divided, divided we will fall."

Conclusion

The explanation for these sentiments surely lies in the desire to retreat from changes associated with globalization. Such strong feelings have been especially marked in rural and regional Australia, where government support for family-based farming has been greatly reduced. Anxiety, coupled with diffuse feelings of resentment, has been the result. Heightening the tension is a sense of injustice based on the grounds that rural Australians have fulfilled their obligations to the state, such as raising families and serving the nation in war, yet have been denied social rights necessary to achieve a reasonable standard of living. Feelings of resentment have been further fueled by challenges to traditional conceptions of Australian identity—challenges posed by policies acknowledging the rights of indigenous and immigrant groups. Country musicians have responded by putting into words what many of their listeners feel. Brian Letton in particular has responded with a series of populist songs, many of which deal with the subject of war, past, present, and future.

His songs about past wars make two key points: that many Australians fulfilled their duties as citizens only to be defrauded of their social rights in return; and that Australian troops may have been sacrificed in vain because the country they fought and died for is in danger of disappearing. Present and possible future wars will be required in order to turn back the tide and protect the Australian heartland from a range of threats. These wars may involve military engagement, but they may also be fought in the economic and cultural arena. "Bringing back those good old Aussie ways" that Letton so passionately desires means protecting the nation from the economic effects of globalization and from cultural changes associated with globalization and postwar immigration. Even he acknowledges, however, that this is likely to be a losing battle.[34]

Notes

I would like to thank Graeme Connors for permission to quote from his work, Brian and Michelle Letton for permission to quote from Brian's songs, and Tracy Coster for permission to quote from Stan Coster's lyrics. I would also like to thank Joel Bateman for research assistance.

1. Paul Taggart, *Populism* (Buckingham: Open University Press, 2000), 96.

2. Elizabeth Van Acker and Giorel Curran, eds., *Business, Government, and Globalisation* (French's Forest, NSW: Longman, 2002), viii.

3. T.H. Marshall, *Citizenship and Social Class and Other Essays* (Cambridge: Cambridge University Press, 1950).

4. J.M. Barbalet, *Citizenship* (Minneapolis: University of Minnesota Press, 1988), 20

5. Bryan S. Turner, "Contemporary Problems in the Theory of Citizenship," in *Citizenship and Social Theory*, ed. Bryan S. Turner (London: Sage, 1993), 12.

6. Bill Chambers, "Things Are Not the Same on the Land," recorded by Slim Dusty, *Live into the 90's.*

7. Barbalet, *Citizenship*, 37, 65.

8. Stan Coster, "Happy Anniversary," performed by Brian Letton on *Footprints.*

9. Ian Gray and Geoffrey Lawrence, *A Future for Regional Australia: Escaping Global Misfortune* (Cambridge: Cambridge University Press, 2002), 3–4.

10. Bill Pritchard, "Negotiating the Two-Edged Sword of Agricultural Trade Liberalisation: Trade Policy and Its Protectionist Discontents," in *Land of Discontent: The Dynamics of Change in Rural and Regional Australia,* ed. Bill Pritchard and Phil McManus, 90–104 (Sydney: University of New South Wales Press, 2000).

11. John Anderson, "One Nation or Two" (address to the National Press Club, Canberra, February 17, 1999), http://www.dot.gov.au/media/anders/speeches/asl_99.htm.

12. Judith Brett, "Pauline Hanson, John Howard and the Politics of Grievance," in *The Resurgence of Racism: Howard, Hanson and the Race Debate,* ed. Geoffrey Gray and Christine Winter, Monash Publications in History 24 (Melbourne, Aust.: Monash University, 1997), 16.

13. Ibid., passim.

14. Michael Roycroft, "The Shame," performed by Raebekah Roycroft, *The Shame;* Graeme Connors, "Let the Canefields Burn," *The Best . . . Til Now.*

15. NFS Publicity, http://www.nfspublicity.com.au/nfs77/7707.htm; cover notes, *The Land of Waltzing Matilda.*

16. Stephen Castles and Alastair Davidson, *Citizenship and Migration* (London: MacMillan, 2000), 67.

17. Michael Leach, "Hansonism, Political Discourse, and Australian Identity," in *The Rise and Fall of One Nation,* ed. M. Leach, G. Stokes, and I. Ward, 42–57 (St. Lucia, Aust.: University of Queensland Press, 2000).

18. Billy Vaughn, "Age of Innocence," performed by Brian Letton on *Footprints;* Brian Letton, "I'm Too Old to Try Something New," *My Australia.*

19. *Australian Bureau of Statistics Yearbook* (Australia, 2002), http://www.abs.gov.au/Ausstats/abs.

20. Leigh Dale, "Mainstreaming Australia," *Journal of Australian Studies,* JAS Archives, http://www.api-network.com/cgi-bin/page?home/index.

21. Brett, "Politics of Grievance," 23–24.

22. Album notes, *My Australia,* LBS Music, http://www.nfspublicity.com.au/nfs77/7707.htm.

23. On the subject of agrarianism, see J. Prest, "Agrarian Politics in Australian History," *Historicus* (November 1970): 7.

24. Russel Ward, *The Australian Legend* (Melbourne: Oxford University Press, 1966), 231.

25. Hans-Georg Betz and Stefan Immerfal, eds. *The New Politics of the Right* (London: MacMillan, 1998), 5.

26. Letton, "Where Have the Old Ways Gone?" *Footprints.*

27. Stan Coster, "Some Things a Man Can't Fight," performed by Brian Letton on *For the Farming Families*; Bill Chambers, "Things Are Not the Same on the Land," recorded by Slim Dusty.

28. Letton, "Will We Still Really Be Australian?" *For the Farming Families.*

29. Quoted in Michael Duffy, "Just Like an Old Stone, If You Start Hanson Up, She'll Never Stop," *Courier-Mail*, February 22, 2003.

30. Letton, "The Land of Waltzing Matilda" and "The Fighting Side of Me."

31. Dale, "Mainstreaming Australia," 16.

32. Brett, "Politics of Grievance," 24.

33. Donald MacRae, "Populism as an Ideology," in *Populism: Its Meanings and National Characteristics,* ed. G. Ionescu and E. Gellner (London: Wiedenfeld and Nicholson), 162.

34. Letton, "Where Have the Old Ways Gone?"

11

"Alternative" to What?

O Brother, *September 11*, *and the Politics of Country Music*

Aaron A. Fox

"All I play is Top 40 music. It's just forty years old."
—Don Walser

Introduction: The Space of the Alternative

The Web site masthead of the influential music publication *No Depression* coyly declares that the magazine is "the alternative country (whatever that is) bimonthly." The formulation is cleverly ambiguous. It could be taken to mean that *No Depression* covers *whatever* "alternative country" is, meaning that whatever the magazine covers is "alternative" by virtue of that coverage. The more prosaic interpretation of the parenthetical hedge, of course, is that the magazine represents a constituency that eschews a firm definition of the boundaries of its interests and refuses the constraints of imposed genre boundaries. Yet a third possibility concerns the grammatical function of the term "alternative," which could be taken to modify "bimonthly" rather than the term "country." Under this rubric, *No Depression* itself is an alternative choice among publications, and "whatever" it covers is something called "country."

Clearly, the idea of "alternative" country is a complicated one, and its complexity is integral to its discursive function as a marker of social identity, musical style, and commercial value. In this essay, I examine contemporary alternative country as part of a broader "alternative" cultural formation. "The alternative" is a compelling figure of culture in modernity, marking a key tactical *habitus* of a certain kind of classed modern subject, at once empowered and confounded by the spectrum of choices offered up for consumption, and just as quickly replaced by new choices. The alternative demands interrogation as a figure of discourse, not as a truth claim or an auratic quality of agents, objects, or institutions. Its attachment to existing, already dense and replete cultural tropes (like "music," "lifestyle," and "medicine") multiplies the difficulties—and the futility—of specifying the content of an alternative essence or of any particular field of alternative practice.

On the surface, a suspicion of "mainstream" and "corporate" cultural formations appears to be a common ideological characteristic of many alternative discourses. But the idea of alternative culture is closely linked to particular idioms of consumption—specifically oriented toward alternative commodities and sites of exchange, constructed in terms of "natural" and "traditional" histories of practice. Thus, a principle, perhaps diagnostic conflict in alternative culture concerns appropriation—the dilution of expressive essence by commodification and the concomitant risk of "selling out." Judgments of alternative authenticity entail complex considerations of the *scale* of any given "alternative" enterprise, as well as the political commitments of the enterprise. Thus Alison Krauss, the crossover bluegrass star, has been widely praised for "staying with" Rounder Records as her sales have gone into the millions, although in the process she has been responsible for a significant expansion of the company.

Emplacement seems to be key as well. If mainstream culture comes from everywhere and nowhere at once, alternative culture stresses connections to particular (usually "rural" and "traditional" places). Thus ice cream from Vermont, medicine from China, and music from Texas are important components of the suite of alternative commodities. But the alternative gaze is also free to wander from place to place, in a classically cosmopolitan fashion. Authentic emplacements are continually in tension with eclectic forms of cultural tourism, and not a little fantasy. Finally, discourses of "purity" and "naturalness" construct alternative identities and commodities in a tense dialectical opposition with an implied, contaminated, artificial character of modern mass culture. Here, technology (or technological obsolescence) comes to the foreground as a central trope of alternative essence.

As in previous epochal formations of bourgeois romanticism, the intellectual and affective languages of alternative culture also emphasize personal authenticity, the idea of a singularity of expression and a uniqueness of individual identity, understood in opposition to the alienating effects of mass culture and rationalization. "Genre" conventions are suspect for the constraints they place on expressive individuality; and as genres of alternative culture have become institutionalized, they have been characteristically eclectic and synthetic, embracing the absence of category as the basis of a new category: "whatever that is." The term's apparently paradoxical crystallization into institutionalized genres of discourse and practice—"alternative rock," "alternative medicine"—returns us to classic problems in genre theory, and the embodiment of both mainstream and alternative identities in suites of commodities and styles of consumption returns us to classic problems in social theory more generally. The dynamics of naturalization, reification, and schismogenesis (Bateson 1936; Feld 1994)—the interplay of emergence and residuality, improvisation and script, performance and text, mimesis and alterity—are reflexively named when the term *alternative* is invoked as a master trope of social, aesthetic, and commercial location. But what are the ideological limits of this reflexivity? What choices or "alternatives" are refused or ignored? Are there alternatives to alternative culture that are *not* mainstream, or at least not the mainstream derided in alternative ideology? And finally, what is this "mainstream" against which alternative discourses are articulated, and into which they are inexorably re-assimilated? Is the mainstream really any less fraught with ambiguity than alternative culture?

Alternative Country: A Personal History

My concern in the remainder of this essay is, specifically, with the discursive and ideological boundaries of alternative country music (now often called "alt.country"—pronounced "alt-country"—in deference to the ironic role of the Internet in constructing a movement that espouses serious doubts about the value of contemporary technology). I argue that the particular ironies of attaching alternative ideology to country music are suggestive for a broader critique of alternative culture, as well as for a more particular critique of recent transformations in the significance of America's vernacular musical traditions. I also consider the implications of the recent emergence of this hitherto subcultural discourse onto the center stage of American popular culture, signaled by the enormous success of the soundtrack album *O Brother, Where Art Thou?* I explore the strange but suggestive conjuncture of *O Brother*'s success and the radical effects of the terrorist attacks of September 11, 2001, on American culture. And finally, I conclude by considering two country music performers whose art would seem to lie beyond the reach of any potential alternative appropriation.

I'd prefer not to face the task of theorizing alternative country, since I am still perplexed by the unmodified term "country." The term has a fiercely complex semantic field, referring simultaneously to a genre of music, a figure of cultural identity, a nationalist ideology, and a structure of feeling that connects communities in places as diverse as South Texas, South Africa, and urban Japan (Fox and Yano, forthcoming). Scholars are just beginning to grasp country's force as a response to global modernity, a response unfolding unevenly in time and place, but always hard on the heels of the equally uneven unfolding of commodity fetishism and the alienation of labor in the global political economy. "Country," in this global sense, was already (before the rise of its alternative other) a trope of alternativity to the modern, albeit a socially specific kind of nostalgic, resistant alternativity first diagnosed as such by Raymond Williams. Williams famously wrote of the trope of "(the) country" as a dialectical response to the figure of "the city," and of the opposition between these emplaced images as "one of the major forms in which we become conscious of a central part of our experience and of the crises of our society" (1973, 289). That the urbanizing "we" of Williams's formulation has expanded to incorporate vast new portions of the world's inhabitants since Williams wrote *The Country and the City* only lends more force to his insight. As Creed and Ching make clear, a signature of postmodern culture and cultural theory has been the tendency to naturalize an urbophilic perspective on this opposition, to see "the country" as a reification only of cultural nostalgia, rather than a lived domain of modern experience (1997).

In the United States, alternative country looms large in the current phase of cultural reflection on "country," vernacularity, and "roots" in the mass media, as the essence of the American national popular has been problematized by all the effects implied by "globalization" and the emergence of a "post-industrial" social order. It looms large, as well, in the history of my own involvement with country music, as a scholar and a musician and a fan. I became interested in country music, as I then understood it, in the mid-1980s, at a time when I had dropped out of college and drifted into a relatively blue-collar existence. During a stint as a household mover, I fell in with a hard-drinking gang of working-class Irish Americans who listened to mainstream country music while we drove trucks full of furniture around New England. I found myself musically engaged by singers like John Conlee and Waylon Jennings, but I was especially impressed by the first recording released by Randy Travis, who emerged on the country music scene in 1986 as an assertive musical traditionalist, whose style offered an implicit critique of Nashville's mainstream country-pop style. (That Travis went on to mainstream superstardom is well known. That his fine *Storms of Life* recording had the feel of an alternative in the 1980s is not always remembered.)

I was surprised by my response to this music. I held a view, common in the eastern, middle-class social world of my upbringing, that country was musically and politically retrograde stuff, overdetermined by the base commercial instincts of an industry that manipulated politically quiescent working-class consumers. When I returned to college, I thought that attending intellectually to "country" would push the envelope of what I was then coming to understand as a new way of thinking about popular culture in the musical academy. (At the time, there was very little serious critical and interpretive scholarly literature on country, though the music had been well documented.) As a middle-class college student trained in art music composition and infatuated with "folk" musical traditions, I saw commercial country music as an extremely mysterious "other," denigrated and dismissed in every cultural discourse with which I was familiar. But I found the music and its cultural meanings compelling.

My first erratic intellectual forays into what I came to understand as the "authenticity" problem were largely guided by artists whose music would now be clearly identified as alternative in sensibility and institutional affiliation, though at the time they were mostly branded as "neo-traditional" acts. In 1986 Steve Earle, for example, had (like Randy Travis) just released his first album (*Guitar Town*) on the Nashville division of a major label (MCA) and was being hailed in some quarters as the savior of an aesthetically *and* commercially moribund style. (In fact, Earle, Travis, and Dwight Yoakam were frequently discussed in those years as representing a coherent neo-traditional musical *movement,* disguising their large differences in approach, heritage, and goals.) Almost twenty years later, after much-chronicled tribulations involving drug abuse, prison, heavy metal music, and a conversion to left-wing politics, Earle has emerged as a leading spokesman for, and elder statesman of, the alternative space, although he still lives in Nashville. The punk/country stylistic and musical fusions of Dwight Yoakam and other Los Angeles–based acts like X and the Blasters, which I thought were the last word in tactical refusal of the mainstream, were in-

Fig. 1. An advertising image for *The Complete Hank Williams* (Mercury Records, 1998).

stead just the first soundings of what became the alternative country formation of today—curiously powerful early entries into a cultural space that could barely be imagined in the late 1980s. The Polygram reissues, during the late 1980s, of nearly the complete Hank Williams catalog were the first reissues to restore Williams's "original" recordings to monophonic sound and to leave the surface noise of the masters intact. The record jacket notes for each volume emphasized the connection between archaic "sound quality" and the "historical importance" of the recordings. These discs were foundational for my generation of country musicians. They have long since been surpassed by the 1998 Mercury boxed set, *The Complete Hank Williams,* issued in a very expensive limited-edition package (fig. 1). But at the time, they were radical and fresh after decades during which Hank's music had been sweetened and smoothed over to maintain its commercial currency.

After college, I spent the late 1980s and early 1990s in Austin, Texas, where I went to graduate school in social anthropology. I was documenting rural, working-class musical and verbal art in a town called Lockhart, thirty miles south and a million miles away from Austin's vibrant club scene, and making my living playing mainstream Top Forty country music in dance halls and bars across the state. But I couldn't avoid noticing the increasing numbers of middle-class musicians of my generation—mostly raised, as I was, on the punk rock canon, and mostly college educated—who, like me, were relocating to Austin from places like Boston, New York, Chicago, and San Francisco. This migration fostered a burgeoning economy of vintage clothing, record, and instrument shops in Austin, and eventually the emergence of a full-scale alternative music industry center. These musicians were interweaving their curatorial musical projects, sourced largely in the growing catalog of reissues of historic country recordings coming mostly from European record companies, with more rooted and local exemplars of "Austin music" (most of them holdovers from the last such phase, when Willie Nelson moved from Nashville to Austin in the 1970s). Increasingly, they were earning record contracts and national exposure playing rock-tinged versions of honky-tonk, western swing, and bluegrass. I was in Austin, that is, to see the idea of alternative country being born as an industry and a self-conscious local musical scene with national commercial aspirations.

In 1995, I moved to Seattle and took my first academic job, in anthropology. There, I began to notice the emergence of the "Americana" music format on college radio stations. In fact, Don Yates, the program director at KCMU in Seattle and a friend from that era, was among the first to use the term "Americana" to describe what he was doing mixing vintage country, alternative country, bluegrass, and blues-rock records on the station's shows. Yates's practice was influential (in part because he created what remains a vitally important Internet listserv for "alt.country" fans and professionals) though not unique. The label stuck as a description of an aesthetic and cultural fusion that was being widely and diversely imagined at college radio stations around the country (where an existing discourse of alternative music was already a well-established effect of the punk rock era) and subsequently became the commercial category that incorporated the various facets of alternative country culture into a viable marketing category, replete with awards shows, record airplay charts, catalogs, tastemakers, and journals.

A moment of insight occurred when I escorted the idiosyncratic Texas yodeler Don Walser into the KCMU studios for an interview by a leather-clad undergraduate with a nose ring and vermillion hair. Walser is a rotund, retired accountant who had a minor career as a country musician in

West Texas in his youth, and who had returned to the profession after his retirement. He played a crucial patriarchal role in the birth of the Austin alternative country scene by facilitating the dialogue between young rock-based musicians and older Texas-based artists, especially as the host of a weekly jam session at a small bar called "Henry's" that had, during the late 1980s and early 1990s, managed to court a hip, youthful, punk crowd without alienating its long-term regular patrons, most of whom were older blue-collar Austinites. As Walser once put it, "I play for both kinds of blue-hairs." Walser's extraordinary charisma and unique yodeling skills had earned him national attention, and he was at the radio station that day, along with Butch Hancock, to promote a show they were doing in Seattle that evening as part of a national tour.

The KCMU disc jockey, as I recall, made a statement to the effect that it would be great if Walser could record his next record on the vintage studio equipment used by Bob Wills in the 1940s. Walser's good-humored reply—that if Bob Wills were alive he would prefer modern digital sound—flummoxed the young interviewer, who was accustomed to the obsessive preference for "vintage" musical technology among most younger alternative country musicians.

In 1997 I moved to New York, and back to academic musicology. But I did keep a practical connection to the country music world by hosting a radio show for several years on a college station in New Jersey, trying to juggle the demands of an audience made up of both truck drivers and college students, and the demands of a station committed to reporting playlists to the Gavin "Americana" charts, but dependent on listener contributions from fans of the Statler Brothers and Conway Twitty. And once again, I seem to have been present for the birth of a new era in the history of alternative country. I refer to the strange combination of the terrorist attacks on New York City on September 11, 2001, and the release of the soundtrack album *O Brother, Where Art Thou?* which I believe are two of the most significant events in the field of country music since World War II. Specifically, I want to argue that they are significant precisely in their conjuncture.

9/11 and Country Music

It may be less obvious why the terrorist attacks of September 11 impinge on this story, so let me begin with that point. I am convinced that whatever the other long-term effects of that day on American culture, the terrorists performed a singular intervention in the American discourse of class identity and the cultural fields (including country music) that articulate with this discourse. In part, I refer to the obvious outburst of nationalism and cultural nostalgia that followed the attack, which was not dissimilar to the cultural effects of the 1991 Gulf War. In the twentieth century, country music was frequently drafted, or enlisted itself, to serve in wartime as a symbolic discourse of nationalist feeling. But I refer here to something more specific and novel about the juxtaposition of the terrorist attacks with a pervasive global postmodernity and a fundamental shift in American social relations that had begun to seem permanent and natural by autumn of 2001. The figure of the heroic, male, blue-collar American worker, the man of few words and strong deeds, had become an almost entirely historical and nostalgic legacy of what Harrison and Bluestone (1988) call "the postwar class compromise" (and which they argue ended in 1977), a residual, sepia-toned ghost on the margins of the postmodern "global" political economy. But in autumn of 2001, this figure loomed up from the rubble of the World Trade Center as a fireman, a cop, a construction worker, and a soldier. The resurrection of this nearly buried figure announced the emergence of a crisis of national identity that would come to center in part around masculinity, whiteness, and the costs of embracing global capitalism. The Internet millionaire and the corporate CEO once again had competition as culture heros. Bill Gates would suddenly have to share symbolic power with the Quecreek miners.

Country music rushed into the discursive opening the attacks created, asserting as in wars past a privileged claim to speak for the nation in the voice of (white) working-class experience. Alan Jackson's "Where Were You (When the World Stopped Turning)" was the most successful country song to deal specifically with September 11 and its effects, in a plaintive, meditative voice that also manages to specify the befuddlement of a working-class perspective that had become detached from geopolitics, though the rhetoric of the song constructs this, in classic nativist terms, as a virtue. There were angry songs, too, especially Toby Keith's "Courtesy of the Red, White, and Blue (The Angry American)," which produced a minor storm of controversy when Keith was excluded from a memorial broadcast on a national television network because, Keith claimed, he had insisted on performing this song, with lyrics like "We'll put a boot in your ass / it's the American way." Country comedian Ray Stevens entered the fray with "Osama Yo' Mama (You in a Heap o' Trouble Boy)," which converted a sentiment similar to Keith's into a personalized attack on the leader of al Qaeda, in a grand tradition of country music war songs.[1]

Some sort of powerful conjuncture was in the air after September 11, a widespread realization that circulated through the media and popular discourses that traditional working-class patriotic nationalism had emerged from the wreckage at Ground Zero as a source of both comfort and critical insight into the risks of globalization and multiculturalism.[2] Laced with themes of denial and compensation, this rediscovery of white, male, blue-collar workers as symbols of a righteous nation was also interwoven with a guilty realization that these same workers had been forgotten and ridiculed in the celebratory discourses of postmodernism, globalization, and technology that had characterized the decade leading up to September 11, 2001. Now, as the president donned a hard hat and stood on the wreckage surrounded by firemen and construction workers, these discourses seemed exposed as mistaken or fraudulent, and once again working-class culture, brave and yet dark, and deeply masculine, seemed possessed of wisdom and worth. Country music stood to gain significantly in stature in this conjuncture, benefitting from a broader reinvigoration of themes of the native, the white, the vernacular, and the folkloric. But as ever, the "working-class" hero who emerged from the rubble became the subject of feverish construction and hegemonic appropriation. And as ever, "country music" came to stand for "working-class" (and "white") identity, which was in turn a metonym for "American" identity, in ways that obscured and misrepresented quite complex fields of social conflict in the service of particular class ideologies and political ambitions.

Anthony deCurtis, writing in the *New York Times,* caught the essence of the conjuncture I am intimating when he observed that Johnny Cash's 1974 album *Ragged Old Flag* was being hurried into reissue to coincide with the three-month anniversary of the terrorist attacks (deCurtis 2002). "Mr. Cash's music," deCurtis writes, "with its patriotic themes and dark undercurrents . . . seems eminently suited to the cultural mood of the country." But what "mood" does deCurtis mean? How could Johnny Cash, who hadn't been a major commercial force in mainstream country music in twenty years, suddenly seem so relevant, not merely an icon of a venerated past but a voice for the present? It is crucial to note that Johnny Cash, whom deCurtis celebrates as the embodiment of a newly rediscovered American authenticity, is simultaneously portrayed as an "outsider" to mainstream country music. Despite Cash's prodigious success as a country artist over the

decades, his long association with the Nashville-based country music industry, and his passionate Christianity, the portrait deCurtis paints of him
stresses the "dark undercurrents" in Cash's persona, music, and biography.
This is an oft-told tale, and one Cash sometimes encouraged in his self-
presentation, focusing on his early embrace of rockabilly elements in his
music, his frequent political and musical acts of defiance against mainstream country culture, and his legion of admirers outside of country music, with Bob Dylan as the exemplary authenticator.[3]

DeCurtis adds an extensive discussion of the latest chapter in this version of Cash's significance, namely, the artist's recent association with punk
rock and hip-hop producer Rick Rubin, who produced Cash's last four
albums, all of which have been marketed strictly as alternative country, and
all of which feature black and white artwork portraying Cash as a forebod-
ing, even avenging dark figure. It is intriguing to observe how Cash was
posed against increasingly dark and elusive backgrounds, from the relatively conventional rustic images gracing his first two records for the American Recordings label, to a darkened backstage corridor on the third, and
most recently with Cash's face emerging enigmatically from black shadows
(fig. 2). With this shift in image came stripped-down acoustic performances,
guest appearances by leading rock artists like Bono and Tom Petty, and
exceptionally bleak and dark songs even for an artist who never shied away
from bleak material.

Cash's four recordings for Rubin's American Recordings label have been
popular and influential among rock and alternative country fans and musicians, whereas they have been virtually invisible from the country mainstream. Cash, of course, played this "dark" character to the hilt throughout
his career, but he simultaneously presented himself as a mainstream American entertainer, emphasizing his Christian faith, his humble background,

Fig. 2. Album cover art for Johnny Cash's *American Recordings* (Lost Highway,
1994); *Unchained* (Lost Highway, 1996); *American III: Solitary Man* (Lost Highway, 2000); and *American IV: The Man Comes Around* (Lost Highway, 2003).

Fig. 3. Album cover art for Johnny Cash and June Carter's *Carryin' On* (Sony, 1967).

his military service, his putative Native American heritage (see below), and his happy family life with wife June Carter Cash (fig. 3).

Cash's renewal of his outsider image was most powerfully signified by a 1998 ad taken out by Rubin's record company in *Billboard*, the paper of record in the mainstream music business, in which Johnny is seen aggressively extending his middle finger to "the Nashville music establishment and country radio" (fig. 4). The picture was taken at a 1970 performance at San Quentin Prison, but had never been used for marketing purposes prior to 1998. (The photo, though, clearly resonated with Cash's album cover for *Bitter Tears* [1964], an expression of sympathy with Native Americans. On the cover of that album, Cash is seen in angry half-profile, giving an approximation of the American Indian Movement's defiant clenched-fist salute [fig. 5]. The *Billboard* ad also prominently features the American Recordings logo—an inverted American flag, signifying a naval vessel in distress. Both the flag logo and Cash's extended digit in this photo also strongly resonate with the cover of *Ragged Old Flag*, where Cash points forcefully with an extended finger to the tattered flag behind him [fig. 6].)

My point—and perhaps deCurtis's point—is that Cash's defiant, rebellious posture *and* his God-and-family patriotism have both become relevant simultaneously in the present moment. Cash's years in the commercial wilderness, and his earnest embrace as the elder statesman of punk-inflected "alternative" country, have become assets that serve his "mainstream" rediscovery as an emblematic "American" vernacular artist, whose conformity to traditional values is contiguous with his politically defiant "alternative" stance. His uncompromising masculinity, his deeply felt empathy with poor, downtrodden, imprisoned, aboriginal and working-class

Fig. 4. A Johnny Cash advertisement
(*Billboard* magazine, March 14, 1998).

Fig. 5. Album cover art for Johnny
Cash's *Bitter Tears* (Columbia/Legacy,
1964).

Fig. 6. Album cover art for Johnny
Cash's *Ragged Old Flag* (Columbia,
1974).

people, his passionate patriotism and religious faith, and his mortality (Cash
suffered from severe health problems before his recent death) combine to
make him a powerful symbol of the post–September 11 zeitgeist. Cash is
big, again. He represents the seam that connects working-class tradition
and the alternative movement. But as emblematic as Cash seemed to be in
the months after September 11, 2001, he was eclipsed by the stunning
success of *O Brother.*

O Brother and the Politics of the Musical Vernacular

O Brother, Where Art Thou? needs little introduction for readers literate in American popular culture. I refer principally to the soundtrack album from 2000's surprisingly popular movie by the Coen brothers, rather than the film itself. The "soundtrack" was conceived as an independent project concurrently with the production of the movie. It features both young bluegrass and roots music revivalists like Alison Krauss and Gillian Welch, and venerable elders, most prominently Dr. Ralph Stanley. The Coen brothers reportedly sank the entire promotion budget for the film into the recording project as an act of curatorial love, and the project, "against all odds," became a spectacular success that has far outdistanced the film itself. It is surrounded by a discourse that suggests this success was an entirely unintended and accidental consequence of the passion and authenticity of the project. It occupied the number 1 position on the *Billboard* country charts for weeks in 2002, and remained on the album charts long afterward. To date, O Brother has sold over six million copies, which would qualify as a significant success for a mainstream country act, especially in the present era of sharply declining album sales in country music and in popular music more generally (and a sales figure previously unimaginable for a recording marketed as alternative country or bluegrass). Even in a year marked by the success of several other musically traditional country projects, the success of O Brother was widely reported to have taken Nashville completely by surprise. O Brother may be the first country album (or as its promoters would have it, bluegrass album) in history to occupy the heights of mainstream commercial success while being critically acclaimed on NPR, in the *New York Times,* and in the world of college radio.[4] Indeed, many sophisticated alternative country fans began to distance themselves from the success of O Brother in embarrassment by early 2002, even as similar and derivative projects choked the advertising pages of No Depression. (*Austin Chronicle* writer Christopher Gray captured the attitude of many purists when he complained, "Things have obviously gotten out of hand when you walk into a record store and see a life-size cutout of Ralph Stanley" [2002].)

Mainstream organs like *Rolling Stone, USA Today,* and *Newsweek* ran glowing articles on O Brother, advancing the claim that country music—or even popular music more generally—had been resuscitated from a moribund state by the soundtrack album. Indeed. *Newsweek* directly invoked the parallel to September 11 that I am advancing here when it declared that

Fig. 7. An advertising image for the *Harry Smith Anthology of American Folk Music* (Smithsonian Folkways, 1997).

the current condition of popular music in the United States constituted "An Aesthetic National Emergency" (Ali and Gates 2002). Reflecting on the spectacle of the 2002 Grammy Awards ceremony (at which *O Brother* scored a surprising number of prizes, including Best Album and Best Male Country Vocal for Ralph Stanley), *Newsweek* singled out the success of *O Brother*—and the ironic centerpiece of that album, Ralph Stanley's stirring a capella rendition of "Oh Death"—as the exception that called attention to the rule of pop's current banality.

The conjuncture I am describing was underway before *O Brother* and September 11. One need only look at the acclaim that greeted the reissue of Harry Smith's *Anthology of American Folk Music* by Smithsonian Folkways in 1997 (originally released in 1952). In its original release, this collection has been widely cited as a key source for the folk revival of the 1950s and 60s. But the *Anthology* reissue project, though a huge critical success in the high bourgeois media (O'Brien 1998), and a big seller by Folkways standards, did not cross over into mainstream popular culture the way *O Brother* did, because the historical recordings on the *Anthology* are too obscure, weird, and low fidelity to be marketable as commercial popular music, and because the beautifully boxed *Anthology* reissue was quite expensive (approximately $75) and self-consciously packaged and promoted as a luxury antique reproduction and a serious scholarly resource (marketing photos prominently featured the extensive book of liner notes) (fig. 7).

Similarly, the much-praised and much-watched PBS series *American Roots Music,* which was first broadcast in 2001 and was smartly packaged with an ancillary book and recordings, seemed to capture an emergent discourse about the vernacular tradition and its relevance to postmodern America. This ambitious project introduced a holistic understanding of twentieth-century vernacular popular styles to a large mainstream audience, but in the earnest high-bourgeois curatorial tones of typical PBS fare. Although it featured extensive coverage of country music, it emphasized the African American contribution to the roots of American popular music in both its narrative rhetoric and its visual imagery. Like the *Harry Smith Anthology* and *O Brother,* the PBS series was also visually designed to evoke antique associations (fig. 8).

These are only the most prominent of a number of examples of bourgeois anxiety about the vernacular heritage that foreshadowed the *O Brother* phenomenon and marked a growing concern with curating the vernacular tradition in an era of fundamental cultural change. (Another case might be the Rounder Records series issuing the complete southern field recordings of Alan Lomax.) But it took terrorists to make the world safe for alternative

Fig. 8. An *American Roots Music* promotional image (Public Broadcasting System, 2001).

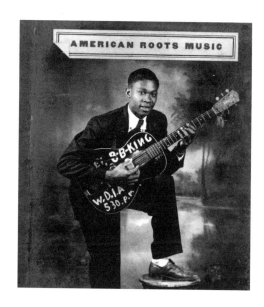

country, and it took *O Brother* to articulate country music—in its postmodern form—as a solution to a nationalist conundrum.

In 1998 Dwight Yoakam's producer and guitarist, Pete Anderson, uncannily anticipated the conjuncture described here when he told the *Hartford Advocate's* Tom LeCompte: "As yet, Americana [the music marketing format] has not been able to translate [radio airplay] chart success into album sales, which it will need to do if it is to ultimately succeed. . . . It will take *Deep Impact*—an asteroid or a tidal wave to change things" (Anderson, in LeCompte 1998). Anderson was flippantly referring to a popular movie in which an asteroid wreaks havoc on the earth, but he was prescient in forseeing the explosive transformation that would produce the cultural opening for *O Brother.* Indeed, it is not obvious to me that *O Brother* would have swept the Grammy Awards or risen to the top of the charts without the historical *aporia*—the "deep impact"—of the terrorist attacks of September 11. With *O Brother,* and in a moment of unprecedented nationalist fervor and anxiety, "alternative country" arrived to save country music and to refashion a cosmopolitan, postmodern version of country's vernacular "roots."

The *O Brother* phenomenon, in other words, depended on a contingent historical conjuncture, overdetermined by a national crisis of identity that might not have emerged into the cultural foreground without the events of September 11, and which is still largely emergent more than two years after the attacks. There are obvious parallels to the way that neo-traditional artists like Yoakam and Earle "saved" country music in the 1980s, or to any of the other roots revivals—reassertions of the vitality of the vernacular heritage—that have periodically revived country music throughout its history as it has drifted in and out of the "pop music" space. These parallels include the influence that the bourgeois folk revival exerted on mainstream country in the 1960s, and stretch back to Ralph Peer's first efforts to sell hillbilly music to a national market in the 1920s (Peterson 1997, 37–51). But something new is at stake in the present conjuncture, and although it is hard to specify, *O Brother* is its calling card.

At Stake

What is at stake here? First, it must be mentioned that *whiteness* has something fundamental to do with the conjuncture, intertwined with a heroic revision of working-class experience in mainstream culture. Among various common features of the *Harry Smith Anthology* and the PBS *American Roots Music* (ARM) projects, the most salient for me is the way both projects advance a laudable, but problematic, liberal vision of American culture as a sepia-toned photo of a gorgeous mosaic. Both projects feature a constant alternation of black and white traditions and artists (ARM also adds an occasional Hispanic note). Implicitly (in the case of the *Harry Smith Anthology*) and explicitly (in the PBS series), we are presented with a vision of vernacular music as a Utopian space—Greil Marcus's "invisible republic" of "old, weird America" (1997)—where black and white contributions commingle without prejudice or disrespect, and with transparent mutual understanding. Racial conflict is located outside of the Utopian space of musical practice itself, and it is safely placed in an artfully burnished past that is both behind us and conclusively narrated from a presentist rather than a historicist perspective. These texts present a modernist bourgeois vision of the folk tradition, a vision that is instantly bothersome for anyone familiar with the social histories indexed by the roots music forms on aural display in these projects. The perspective leads to certain critical incoherencies in both projects, and especially in the PBS series, incoherencies that are probably obvious, if not particularly formulable, for even the most casual viewer or listener. To paraphrase Eric Lott, these projects mostly give us the Love, but they leave out the Theft (Lott 1993). Or rather, they attempt to redress an undeniable history of theft and conflict through a nostalgic politics of authenticity (for an extended exemplification of this point, see Fox 2004).

O Brother, however, moves the discourse of the vernacular into a more elusive, postmodern space. The album shrewdly limits "roots music" to a narrower, sonically whitened space (leaving aside the largely unknown but critically important history of African American string band, balladry, and fiddle traditions hidden in the canonical narrative of the album's dominant bluegrass texture). African American music is represented, but in a different kind of archaic space from the bluegrass styles that dominate the album. Black music is literally marginal—the first and penultimate tracks on the record aurally invoke the chain gang and the spiritual, respectively.[5] Chris Thomas King's "Hard Time Killing Floor" is the lone blues track on the album, and it has not been treated by reviewers as fundamental to the project's meaning, nor has it received the airplay of the tracks that are styled more as hillbilly and bluegrass. The album invokes an American roots tradition that leaves racial conflict and African American grievances out of the

Fig. 9. Dorothea Lange's "Migrant Mother. Nipomo, California." (Lange, Dorothea, photographer, "Destitute Pea Pickers in California. Mother of Seven Children. Age Thirty-Two. Nipomo, California." February, 1936. America from the Great Depression to World War II: Black-and-White Photographs from the FSA-OWI, 1935–1945, Library of Congress.)

picture for white listeners—including the largely white markets for mainstream commercial country music and the bourgeois market for NPR-approved high culture. Likewise, Native American identity is represented on *O Brother,* but in the form of a John Hartford instrumental entitled "Indian War Whoop" that panders to obvious and banal stereotypes of Indianness and locates that Indianness on the cinematic margins of the America being sonically conjured here. Although the movie to which the soundtrack refers makes racism and racial violence a central theme of its narrative, that theme cannot easily be recovered from the music alone. *O Brother,* in other words, represents a specifically white claim on the postmodern revision of vernacular cultural roots.

A second issue concerns the management of irony on *O Brother* and in alternative country more generally. In this respect, the project's handling of whiteness is no more progressive than its representations of black or Native American agency. Since the early 1990s, commentators on alternative country have frequently noted a variety of constitutive and performative ironies as central to the formation of the genre, though the meaning of these ironies is hotly disputed within the alternative country community, and the imputation of irony is sometimes hotly denied by alternative country partisans. The obvious ironies of alternative country have mostly involved forms of appropriation and presentation that are suggestive of Lott's description

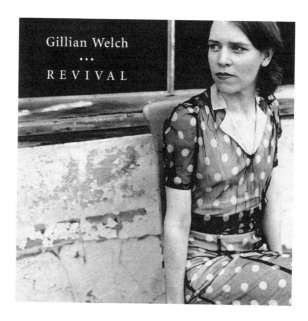

Fig. 10. Album cover art for Gillian Welch's *Revival*
(Acony Records, 1996).

of blackface minstrelsy (1993). Hyper-modern, technologically sophisticated, well-capitalized, urban, cosmopolitan, well-educated deployments
of archaic, low-tech, shoestring, rural, and ignorant images and expressive
styles have been definitive features of alternative country since Exene
Cervenka and John Doe (as the Knitters) caterwauled grotesque imitations
of Kitty Wells and Hank Thompson (both technically polished country
singers) in 1985 (on *Radio Tokyo Tapes*, vol. 3, PVC Records).

New heights of problematic minstrelsy were reached when Gillian
Welch, the daughter of successful television and film composers, and a
graduate of the University of California at Santa Cruz, appeared on the
cover of her debut album in a plain cotton dress and with a grim expression that evokes a famous Dorothea Lange Depression-era photograph ("Migrant Mother, Nipomo, California," 1936 [fig. 9]). The intentionality of the
gesture might be inferred from the fact that Welch studied photography
seriously in college. Significantly, *Revival* (the name makes a cultural claim
that resonates with my argument) was produced by T Bone Burnett, who
also produced the *O Brother* soundtrack, and who employed Welch as one of
the major alternative country stars on the *O Brother* recording.

Of course, this sort of theater of poverty is not unique to alternative country, and one could argue that mainstream country has frequently been characterized by a similarly constitutive ironic gaze at working-class, southern, rural identity. The ironies of alternative country, in other words, are second-order tropes, ironizing an already ironic country music history. The interplay of respectful and disrespectful appropriations of signs of poverty, and the injuries of class—of Love and Theft, again—in mainstream country is a complex topic in itself. One could simply invoke the early repertoire of hillbilly singers, and look back to figures like Bradley Kincaid to begin to tell a complicated story about the intertwining of cosmopolitan and rustic identities in country music history. A host of scholars have considered the issue of authenticity in country music, and almost all such discussions center around questions of how irony is interpreted and intended within country's diverse constituencies of producers and consumers (Ching 1993, 2001; Dawidoff 1997; Fox 1992; Jensen 1998; Malone 2002; Peterson 1997).

The majority of mainstream country stars, however, have been, until recently, products of working-class and rural or small-town backgrounds, and their music has been marketed substantially to working-class fans. As the canonical site of working-class social experience has shifted over the course of the last century, country has shifted with it, handling the important task of looking back nostalgically, and inevitably ironically, to a social "lifeworld" that was not utterly imagined for country's working-class constituency. This lifeworld—centering on rural sociality and the moral significance of poverty—has never been utterly disavowed, but it has historically been portrayed in both bitter and nostalgic terms, and its setting has been updated in complex ways as country's rural constituency has become an urban, blue-collar constituency, and latterly an increasingly suburban, female, and service-economy constituency. The meaning of country's class minstrelsy must be contextualized accordingly. In this light, the minstrelsy of O Brother—its constitutive irony—is both bothersome and distinctly postmodern, even when the album features star turns by revered working-class musicians like Ralph Stanley, whose performance on the record drew massive critical and popular acclaim and earned a Grammy Award. Stanley's "O Death" also spoke directly to the post–September 11 mood of the country, with its religious fervor and its grim subject. It is hardly surprising that this track, in particular, caught the nation's attention. But the framing of Stanley's contribution with such a heightened sense of reverence is a distinctly revisionist aspect of this project. For Stanley is made to speak only for the past in this appearance. The presentation of his contribution as a solo a capella performance marks the moment as set apart from the otherwise richly textured recording.[6] Stanley, one of the great instrumental innovators in country music history, a leading and progressive bandleader in the bluegrass tradition, and an artist who made his living earlier in his career selling his nostalgic mountain music (which was born along with rock and roll) in modern overdrive to Appalachian migrants working on the shop floors of northern cities, is here presented as a living relic, alone on a premodern pedestal, the embodiment of (white) rural, folk purity.

That this is already the predominant symbolic meaning of "bluegrass" in contemporary culture is worth mentioning; but again, this is a second-order appropriation. A slyly invented tradition already evocative of an authentic vernacular folk object is here reinvested with the status of a postmodern myth, marked by consciousness of its inventedness yet signifying a new kind of authenticity by virtue of its very self-consciousness. A delicate balance, to be sure, is thereby achieved. And this delicate balance is emblematic of the conjuncture I am describing as "alternative."

What's Left Out?

Alternative to what? It's clear that one answer to this question is something commonly called "mainstream country music" and metonymically summarized with the name "Nashville." Robert Oermann's liner notes to *O Brother* make this point more succinctly than the hundreds of reverent articles that have appeared to laud the project: "There is another Nashville, with a kind of music so distant from what the city's commercial center cranks out as to be from a different planet. It thrives in the community's nooks and crannies like a cluster of quietly smiling mountain wildflowers in the shadow of those cultivated hothouse blooms that flaunt their colors on radio stations from coast to coast" (2000). How different would it sound to suggest that these "mountain wildflowers" thrive, in fact, in the studios of NPR and college radio stations, on PBS stations, on the Internet, in the *New York Times,* and now on the Grammy Awards show and the *Billboard* charts? More polemically, what do we make of the fact that the "hothouse flowers" take root—and drop their blossoms—in the bars, homes, and pickup trucks of the southern white working class, and that they are cultivated *from* cuttings taken from the small towns and trailer parks of flyover country? These are different planets, indeed, but it's not as clear to me as it seems to be to Oermann that the mainstream Nashville planet is closer to the sun than the other. The rhetoric of alternative authenticity in Oermann's prose belies a specific judgment of taste, one rooted in bourgeois and cosmopolitan cultural ideologies of value.

What does alternative country actively exclude? I conclude here by considering briefly two kinds of musical practice that don't make the ideological cut. Consider, for a moment, the strange affinities between a local working-class country musician toiling in relative obscurity in the VFW halls and honky-tonks of South Texas, and the pop-country mega-star Shania Twain. As far as alternative country is concerned, the former exists only in the nostalgic imaginary, and the latter represents the most vilified and despised exemplar of the "hothouse flower," once called, by Steve Earle, "the highest paid lap dancer in Nashville."

And yet a working-class barroom singer like Randy Meyer, an artist from whom I learned most of what I know about country music as a class-specific art form, and a multi-platinum diva like Shania Twain have more in common with each other, from a working-class perspective, than either has with *O Brother.* Both Meyer and Twain are children of poverty. Meyer grew up around Austin, Texas, as one of six children of a journeyman carpenter; Twain grew up as the adopted daughter of an Ojibway Indian father in rural Ontario, Canada. Meyer devoted his musical career to articulating the cultural values of the blue-collar urban fringe community in which he was raised, singing contemporary commercial "hard" country (by artists such as Merle Haggard) in small bars for most of his life. The persona he cultivated was aggressively masculine, fiercely independent, and intensely sentimental. Although he was a technically masterful singer, and a charismatic stage performer, Meyer made only a few independent recordings in the 1970s, and remained an obscure local artist throughout his life.

Twain famously set her sights on superstardom at an early age, but in terms that were set by her rural, working-poor and largely Native American community. The persona she embodies is aggressively feminine, and in her view feminist; but this is a working-class feminism that has made her spectacularly popular not only as a pinup idol for men but as a fantasy role model for millions of working-class American girls (and sometimes dismissed as "belly button feminism" by her critics). She sings songs that have been derided as formulaic pop by alternative country fans and many critics of contemporary country music, although she has also been criticized by country music industry insiders for breaking with country production conventions in her collaboration with her producer (and husband) Mutt Lange, best known for his work with arena rock acts like Bryan Adams and Def Leppard. With hits such as "Any Man of Mine" and "Man, I Feel Like a Woman," Twain has projected a confident, assertive femininity. But she has done so in highly stylized and conventional terms, eschewing the ideology of distinctively personal expression that dominates alternative country discourse. Although she writes or cowrites much of her own material, she has not been taken seriously as a songwriter, and her aggressive presentation of her embodied sexuality—she drew fire in the 1990s as one of the first women performers in country to bare her midriff—has made her a target of derision among some feminist critics of popular music, as well as a highly lucrative object of male desire beyond country music's core audience.

Both Meyer and Twain express an entirely unironic *effort* in their performances, a commitment to values of discipline, self-denial, religiosity, convention, and craft, and both thereby refuse the canonical bourgeois affect identified by Bourdieu as *ease,* an aesthetic stance that announces "objective distance from necessity and those trapped within it" (1981, 55). The demonstration of effort—the lack of ease—in mainstream country music is profoundly gendered. Twain's performative persona embodies what sociolinguists call *hypercorrection*: her visible efforts are directed too obviously to upward mobility, self-regulation, and a concern with what one's social betters might stigmatize. That she has succeeded in massively improving her class position confirms her performance of working-class femininity, and earns her the kind of bourgeois scorn reserved for working-class women who don't realize that they are making fools of themselves and that money does not liberate. Steve Earle's comment nicely summarizes this dismissal, and it may be relevant to mention that he is the son of an air traffic controller.

Meyer, on the other hand, embodies the phenomenon sociolinguists call *covert prestige,* a cultivated refusal to engage with any bourgeois norms of bodily disposition, language, or ideology that defines traditional working-class ideas of masculinity. Currently a heroic image, this kind of working-class masculinity has also been the object of bourgeois scorn in American culture, in the figure of the hard-drinking, racist, inelegant "redneck." That Randy Meyer, were he alive, would reject Shania Twain as an artist, or that Shania Twain would consider Randy Meyer a relic of her own kind of past only amplifies the point. For artists like Meyer and

Twain, the ideological categories within which they craft their respective arts offer few if any alternatives to gendered musical conventions. Their socially located performance styles are overdetermined by working-class identity politics, and by each artist's working-class background. Conversely, *O Brother* embodies bourgeois ease: the freedom to cultivate, curate, dabble in, and reconfigure the alternatives offered up in the commodity form by modern American culture. The social crossing, passing, and constitutive irony of the project—indeed, its ability to simply (and massively) occupy the space of the vernacular at a crucial moment in American history when the vernacular is suddenly an object of renewed, if nostalgic, affection—complement the claim to adjudicate the boundaries of vernacular authenticity assumed by the *O Brother* project.

Johannes Fabian has famously said of anthropology that the discipline "emerged and established itself as an allochronic discourse; it is a science of other men in another Time. It is a discourse whose referent has been removed from the present of the speaking/writing subject. This 'petrified relation,'" he writes, quoting Marx, "is a scandal" (1983, 143). *Mutatis mutandis*, the *same* could be said of the present condition of some contemporary alternative constructions of the vernacular. It is not as simple as deciding whether any particular gesture of cultural minstrelsy is respectful or not, authentic or not, musically articulate or not, popular or not, commercial or not. I am passing no judgments on any of those questions. Rather, I am interrogating the class politics of alternative identities, products, and expressions, and the significance of those politics in the present, fraught historical conjuncture in which class might once again begin to matter in American culture in a more explicit and conflicted way than it has for the past few decades. I don't listen to Shania Twain for pleasure, though I don't listen to *O Brother* either. Personally, I prefer Randy Meyer, which is, ironically, most likely an effect of my own cosmopolitan habitus. I am not implying that working-class mainstream country fans can't appreciate *O Brother,* or that cosmopolitan alternative country fans might not find pleasure or meaning in music performed by Meyer—the unironic rube—or Twain—the hothouse flower. Obviously many people who do not listen to NPR or read the *New York Times* are buying and listening to *O Brother,* but that does not obviate the point I am making either. That point, in summary, is that the question "'alternative' to what?" cannot be answered by listing off styles, genres, institutions, or practices, and perhaps might best be rephrased as "alternative to—and for—whom?"

Notes

1. As far as I know, Steve Earle's "John Walker's Blues" was the only alternative country song to enter the conversation, when it was derided in the media for seeming to sympathize with the political views of John Walker Lindh, the "American Taliban." (It also appears to be the only country song dealing with September 11 not to use a parenthetical subtitle. And it represents what is probably the only example of Qur'anic recitation in the history of country music.) *No Depression* also ran an editorial in its November-December 2001 issue entreating readers to "urge your elected leaders to wage peace with the same ferocity they seem to be willing to wage war," though publisher Grant Alden also acknowledged that "some—perhaps many" of his readers might not share his politics. Beyond country music, working-class experience gained a renewed nationalist metonymy in Bruce Springsteen's *The Rising,* widely understood to be the most profound popular musical statement on the terrorist attacks in large part because of Springsteen's established identity as the voice of what had come to seem like an archaic industrial working-class culture. Springsteen's songs, however, disappointed many of his fans. They are mostly meditations on personal loss, and lack his famously ethnographic attention to the texture of working-class life.

2. The almost giddy national fascination with the Quecreek, Pennsylvania, coal mine disaster and the subsequent miraculous rescue of nine trapped miners in August of 2002 reflected and amplified this mood. The miners were quickly claimed as heroes, by right-wing nationalists especially, many ironies aside.

3. Indeed, deCurtis's article about *Cash* appeared on the same front page of the Sunday "Arts and Leisure" section of the *New York Times* as Jon Pareles's obituary for "outlaw" country star Waylon Jennings, who is celebrated in exactly the same terms (Pareles 2002).

4. A case could be made for Alison Krauss's 1995 *Now That I've Found You,* which was the first independent-label bluegrass record to get to the top of the country charts in the modern era. Krauss's success clearly foreshadowed the moment I am discussing, but her breakthrough album was produced to sound like a mainstream country record, whereas *O Brother* has a much rawer and less radio-friendly sound.

5. "Po Lazarus," the opening track on the album, is an actual field recording of James Carter and a gang of prison laborers made by Alan Lomax in 1959. The penultimate track, "Lonesome Valley," is performed by the Fairfield Four, an Alabama gospel quartet that achieved its major popular success in the 1940s and 50s.

6. "Oh Death" has a long and complex history in the vernacular tradition. Stanley's a capella performance is an unusual break from the typical instrumental versions of the song, such as the first recording of the song by the Stanley Brothers in 1964 (on *Hymns from the Cross*). Stanley's unadorned vocal performance evokes the singing

practices of the Primitive Baptist Church, of which he is a devout member. A case could be made that the song's lyrics also reflect distinctive theological concerns of Primitive Baptist believers. The representation of religion on *O Brother* is an important subject, but one that is beyond the scope of this essay.

References

Ali, Lorraine, and David Gates. Looking grim at the Grammies. *Newsweek,* March 11, 2002.

Bateson, Gregory. 1936. *Naven.* Reprint, Stanford: Stanford University Press, 1958.

Bourdieu, Pierre. 1981. *Distinction: A social critique of the judgment of taste.* Cambridge, MA: Harvard University Press.

Ching, Barbara. 1993. Acting naturally: Cultural distinction and critiques of pure country. *Arizona Quarterly* 49, no. 3: 107–25.

———. 2001. *Wrong's what I do best: Hard country music and contemporary culture.* New York: Oxford University Press.

Creed, Gerald W., and Barbara Ching. 1997. Introduction: Recognizing rusticity. In *Knowing your place: Rusticity and identity,* ed. G. Creed and B. Ching, 1–38. New York: Routledge.

Dawidoff, Nicholas. 1997. *In the country of country: People and places in American music.* New York: Pantheon Books.

DeCurtis, Anthony. Music: An American original returns. *New York Times,* Feb. 24, 2002. http//query.nytimes.com/search/article-page.html?res=9B05E1D7163EF 937A15751C0A9649C8B63.

Fabian, Johannes. 1983. *Time and the Other: How anthropology makes its object.* New York: Columbia University Press.

Feld, Steven. 1994. From schizophonia to schismogenesis: The discourses and practices of world music and world beat. In *The traffic in art and culture,* ed. George Marcus and Fred Myers. Berkeley and Los Angeles: University of California Press.

Fox, Aaron A. 1992. The jukebox of history: Narratives of loss and desire in the discourse of country music. *Popular Music* 11, no. 1: 53–72.

———. 2004. White trash rhetorics of the abject sublime. In *Bad music,* ed. C. Washburne and Maiken Derno. New York: Routledge.

Fox, Aaron A., and Christine Yano. Forthcoming. *Songs out of place: Country musics of the world.* Durham: Duke University Press.

Goodman, David. 1999. *Modern twang.* Nashville: Dowling Press.

Gray, Christopher. Down from the mountain and into Wal-Mart: *O Brother. Austin Chronicle,* June 19, 2002. http://www.austinchronicle.com/issues/dispatch/2002 -07-19/music_feature.html.

Harrison, Bennett, and Barry Bluestone. 1988. *The great U-turn: Corporate restructuring and the polarizing of America.* New York: Basic Books.

Jensen, Joli. 1998. *The Nashville sound: Authenticity, commercialization, and country music.* Nashville: Country Music Foundation and Vanderbilt University Press.

LeCompte, Tom. Take this song and shove it. *Hartford Advocate,* March 28, 1998. http//www.hartfordadvocate.com/articles/shovesong.html.

Lott, Eric. 1993. *Love and theft: Blackface minstrelsy and the American working class.* New York: Oxford University Press.

Malone, Bill C. 2002. *Don't get above your raisin': Country music and the southern working class.* Urbana: University of Illinois Press.

Marcus, Greil. 1997. *Invisible republic: Bob Dylan's* Basement Tapes. New York: Holt.

O'Brien, Geoffrey. Recapturing the American sound. *New York Review of Books,* April 9, 1998. http://www.nybooks.com/articles/article-preview?article_id=889.

Oermann, Robert. 2000. Liner notes. *O brother, where art thou?* Universal Records. http://www.obrothersoundtrack.com/soundtrack.html.

Pareles, Jon. Waylon Jennings, singer, songwriter and outlaw of country music, dies at 64. *New York Times,* Feb. 14, 2002. http://query.nytimes.com/search/article-page.html?res=9B02EFDE143FF937A25751C0A9649C8B63.

Peterson, Richard. 1997. *Creating country music: Fabricating authenticity.* Chicago: University of Chicago Press.

Peterson, Richard, and Bruce A. Beal. 2003. Alternative country: Origins, music, worldview, fans, and taste in genre formation. http://people.vanderbilt.edu/~steve.lee/country.htm.

Peterson, Richard, and Steven Lee. Internet-based virtual music scenes: The case of P2 and alt.country music. http://people.vanderbilt.edu/~steve.lee/p2paper.htm.

Tichi, Cecelia. 1998. *High lonesome: The American culture of country music.* Chapel Hill: University of North Carolina Press.

Williams, Raymond. 1973. *The country and the city.* Oxford: Oxford University Press.

12

Ulster Loyalism and Country Music, 1969–85

David A. Wilson

When I was living in Belfast during the mid-1980s, I shared an apartment with some supporters of Sinn Féin, the political wing of the Irish Republican Army. They were a lively, energetic group of people, who thrived on political arguments in the local pubs. One of their customs, however, was rather surprising. After a full night of drinking, they would come home, play Ulster loyalist paramilitary music cassettes, and fall around the room laughing. The cassettes contained a wide variety of songs. Some were based on traditional Irish melodies, many were taken from marching tunes, and a few were drawn from mainstream English popular music. What was particularly striking, though, was the presence of American songs in general and country songs in particular, imported into loyalist Ulster, and given new lyrics. The songs were full of vitriolic anti-Catholic and anti-Irish nationalist sentiments, and were so extreme that to Sinn Féin ears they had passed beyond offensiveness into the realm of black comedy.[1]

My apartment mates viewed themselves as anti-sectarian, progressive, and enlightened people, locked in combat with the forces of loyalist bigotry; the songs appeared to confirm both their own self-image and their characterization of the enemy. And yet their enjoyment of loyalist paramilitary country songs actually reflected and reinforced a more subtle form of ethnic stereotyping. From their perspective, the songs were yet another demonstration that Ulster loyalists had no culture of their own; cultural derivation appeared as a product of cultural deprivation, not to mention

depravation. Something else was going on, as well; the listeners were unconsciously engaging in one of the oldest ethnic pastimes in Ireland—focusing on the most objectionable features of their opponents, and viewing the whole through the prism of the part. After all, it is always easier to justify your own side's violence by pointing to the physical, verbal, and cultural violence of the other.

Both these issues—the cultural derivation argument and the "worst feature" perspective—require further investigation. On the cultural question, it is important to note that the popularity of country music in Ireland is by no means confined to Protestant loyalists. Not only are American country artists played regularly on Irish radio stations, north and south, but homegrown singers such as Big Tom have enjoyed an enormous following. Arguably, country music is more popular in the Irish Republic than is so-called Celtic music—although the two are far from being mutually exclusive categories, and one finds Gaelic *sean-nós* (old style) singers such as John Beag Ó Flatharta writing songs such as "Scriosta ag an Ól" ("Destroyed by Drink") to a tune reminiscent of "The Wabash Cannonball."[2] The difference, though, is that American country songs do not generally find their way into the nationalist musical repertoire. Many Irish republicans are cultural as well as political nationalists, and self-consciously identify with indigenous song traditions rather than the "filthy modern tide" washing in from overseas.

Yet much of the American music that is so popular today was itself influenced by earlier Irish traditions, and is thus not quite as "foreign" as it may first appear. A classic example is "The Cowboy's Lament," better known as "The Streets of Laredo." Although it seems to be a quintessentially American cowboy song, it actually originated in eighteenth-century Ireland as "The Bard of Armagh," and was integrated into the Irish nationalist tradition as "Bold Robert Emmet" before crossing the Atlantic. Similarly, the American music-hall song "Sweet Betsy from Pike" was based on "The Ould Orange Flute," one of the major songs in the Ulster unionist tradition; the sectarian message of the original was replaced in America by a comic tale about the adventures of Betsy and her lover Ike. In both these examples, Irish songs of nationalism and Orangeism became Americanized and depoliticized.

The reverse pattern also occurred; nonpolitical songs from Ireland were rewritten as nationalist American pieces. During the early nineteenth century, three United Irish exiles in the United States, John Daly Burk, John McCreery, and Thomas Robinson, set out to publish a songbook that would transform the ancient melodies of Ireland into the modern patriotic music of the United States. Out of this venture came McCreery's "The American Star," set to the tune of "Captain O'Kane"; during the War of 1812, it rivaled "The Star-Spangled Banner" in its popularity.[3] In some cases, Irish melodic structures, rather than specific tunes, influenced American patriotic music. "The Battle Hymn of the Republic" does not have an Irish melody, but it replicates the structure of an Irish jig, with its six-eight time and its repetitive pattern running through an *aa/bb* eight-bar arrangement.

When Ulster loyalists began drawing on American melodies for their own songs, and incorporating country music into their own patriotic repertoire, they were repeating the same process that had occurred with Irish music in the United States. If it is indeed the case that the loyalists have customarily identified with people other than themselves, their choices are revealing—the British and the Americans. But they have never fully trusted the British, and have long feared that British politicians would sell them out to their Catholic enemies. Although the loyalists have been acutely aware of the power of the Irish American nationalist lobby, they have taken great pride in the contribution of Irish Protestants to the political and religious culture of the United States. In 1829 many Irish Protestants expressed shock and anger when the British politician Robert Peel completed the emancipation of Catholics in Ireland. But that same year, many of them

were delighted when the son of emigrants from Carrickfergus, Andrew Jackson, became the first Irish president of the United States. Ironically, the hyper-loyal Irish Protestant subjects of the British Crown have had a strong emotional identification with American republicanism, the Wild West, and cowboys—with the Catholics cast in the role of Indians.

Precisely because hyper-loyalist anti-Catholic sentiments permeate the songs of Ulster loyalists, we need to guard against the fallacy of tarring all Northern Ireland's Protestants with the paramilitary brush. Some of the songs do indeed display a visceral and vicious sectarianism, and their composers would certainly be prosecuted under hate laws in North America. It is also probable that some non-paramilitary Protestants would have shared such sentiments at various low points of the Troubles; atrocities often bring out extreme reactions within targeted communities. But the fact remains that the vast majority of Northern Ireland's Protestants have consistently refused to vote for the political representatives of paramilitary organizations, and there has been a strong liberal component within the Ulster Protestant tradition.[4]

In examining the songs of loyalist paramilitaries, we are exploring the musical world of an embattled minority with a highly local sense of consciousness—the Protestant working-class housing estates of places like Belfast, Londonderry, and Portadown, with their long historical memories, short pockets, deep resentments, and wide insecurities. Many of the songs celebrate loyalist enclaves, and specific streets. The song "Shankill," set to the tune of "The Banks of the Ohio" and replete with references to the "IRA scum" and "vermin," praises the loyalist district in West Belfast; similarly, the song "East Belfast," based on the Irish-influenced "Battle Hymn of the Republic," praises the steadfastness of the loyalists on the Newtownards Road.[5] The loyalist cassettes are for local consumption only; recording standards are amateurish, and the content totally disregards notions of spin, image, and media manipulation. Loyalist songs are products of a marginalized and self-referential world, and cannot be taken as representative or typical of Protestant culture in general.[6]

Above all, the paramilitaries who operate in such localities have seen themselves as men at war with the Irish Republican Army and its Catholic supporters. Their central symbols go back to the seventeenth century, when the Protestant Apprentice Boys withstood the Catholic siege of Londonderry in 1689, and when the Protestant King William of Orange defeated the Catholic forces of King James II on the twelfth of July, 1690. Drawing on a long tradition of resistance to Irish nationalism and republicanism, loyalists developed a deep distrust of Irish Catholics, and believed that their own loyalty should be rewarded by preferential political, economic, and legal treatment. After the partition of Ireland in 1920, most Ulster Protestants were determined that Catholics would never be in a position to vote the Northern Irish state out of existence, and viewed any challenge to the status quo as a challenge to the state itself. When the Civil Rights Association emerged in 1967–68, loyalists were not impressed with its claims to be a nonsectarian and non-nationalist organization; the graffiti on Belfast walls proclaimed that "CRA = Crafty Romanist Agitators."[7]

In the loyalist view, "concessions" to Catholics would only lead to more demands; the best response to the civil rights movement, they believed, was straightforward repression. When the Northern Irish government, under pressure from Britain, introduced a series of civil rights reforms, loyalist attacks on Catholic ghettos increased in intensity. After the British army came to Northern Ireland in August 1969 to protect Catholics from loyalist pogroms, Protestant extremists reacted with fury. As one loyalist song (based on a popular Irish nationalist melody) put it:

> I have often thought and wondered what the outcome might have been,
> If the army hadn't come in to protect the scum in green.

Well they shouted all their insults, they threw their petrol bombs and shot,
But on the sixteenth night of August we should have shot the lot.[8]

The combination of nationalist expectations of change and experiences of loyalist violence created conditions in which the IRA was able to expand its base of support and to launch its guerrilla war for the unification of Ireland. For the loyalists, the rise of the IRA vindicated their original argument that concessions would open the door to republican terrorism. The loyalists were convinced that successive British governments were mistakenly trying to reach a compromise with republicans who would accept nothing short of total victory; British politicians, from this perspective, were inadvertently aiding and abetting the IRA. The loyalist conclusion was clear: if the forces of the Crown would not be permitted to do the job, the men of paramilitary organizations such as the Ulster Defence Association (UDA) and the Ulster Volunteer Force (UVF) would do it themselves.

The loyalists believed that if you scratched a Catholic, you would find an IRA supporter; if the IRA were the fish, to use Mao's famous metaphor, the Catholics were the water that sustained them. One way to poison the water, the argument ran, was to make Catholics realize that the price of supporting the IRA was unacceptably high. This was to be done not only by targeting known or suspected IRA volunteers, but also by torturing and killing individual Catholics. Although most Catholic victims were selected at random, the strategy of anti-Catholic violence was anything but random or senseless. The loyalist paramilitaries regarded themselves as soldiers, fighting a duplicitous and unseen enemy who was out to destroy their country and see it go to hell. And if a dirty war was the only way to save Northern Ireland, then a dirty war it would be.

While the civil rights marchers of the late 1960s were inspired by the marches of Martin Luther King, loyalist paramilitaries identified with white South Africans and with American troops in Vietnam. It was no coincidence that a popular loyalist song of the early 1970s, "Orange Wings," was based on the militaristic "Ballad of the Green Berets," Barry Sadler and Robin Moore's hit record of 1966. Both the original song and its loyalist derivative glorified the men who were prepared to kill and die for their country. The loyalist version began and ended with the words:

With Orange Wings upon our breasts
We are the men of Ulster's best

> Ten thousand men will fight today
> And all are men of the UDA.[9]

The loyalist paramilitaries saw themselves as elite combat troops fighting for God and Ulster, law and order, and the faith of their forefathers. There is, however, an instructive difference between the two songs: while the "Ballad of the Green Berets" speaks in general terms about combat, courage, death, and determination, "Orange Wings" describes in detail how the UDA gave the Catholics a hammering on the streets of Belfast. The conflict in Northern Ireland was much more immediate, intimate, and in-your-face than the conflict in Southeast Asia. Vietnam was thousands of miles away, even though television brought it into the living rooms of the nation. Violence in the ghettos of Belfast and Derry was taking place in the neighborhood, and petrol bombs were bringing it directly into the living rooms. The enemy in Vietnam appeared foreign and strange to most Americans; the enemies in Northern Ireland knew each other only too well.

The military ethos of loyalism served the dual function of providing popular legitimization for illegal paramilitary organizations and of justifying as acts of war the murder and maiming of the "enemies of Ulster." Loyalist splinter groups with names like the "Red Hand Commandos" were responsible for some of the worst anti-Catholic atrocities in the Troubles. Their leader, John McKeague, compiled a songbook in 1971 that encouraged the killing of "Taigs" (a derogatory term for Catholics), advocated the destruction of the Catholic Falls Road district of Belfast, and celebrated the loyalist strongholds of the Shankill Road and Sandy Row. His most notorious song was based on "I Was Born Under a Wandering Star," the Alan Jay Lerner composition that Lee Marvin had sung in the 1969 film *Paint Your Wagon*. McKeague changed the title to "I Was Born Under the Union Jack":

> I was born under the Union Jack,
>   I was born under the Union Jack.
> Do you know where Hell is?
>   Hell is up the Falls,
> Kill all the Popeheads, and we'll guard Derry's walls.
>
> I was born under the Union Jack. . . .
> Falls was made for burning!
>   Taigs are made to kill.
> You've never seen a road like the Shankill.

> I was born under the Union Jack. . . .
> If Taigs are made for killing
>   Then blood is made to flow.
> You've never seen a place like Sandy Row.
>
> I was born under the Union Jack. . . .
> If guns are made for shooting
>   Then skulls are made to crack.
> You've never seen a better Taig, than with a bullet in his back.[10]

Anti-Catholic lyrics were nothing new in popular loyalist culture. Long before McKeague put pen to paper, one of the best-known songs in the loyalist repertoire was a version of "Home on the Range" that presents an Orangeman's picture of paradise:

> No, no Pope of Rome
> No chapels to sadden my eyes
> No nuns and no priests and no rosary beads
> And every day is the Twelfth of July.[11]

McKeague, however, took sectarianism to its extreme form. Under the pressure of intense loyalist-republican hostilities between 1969 and 1971—which would undoubtedly have produced a full-scale civil war in the absence of the British army—the anti-Catholicism of "No Pope of Rome" had hardened into hatred and escalated into a call for ethno-religious genocide.

In the view of loyalist leaders such as Alan Wright, Rome was using Irish republicanism as part of its plan for universal domination; once the forces of Rome had battered down Protestantism in Ulster, Wright believed, they would take over the British Empire and then the world.[12] It is a truism that religion and politics are inseparable in Ireland, but it needs to be remembered that their relative importance differs within each community. Catholics, it has been said, fear Protestant politics, while Protestants fear the Catholic religion;[13] one of the key loyalist slogans proclaims that Home Rule Is Rome Rule. Within loyalist culture, this outlook has produced an unstable compound of defiance and defensiveness, faith and fear, righteousness and retribution. The mixture of religion and politics is clearly illustrated in the loyalist version of "The Deck of Cards," an American hit that was recorded by such artists as Tex Ritter and Ernest Tubbs. In the original, the message is entirely religious: During the North African campaign in World War II, a soldier who takes out a deck of cards during a religious service is arrested and ordered to explain himself. He replies that each of the cards possesses deep religious significance; the ace reminds him of the one God, the deuce of the Old and New Testaments, the three of the Father, Son, and Holy Ghost, and so on. In the Ulster Volunteer Force's rendition, the form remained the same but the content was radically altered.

Over the humming of the Twenty-third Psalm, the narrator tells the story of a grandfather who encounters his ten-year-old grandson playing with a deck of cards, and asks for an explanation; straight away, the theme of generational continuity is established. The boy, who turns out to be remarkably precocious, says that the ace reminds him of the one God, "the God of our forefathers," and that the two reminds him of the two testaments, "the foundations of our beloved Protestant religion." By the time we come to the three, however, we enter very different territory; instead of the Holy Trinity, the boy thinks of "three letters, UVF, the Ulster Volunteer Force, whose gallantry in battle is world-renowned, and whose one aim is to defend Ulster against its enemies."

From this point, political imagery possesses the scene; the six stands for "the land of our birthright, Ulster, with its six counties proud and true," and the seven "reminds me that seven days a week, we must be on our guard against the enemies of Ulster." The character of those enemies is spelled out as we proceed through the deck; the nine triggers memories of "1969, when the treacherous rebels thought they had us beaten," and the ten calls to mind "the tenth day of March, 1971, when three young Scottish soldiers were brutally murdered and left lying in a ditch on a lonely country road." When religious imagery returns, it is thoroughly politicized: "When I think of the Jack, it reminds me of the Devil, and his band of followers, the IRA"; the king, in contrast, is "God Almighty," and the UVF's motto is "In God Our Trust." The defense of Ulster is sanctioned by the cause of God, the struggle is one of good against evil, and the treachery and cruelty of the enemy are illustrated through specific examples. In the end, the narrator assures us that the story is true, "for I was that little boy"—which means that he must have grown up at a remarkably rapid rate.[14]

One of the key words in the UVF version of "Deck of Cards" is "forefathers"; along with military and religious justifications for violence, the loyalists sought a historical warrant for their actions and, indeed, their existence. Most of the marching songs in the Protestant tradition go back to the nineteenth century, and celebrate the seventeenth-century "deliverance" from

Catholicism. But Edward Carson's leadership of the Protestant resistance to the Home Rule Bill of 1912, and the Protestant blood sacrifice at the Battle of the Somme in 1916, emerged as central twentieth-century symbols of inspiration, and required new tunes and new words. A melody based on George Jones's "He Stopped Loving Her Today" (complete with talking break in the middle) was transformed into "Our Flag"; the song commemorates the founding of the Ulster Volunteer Force in 1912, and stresses the importance of passing the flag from fathers to sons.[15] Similarly, a generic "country-and-Irish" song, "Billy McFadze[a]n," praises a young UVF man who died for his comrades and won the Victoria Cross at the Somme; his courage was clearly intended as a model for the current generation.[16] The past was pressed into service for the purposes of the present, and the songs moved easily and effortlessly from 1689 to 1969. This is particularly apparent in "The Heroes of the UVF," based on the ubiquitous "Battle Hymn of the Republic":

> Now they chased King James and all his gang from the gates of Derry's
> walls
> They chased the IRA up the Crumlin and the Falls
> And they'll rally round the Shankill when the voice of duty calls
> Who? The heroes of the UVF.
>
> Glory glory to the Red Hand
> Glory glory to our own land
> Glory glory to that gallant band
> Who? The heroes of the UVF.[17]

This is a form of historical consciousness that divides the world into heroes and villains, that is much more interested in using rather than understanding the past, and that is informed and imprisoned by a pervasive sense of siege. Even when the loyalists adopted a forward-looking song of hope and progress like Bob Dylan's "The Times They Are A-Changin'," they managed to transform it into an anthem for the status quo ante-1968:

> Come all you young brethren [sic] and listen to me,
> And pledge that your country stays loyal and free.
> And step proudly forth each twelfth of July,
> And let Dublin know now that Ulster won't die.
> And if you love your country you'll stand up and cry
> That the times they are a-changin'. . . .

> Now Armagh and Antrim, Londonderry and Down
> Tyrone and Fermanagh remain true to the crown
> They remember Lord Carson, his famous reply
> "No home rule for Ireland," and Ulster won't die
> And if you love your country you'll stand up and cry
> That the times they are a-changin'.[18]

For loyalist listeners, the song's definition of change would have been quite clear: The Irish Catholics are doing everything in their power to destroy our state, and we've been letting them get away with it. From now on, things are going to be different; we're going to follow the example of Lord Carson in 1912, fight the foe and save our country. This was not quite what Bob Dylan had in mind.

Insofar as the future figures into the equation, it is one in which the brave loyalist heroes wipe out their enemies and enjoy life under the British Crown. "The Ulster Story," set to "Red River Valley," emphasizes the immediate objective of destroying the IRA:

> So take heed all you treacherous rebels
> Lay down arms now before it's too late
> O you never will rule over Ulster
> And death surely will be your fate.[19]

The song "Victory Is Ours" imagines the day of deliverance, when the men of the UVF prevail. The words are set to the tune of "Billy Don't Be a Hero"; the original title would hardly have been appropriate for a loyalist community that venerates King Billy and celebrates heroism:

> Fathers and sons were standing together
> Hand in hand against the foe
> Ready to pledge their lives for their country
> The UVF was set to go
> The rebels didn't know what had hit them
> They lost their nerve and ran away
> But we stood firm and cried "No Surrender"
> The UVF had won the day.
>
> We were watching the heroes, cheering and singing along
> They were flying the colours red white and blue in a throng
> As the drum rolled out a command

We saluted Ulster's Red Hand
Marching onwards to freedom
Victory is ours.[20]

In some songs, the culture of heroism glissades into the cult of the hero; there are dreams of a modern-day King William or Lord Carson who will unite the loyal people of Ulster and usher in a kind of Protestant millennium. A good example is "U.V.F. Hero," which is set to the tune of "The Wind beneath My Wings," a song made famous by Bette Midler. In the loyalist version, the people are confidently awaiting the arrival of the hero "who's been sent to set us free"; like a sheriff coming into an unruly town in the Wild West, the hero wears a badge (an "Ulster badge") and gathers a posse ("an army of men to follow you") to drive out the bad guys:

The hero will purge the rebel band
And we will reclaim our glorious land
And when we have got the rebels running
Surrendering to our mighty flag
The red, white and blue will fly on high
And Ulster is Free will be our cry

And our flag will fly on high forever
And our songs will sing our victory song
Our voices will rise with one accord now
For we have been silent for too long.[21]

The IRA defeated, the Catholics submissive, and the Protestants back on top, honored and revered as the most loyal subjects under the Crown—it was all utterly unrealistic, and was progressively undermined by the sequence of events between the Anglo-Irish Agreement of 1985 and the Good Friday or Belfast Agreement of 1998. But the atavism expressed in the loyalist songs remains an important aspect of life in the loyalist ghettos, simmering beneath the political surface, and threatening to erupt if conditions change. Its power should not be underestimated.

The songs were part of a conscious and continuing attempt to contribute to a distinctly loyalist culture. As the dedication to the *Songs of the U.V.F.* put it:

This Loyalist tape is the first step on the long road of re-establishing the Loyalist tradition of recounting in song, stories of patriotism, courage,

sacrifice and resolve relating to our heritage of freedom and British way of life. The . . . ballads are new and hitherto unheard and they are a further addition to that vast reservoir of words and melodies which, like the Ulster Loyalists themselves, have withstood the twin barbs of time and violent onslaught.

Preaching to the converted, and sung in crowded, smoke-filled loyalist drinking clubs, the songs attempted to boost the morale and reinforce the solidarity of communities who believed that the whole world was against them—Irish Catholics and their Third World sympathizers, untrustworthy and unreliable British politicians, the powerful Irish American lobby, liberal media types, and condescending academics. In their attempt to respond to the contemporary musical tastes of their constituency, loyalist songwriters drew largely—but not exclusively—on American songs and country music traditions that were themselves partly influenced by earlier Irish ballads. None of the melodies in *Songs of the U.V.F.* were original; all would already have been well known to their listeners. The words may have been "new and unheard," but their message turned out to be as familiar as the melodies; indeed, this goes a long way toward explaining their local popularity.

In this highly charged and quintessentially male world of religion and politics, the songs venerated patriotism, militarism, heroism, struggle, and sacrifice. Popular contemporary American tunes became a means by which communal historical "memories" were transmitted to the next generation; the Siege of Derry, the Battle of the Boyne, Lord Carson, and the Somme all

fit easily within an American country music framework. Equally important, the songs express communal hatred of the IRA—indeed, one loyalist
cassette is simply titled *We Hate the IRA*—and their real or perceived supporters. In its extreme form, this hatred assumed genocidal proportions.
Against the background of a chronic, low-grade civil war, in which an unseen enemy could strike at any time before disappearing back into its host
community, loyalist songs began to assume a quasi-apocalyptic tone. With
the help of God, loyalist paramilitaries would wipe out their enemies, and
Ulster would become the "wee spot in Europe" where Britishness and Protestantism would reign supreme, and where loyalists would receive the respect, value, and appreciation that they truly deserved.

To a considerable extent, the medium matches the message. Short songs
with a verse-chorus structure are well suited to a simplistic, fundamentalist, black-and-white view of the world, while strong melodic lines keep
words in heads. This kind of structure, of course, is by no means confined
to country music, and the loyalists were quite promiscuous in their cultural borrowings. Nevertheless, the significant seam of country music that
runs through the loyalist repertoire attests to the importance of American
culture in Northern Ireland. The way in which the loyalists have used that
cultural influence for their own ends is also highly revealing. It has often
been argued that Americanization entails homogenization, and that tradi-

tional cultures are being eroded by secular, liberal capitalist values and practices that find their clearest expression in the United States. The experience of working-class loyalist communities in Northern Ireland suggests otherwise; instead of cultural erosion, there has been a cultural synthesis between American music and distinctively Irish or Ulster themes. Within that synthesis, the local traditions have clearly preponderated; American forms have been filled with Ulster loyalist content. In the end, perhaps it was Karl Marx who got it right: "The tradition of all the dead generations weighs like a nightmare on the brain of the living."[22] Far from reducing the burden of history in Ireland, American country songs have actually been used to increase the weight.

Notes

1. A few words are required about definitions—always an ideological minefield in Irish history. "Ulster" traditionally refers to the ancient nine-county province of Ulster; in Northern Irish Protestant parlance, it has come to mean the six-county state of Northern Ireland that was established in 1920. For reasons of convenience, I am here employing the Protestant loyalist usage. On the question of "country" music, I have taken an ecumenical position that moves from songs such as "Red River Valley" to Bob Dylan's "The Times They Are A-Changin'."

2. John Beag Ó Flatharta, *An tAncaire—Fiche Amhrán 1980–1990*, Conomara, 1990.

3. David A. Wilson, *United Irishmen, United States: Immigrant Radicals in the Early Republic* (Ithaca, NY: Cornell University Press, 1998), 110–11.

4. See, for example, Arthur Aughey, *Under Siege: Ulster Unionism and the Anglo-Irish Agreement* (London: Palgrave Macmillan, 1989).

5. Ulster Volunteer Force, *In God Our Trust* (Belfast, [1974]).

6. On the political culture of Ulster loyalism, see Sarah Nelson, *Ulster's Uncertain Defenders: Protestant Political, Paramilitary and Community Groups and the Northern Ireland Conflict* (Belfast: Appletree Press, 1984); Steve Bruce, *God Save Ulster: The Religion and Politics of Paisleyism* (Oxford: Clarendon Press, 1986); Richard Davis, *Mirror Hate: The Convergent Ideology of Northern Ireland Paramilitaries* (Brookfield, VT: Dartmouth Publishing, 1994); Peter Shirlow and Mark McGovern, eds., *Who Are 'the People'? Unionism, Protestantism and Loyalism in Northern Ireland* (London: Pluto Press, 1997); and Peter Taylor, *Loyalists* (London: Bloomsbury, 1998).

7. Conor Cruise O'Brien, *States of Ireland* (London: Hutchinson, 1972), 152.

8. "The Night We Burned Ardoyne," *Ulster Defence Association Songs*, http://www.prideofthehill.co.uk/songsuda.htm.

9. "Orange Wings," ibid.

10. *Orange-Loyalist Songs* (n.p., 1971), Northern Ireland Ephemera Collection, Linenhall Library, Belfast.

11. Heard by the author on the streets of Portadown, July 12, 1986.

12. Personal interview with Alan Wright, June 23, 1988.

13. Personal interview with John Morrow, June 6, 1988.

14. *United We Stand: Old Songs of the Volunteers* (Belfast, n.d.).

15. *Songs of the U.V.F., Vocals by the Platoon* (Belfast, n.d.).

16. Thistle Accordian Band, Antrim Volunteers Flute Band, *We Hate the IRA* (Belfast, n.d.).

17. Ibid.

18. *Orange-Loyalist Songs, Songs of the U.V.F.*

19. *United We Stand.*

20. *Songs of the U.V.F.*

21. Ibid.

22. Karl Marx, "The Eighteenth Brumaire of Louis Bonaparte," in Karl Marx and Friedrich Engels, *Selected Works* (London: International Publishers, 1970), 96.

13

In Whose Name?

Country Artists Speak Out on Gulf War II

Randy Rudder

How could fifteen little words cause such an uproar? In March of 2003, as the United States prepared to invade Iraq, the Dixie Chicks' lead singer, Natalie Maines, declared from a stage in London: "Just so you know, we're ashamed the President of the United States is from Texas." This simple sentence thrust Maines and her fellow Chicks, Martie Maguire and Emily Robison, into a media firestorm that was in some ways a publicist's dream, but an artist's nightmare. Within weeks, radio stations were pulling their songs from playlists and fans were staging CD-smashing parties.

Why was there such a vitriolic response to the Chicks? After all, hadn't many rock singers and Hollywood actors said far more disparaging things about the president? Actor Jennifer Aniston, for example, in her erudite analysis of the situation brewing in the Middle East, pronounced the commander in chief a "[expletive] idiot."[1] The Pretenders' lead singer, Chrissie Hynde, in her best masochistic rant, cried, "we deserve to get bombed. Bring it on. . . . I hope the Muslims win."[2] Danny Glover informed us that "We know Bush is a racist, but now the world is finding that out."[3] Dozens of other Hollywood activists went on record calling Bush a Fascist or a Nazi. And Steve Earle wrote a song dedicated to the "American Taliban," John Walker Lindh, and began some of his shows shouting the Shahada, the Muslim declaration of faith—in Arabic. Let's face it, for pure sound-bite potential, it's hard to top those. So why the furor over Maines's simple opine?

One reason could be that this came from a *country* artist, after all. We're used to it from actors and rock 'n' rollers, but country has a more conserva-

Fig. 1. The Dixie Chicks. Natalie Maines's simple opine on a British stage set off a firestorm of controversy that turned many country fans against the act. (Photo by Alan Mayor.)

tive demographic, doesn't it? Aren't we a little more patriotic than those left-wingers? Don't we have better manners than to slam the president on foreign soil, whether we agree with him or not? Weren't we taught to be more polite and less confrontational, and to avoid discussing politics and religion? Well, *weren't* we?

Some of the Chicks' own lyrics have been nearly as controversial as the comments made in London. When the trio released the single "Goodbye Earl" and the accompanying video, filled with mirth and merrymaking about killing an abusive spouse, a few eyebrows in country music were raised. The position of advocating violence for violence is a tenuous one, even when the song is allegedly playful, as "Goodbye Earl" is. Gretchen Peters is one of the few other songwriters willing to take on the topic of spouse abuse, in her song "Independence Day" (a huge hit for Martina McBride). However, even in "Independence Day," the singer is quick to point out, "Well I ain't saying it's right or it's wrong, but maybe it's the only way," when the victim of abuse burns down the house.

The Chicks probably didn't win any new fans from the gospel music field either when they released the single "Sin Wagon," which closes with a tag that is a play on the gospel standard "I'll Fly Away." The release also led to a lawsuit from the publisher of "I'll Fly Away."

But none of these peccadillos raised as much of a ruckus as those fifteen little words about the president. Maines's comment seemed even more ironic in light of the fact that the Chicks' single airing at that time was a tune called "Travelin' Soldier." The group even performed the national anthem at a recent Super Bowl.

As Internet chat rooms and discussion boards filled up for nearly four months, defenders and critics of Maines weighed in. What seemed to rankle most of the band's detractors was the fact that, when pressed for more details as to exactly why she was embarrassed, Maines made vague responses. That her comments were made on foreign soil was another factor. Maines later admitted, in fact, that she had probably gotten swept up by the antiwar fervor in Europe and had spoken out of school.

What followed shortly after was what appeared to be a scripted apology (possibly at the urging of her label or management) via a press release, and a perplexing clarification in a *Primetime* interview a month later with Diane Sawyer. In the Sawyer interview, Maines appeared to be concomitantly apologetic and unyielding. At one point, Maines said, "I think it came down to, it was . . . that it was in a foreign country and it was that it was an off-the-cuff statement. And I think the way I said it was disrespectful. The wording I used . . . that was disrespectful."

"I hear something not quite . . . wholehearted" was Sawyer's response, to which Maines replied, "It's not because it's not genuine. It's because I'm on guard now. . . . Am I sorry that I asked questions and that I don't just follow? No."

Maines added later in the interview, "We support the troops 100 percent. We have said that from day one. . . . There is not a correlation between not wanting a war and not supporting the troops who are doing their job. . . . Martie and I have family in the military." Maines went on to say that she probably spoke the famous line "out of frustration. At that moment, on the eve of war, I had a lot of questions that were unanswered."[4] Maines, however, never elaborated on what those questions were.

Other critics of the Chicks ranged from servicemen to DJs to columnists like veteran music journalist Chet Flippo, who went on record against the Chicks in his March 24 CMT.com column, "Shut Up and Sing." "She [Maines] could not have made a stupider mistake," the former *Rolling Stone* and *Billboard* writer noted. "First of all, if she really has strong convictions about the war, she should spell them out. And stand up for them. Most sensible people will respect her right to do that. But don't make what amounts to a personal attack on Bush." Flippo added that he also felt the apology that was forthcoming seemed insincere, adding,

> Country music fans are largely conservative and patriotic . . . and the U.S. was only days away from a possible war. What do you expect country fans to say when a country star dumps on the president? That tells me that none of them—Chicks, PR, label, management—knows anything about the country music audience. And that audience is tolerant of artists' mistakes and foibles: drunkenness, drug use, adultery, no-shows and any amount of indulgent behavior. What that audience will not tolerate is an artist turning on them. . . . You're an artist? And you have a message? Hey, put it in a song. We'll listen to that. But otherwise, shut up and sing.[5]

Flippo received hundreds of responses from readers both agreeing and disagreeing with his stance. One of the opponents was his friend and fellow author Bill Malone, who took Flippo to task the next week in a response that CMT.com also published.

> In my opinion, you had every right to question the wisdom, timing, and context of Natalie Maines' remarks, but after having done that, you should have asserted her right to express her opinions. . . . Old friend, I am sorely offended by your attempts to argue that the country music audience is monolithic, or that some of us are more patriotic than others because of our attitudes toward the current president. . . . Some of us vehemently oppose the war that Bush has instigated and, like Natalie Maines, we worry about

the consequences that the war will have not only for men and women who have to fight it, but also for other people who may suffer from its ravages.[6]

Malone closed by writing that the Chicks' audience is likely made up at least in part by the same nontraditional fans who made *O Brother* such a huge success, and that the Chicks have also brought good acoustic music with strong harmonies to an audience that has had little exposure to it.

The real issue in the minds of most Americans who followed the Chicks story was not whether Maines had a right to speak her mind. She did. It was not whether the record buyers had a right to smash a few CDs. They did. It was not even whether a few DJs, in order to appease their listeners, pulled the Chicks' music from the station playlists. The real issue to many was whether or not the corporate conglomerates, such as Clear Channel Communications, Cumulus Media, and Cox Communications (which together make up a large majority of radio stations in America) issued a proclamation from on high to suspend the trio's music solely based on the band's perceived controversial opinions. Although censorship by its strictest definition is something initiated by the government rather than private corporations, legislators have always recognized the tremendous power of the media and the potential for abuse, and therefore until recent years regulated broadcasters through the Fairness Doctrine and other regulations addressing equal time for candidates and viewpoints and ownership of media. (Whether or not those regulations interfere with the free market is not the focus of this piece.)

A related concern was whether DJs acted alone in staging CD-smashing events and pro-war rallies, such as the Rallies for America, or were encouraged to do so by management. Some executives of Clear Channel, which is headquartered in San Antonio and owns 1,250 stations, had business dealings with Bush in the past, which raised further concerns about their ability to remain neutral. NPR's Bob Edwards aired his concerns in a speech that ran in the *Louisville Courier-Journal*: "The backlash against the Chicks is spearheaded not by fans, but by Clear Channel Radio, owner of 1,250 radio stations. Clear Channel is based in Texas. Clear Channel loves George W. Bush," Edwards asserted. "Is Clear Channel's move on those Dixie Chicks an expression of patriotism or a business decision? Should Clear Channel have the right to ban the Chicks from its 1,250 stations? I think what individuals do is fine—burn the CDs if you want. What industry does is another matter." Edwards added, "Clear Channel can say the Dixie Chicks are tools of Saddam if it wants to, but it should not be allowed to kill the livelihood of any recording artists based on politics."[7]

Legitimate concerns to be sure—if true. However, for all the alleged or even known connections between the Bushes and Clear Channel, the company does not appear to be guilty of any organized conspiracy. First, Clear Channel's concert division was sponsoring the current Chicks tour, so it would be unlikely that it would cut its own financial throat by encouraging its stations to boycott the artists they were promoting, ideology be damned.

Further, the organization Accuracy in Media, in response to Edwards's piece, asserted that he had no basis for his claims that Clear Channel ordered songs pulled and that, "according to the Mediabase Airplay Monitor Service, Clear Channel played the Dixie Chicks songs more often—a full 10,069 times—than any other major broadcaster in the two weeks following the controversial statements made by the lead singer." Cliff Kincaid of AIM's publication *Media Monitor* added, "Did Clear Channel destroy Chicks' CD's? There's no evidence of that at all. Instead, consumers did so, and that's their right."[8]

The situation with Cumulus, however, was not so cut and dry. Cumulus president Lewis J. Dickey admitted the company pulled the trio's music, although it reversed its position shortly after.

Even so, the issue was serious enough to raise concerns in the Senate. In July of 2003 hearings were held on Capitol Hill by the Senate Commerce Committee to assess whether or not broadcasters really did abuse their power in limiting free speech. John McCain, who oversees the FCC, was one of the parties who questioned Cumulus. McCain stated emphatically that he was offended as much as any veteran by Maines's comments; however, he defended her right to hold her position without undue economic burden to her career. McCain reiterated the concerns of others on the committee when he said, "If a local station made a decision not to play a particular band, then that is what localism is all about. But when a corporate decision is made that [stations] will not play a group because of a political statement, then that comes back to what we're talking about with media consolidation."[9]

Dickey said that the initial decision "had come as a result of a 'hue and cry' from local listeners and requests from local programmers for direction. . . . This was no censorship from Cumulus," Dickey asserted. "The listeners did this."[10]

However, a *Hollywood Reporter* story claimed that the decision was made from the Cumulus corporate headquarters. Dickey's rebuttal? "Our program directors knew what they wanted to do. They were looking to us for guidance, so we put in a framework to make the decision," he said, which sounds like a distinction without a difference.

What appears to have happened is that Cumulus essentially issued a statement that "allowed" local program directors the prerogative of banning the Chicks' music if they felt the need to do so. Also, one of the CD-smashing rallies in Louisiana was sponsored by KRMD, a Cumulus station. "It would not be done the same way," Dickey said to the committee when asked what he would do if the situation arose again.[11]

Dixie Chicks manager Simon Renshaw, testifying before the committee on behalf of the Recording Artists' Coalition, commented on the matter. "Even the perception of a radio network using power in this way clearly demonstrated the potential danger of a system of unchecked consolidation that ultimately undermines artistic freedom, cultural enlightenment, and political discourse." Renshaw added, "What happened to my clients is perhaps the most compelling evidence that radio ownership consolidation has a direct impact on diversity of programming and political discourse over the airwaves."[12]

As if the media whirlwind surrounding Maines's comments wasn't quite enough publicity for the band, the girls posed semi-nude on the cover of the May 2, 2003, issue of *Entertainment Weekly*. Epithets such as "Dixie Sluts" and "Traitors" covered the girls' bodies. "We wanted to show the absurdity of the extreme names people have been calling us," Maines explained. "How do you look at the three of us and think 'Those are Saddam's Angels'?" Maines said in the *EW* interview. "I hope people don't look at this and go 'Oh isn't that nice? They're trying to get more attention.' Trust me— we never wanted this much attention." The group said the longer feature gave them an opportunity to express their point of view in more detail, and perhaps more accurately, than did the Diane Sawyer show, which aired live. "I was more worried about how it affected our families," said Emily Robison. "They had done a cute little hometown story on [my father] in North Carolina right before this happened, and then these horrible, hateful letters started coming in to the school where he teaches, calling my dad a traitor." Maguire said, laughing, "My grandfather [a staunch Republican] is catching a lot of s—t at the nursing home."[13]

The Chicks knew they would face some opposition, but when death threats began being directed toward them, they were stunned. "One of those radio talk show hosts said, 'Well what did they expect?' My answer was: Not That! Didn't expect death threats! Didn't expect to have 24–hour security at my house. Violence doesn't cross my mind when I don't like what someone said," Maines explained.[14]

Apparently, it wasn't just fans who were upset at the Chicks during the whole brouhaha. Several other country artists voiced their opinions about Maines, including Travis Tritt, who told Fox News, "I think the comments were made primarily because it was in front of an audience that agreed with them. But I think if you make those statements over there versus over here, it is sort of cowardly, and I think it was a cheap shot." Tritt added, "The last thing in the world that those people [the troops] need to hear every time they turn on the television or the radio is some half-cocked entertainer coming off and making statements against the actions that they're doing under the direction of our Commander-in-Chief." Tritt closed by saying, "If the Dixie Chicks really wanted to do something to prove just how sorry they are about those statements, they would volunteer to go and perform at some military base."[15]

Perhaps the most interesting feud that spawned from Maines's statement was the resulting duel between Natalie and country singer Toby Keith. It's hard to say just when this fight began (or when it may end), but it definitely heated up when Maines told *L.A. Daily News* writer Fred Shuster what she thought of Keith's pro-war song, "Courtesy of the Red, White, and Blue." "I hate it," she said. "It's ignorant and it makes country music sound ignorant. It targets an entire culture—and not just the bad people who did bad things. You've got to have some tact. Anybody can write, 'We'll put a boot in your ass.'"[16]

After 9/11, Keith had written the song as a tribute to his father, who was killed in an auto accident in 2002. "Courtesy of the Red, White, and Blue (The Angry American)" was a last-minute addition to his *Unleashed* album, according to Keith. He initially hadn't planned on recording it, but encouragement from his fans and his record label convinced him to do so.

During the summer of 2002, ABC anchor Peter Jennings had misgivings about the song being sung on an ABC-TV Fourth of July special. Peter Jennings hosted the show, but objected to the song's "angry" tone and vetoed it. As a result, Keith did not appear.

Keith responded to Maines's disparaging remarks about his songwriting skills in an interview with CMT.com in December of last year. "That's what I do—I write songs. And I've had a string of number ones that I don't think

Fig. 2. Toby Keith, the angry American. Keith's "Courtesy of the Red, White, and Blue" resulted in his being "uninvited" to host a holiday TV special. (Photo by Alan Mayor.)

anybody can take away from me. I have been BMI's Songwriter of the Year. I am a big-time songwriter and, first and foremost, a songwriter. So, I'm in the big-league of that. By you asking me [my reaction], that's like asking Barry Bonds what he thought about what a softball player said about his swing."[17]

In March, Keith commented on Natalie's remarks about the president. "She's come after me before. She's got a big mouth," he said. As the conflict in Iraq escalated, so did the feud between Keith and Maines, culminating with Natalie's appearance via satellite at the Academy of Country Music Awards in May. Maines wore a T-shirt with the letters "F.U.T.K.," which most in the audience read to mean "F—k you Toby Keith." Her publicist later said the initials stood for Freedom, Understanding, Tolerance, and Knowledge. Keith had his revenge, however, when he walked away with the evening's most coveted award, Entertainer of the Year.

As for the Chicks, they appeared to end their summer relatively unscathed. After the initial dip in sales in March, the Chicks' CDs began selling again. Tour attendance appeared to be affected only minimally. The Chicks' first U.S. concert following the remarks was in South Carolina, where only a few protesters showed up. By the end of the U.S. tour in August, their final show in Nashville was a sellout. *Washington Post* writer Anne Hull wrote of that last show, "To be a Dixie Chicks fan now requires more than mere affection. It means having your patriotism challenged. It means getting cussed when you call the country radio station to complain about the boycott on Chicks songs. It means dinner-table squabbles with your soldier cousin who just returned from Iraq, with the whole family wondering why you can't just be like Kenny Chesney." The atmosphere that evening at the Gaylord Auditorium in Nashville was far from combative, although some rowdy boyfriends took the opportunity to don anti-Chicks shirts as they accompanied their dates to the show. Hull continued: "Aside from a lone protester with a sign, the 18,000 others who will see the show seem to have suspended a grudge, if they had one. Lots of moms and dads are in tow. Some say they used the Dixie Chicks flap as a civics lesson at home, talking about free speech or the consequences of disrespecting the country. 'It was tacky,' says Bernadette O'Daniel of Lebanon, Ky., standing with her daughters. 'But we're all entitled to our opinions. You're talking to someone who opens her mouth all the time.'"[18]

Ever wanting to push the envelope, however, the Chicks weren't content to let the evening escape controversy, once again possibly misreading their audience. The Chicks discovered that just because their fans stood with them on the war issue didn't necessarily mean they agreed with them on everything. At one point in the show, the Chicks showed a video montage of demonstrators. The reaction was far from thunderous. "I was just disgusted when I left," a radio talk show caller reported the next day. "They showed videos of protesters fighting for abortion and gay marriage." The host of the show, Steve Gill of radio station WTN in Nashville, said, "These nitwits have still not gotten the lesson that people want to hear their music and not their political agenda."[19]

If they gave a trophy at this year's CMA Awards for Most Misunderstood Artist, it would have to go to Darryl Worley. When Worley wrote his single "Have You Forgotten?" he had just finished visiting the troops in Afghanistan. When he came back to the states, he and cowriter Wynn Varble got together and wrote the song. Worley debuted it in January at the Opry.

"Have You Forgotten?" has references to bin Laden and 9/11. The lyrics also read, "I hear people saying, 'We don't need this war' / But I say there's some things worth fightin' for." Of course, when Worley wrote the song, he was referring to the war on terrorism in general and Afghanistan in particular, but by the time the song was recorded, shipped, and getting airplay, we had gone into Iraq. A slew of criticism from opponents of the war alleged that Worley had been reactionary and played on the nation's sentimentality with his references to 9/11. Furthermore, they asserted, there hadn't been a clear connection established between bin Laden and Hussein. Worley's critics claim he made leaps of logic and, despite his efforts to explain, he never seemed to get his point across.

Interestingly, Worley actually fell victim to the same alleged censorship that the Dixie Chicks experienced when his song was pulled in some markets whose program directors were antiwar. The song debuted at number 43 and eventually reached number 1, where it stayed for several weeks.

Most supporters of the war in country music never really got into the "Does Saddam still have weapons of mass destruction or doesn't he?" debate, although Bush sold that as the primary justification for attacking Iraq. For many pro-war country artists, Hussein's invasion of Kuwait, his use of chemical weapons against thousands of Kurds, his refusal to cooperate with UN weapons inspectors throughout the 1990s, his slaughter of a million innocent Iraqi men, women, and children, and the discovery of terrorist training camps in Iraq was more than enough proof that this was a man who needed to be dealt with. Whether or not he possessed biological and chemical weapons was only a small part of a large dossier of offenses.

Pro-war conservatives were attacked regularly in the media during the spring of 2002 as antiwar protests were held across America. In July of 2003, a Berkeley study of conservatives stopped just short of calling con-

Fig. 3. Darryl Worley, country's most misunderstood artist. Worley's "Have You Forgotten?" was written after he visited troops in Afghanistan, but critics attacked the song's content because of what they felt were faulty connections between Osama bin Laden and Saddam Hussein. (Photo by Alan Mayor.)

servatism a mental illness; the study cited five primary characteristics of the conservative mind: fear and aggression, dogmatism and intolerance of ambiguity, uncertainty avoidance, a need for cognitive closure, and terror management. The article, "Political Conservatism as Motivated Social Cognition," was published in the American Psychological Association's *Psychological Bulletin*. One of the study's authors, Professor Jack Glaser of the Berkeley School of Public Policy, wrote that conservatives don't feel the need to jump through complex intellectual hoops in order to understand or justify some of their positions. "They are more comfortable seeing and stating things in black and white in ways that would make liberals squirm," Glaser said.[20] If there is one country artist who possesses this "intolerance of ambiguity," it's got to be Charlie Daniels.

Daniels is famous for his war anthems such as "In America," "Simple Man," and most recently, "This Ain't No Rag, It's a Flag." In "An Open Letter to the Hollywood Bunch," initially posted on his Web site, Daniels minces no words:

Fig. 4. Charlie Daniels minced no words in his Web site criticism of Hollywood activists and what he felt was their naive view of global issues. (Photo by Alan Mayor.)

Ok, let's just say for a moment you bunch of pampered, overpaid, unrealistic children had your way and the U.S.A. didn't go into Iraq. Let's say that you really get your way and we destroy all our nuclear weapons and stick daisies in our gun barrels and sit around with some white wine and cheese and pat ourselves on the back, so proud of what we've done for world peace.

Let's say that we cut the military budget to just enough to keep the National Guard on hand to help out with floods and fires.

Let's say that we close down our military bases all over the world and bring the troops home, increase our foreign aid and drop all the trade sanctions against everybody.

I suppose that in your fantasy world this would create a utopian world where everybody would live in peace. After all, the great monster, the United States of America, the cause of all the world's trouble would have disbanded it's horrible military and certainly all the other countries of the world would follow suit.

After all, they only arm themselves to defend their countries from the mean old U.S.A.

Why you bunch of pitiful, hypocritical, idiotic, spoiled mugwumps.

Get your head out of the sand and smell the Trade Towers burning.

Do you think that a trip to Iraq by Sean Penn did anything but encourage a wanton murderer to think that the people of the U.S.A. didn't have the nerve or the guts to fight him? . . .

You people need to get out of Hollywood once in a while and get out into the real world. You'd be surprised at the hostility you would find out here. Stop in at a truck stop and tell an overworked, long distance truck driver that you don't think Saddam Hussein is doing anything wrong.

Tell a farmer with a couple of sons in the military that you think the United States has no right to defend itself.

Go down to Baxley, Georgia and hold an anti-war rally and see what the folks down there think about you. . . .

Sean Penn, you're a traitor to the United States of America. You gave aid and comfort to the enemy. How many American lives will your little, "fact finding trip" to Iraq cost? You encouraged Saddam to think that we didn't have the stomach for war.

You people protect one of the most evil men on the face of this earth and won't lift a finger to save the life of an unborn baby. Freedom of choice you say?

Well I'm going to exercise some freedom of choice of my own. If I see any of your names on a marquee, I'm going to boycott the movie. I will completely stop going to movies if I have to. In most cases it certainly wouldn't be much of a loss.

You scoff at our military whose boots you're not even worthy to shine.

They go to battle and risk their lives so ingrates like you can live in luxury.

The day of reckoning is coming when you will be faced with the undeniable truth that the war against Saddam Hussein is the war on terrorism.

America is in imminent danger. You're either for her or against her. There is no middle ground.

I think we all know where you stand.

What do you think?

God Bless America[21]

Several country music artists voiced their opposition to the war via the organization Musicians United to Win Without War, which was founded by Talking Heads member David Byrne. Roseanne Cash, Steve Earle, Emmylou

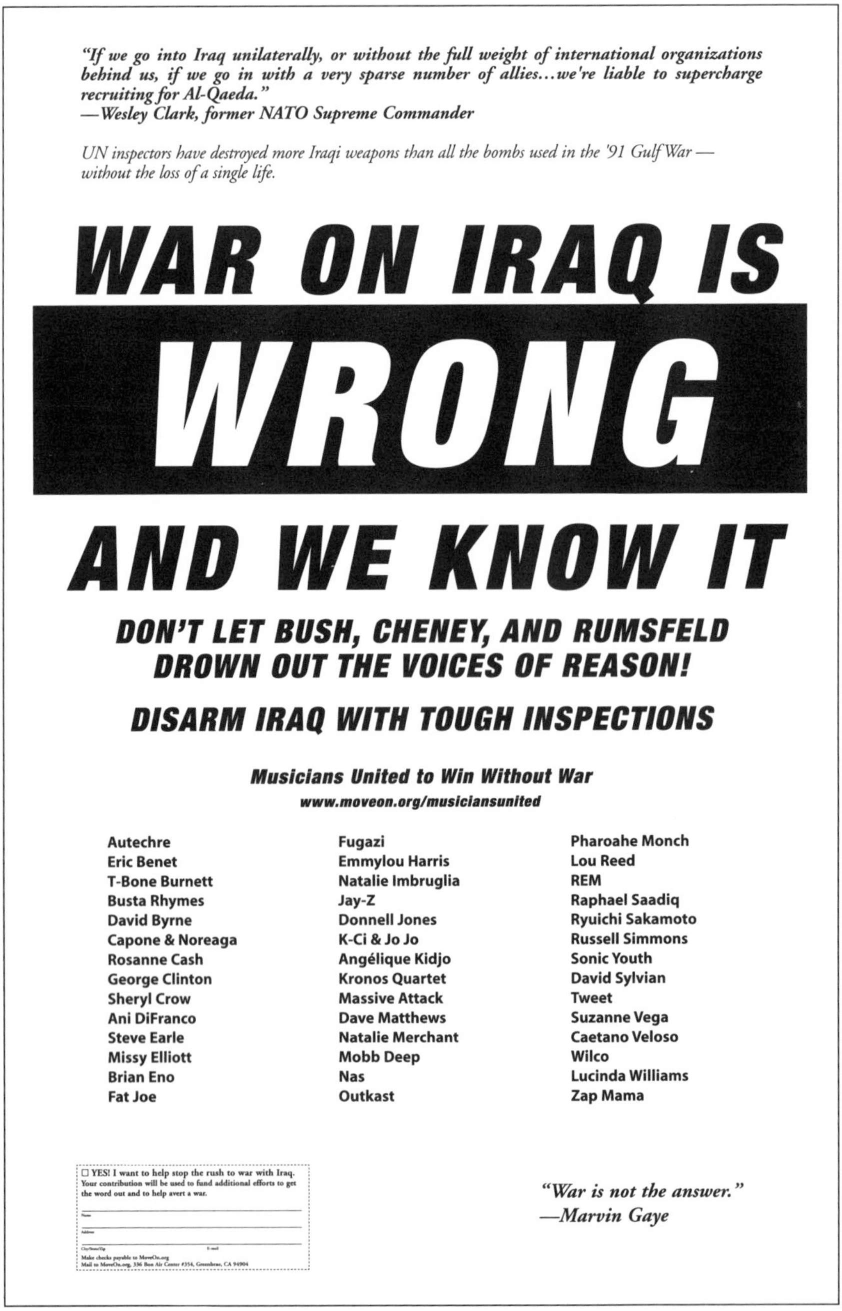

"If we go into Iraq unilaterally, or without the full weight of international organizations behind us, if we go in with a very sparse number of allies...we're liable to supercharge recruiting for Al-Qaeda."
—*Wesley Clark, former NATO Supreme Commander*

UN inspectors have destroyed more Iraqi weapons than all the bombs used in the '91 Gulf War — without the loss of a single life.

WAR ON IRAQ IS
WRONG
AND WE KNOW IT

DON'T LET BUSH, CHENEY, AND RUMSFELD DROWN OUT THE VOICES OF REASON!

DISARM IRAQ WITH TOUGH INSPECTIONS

Musicians United to Win Without War
www.moveon.org/musiciansunited

Autechre	Fugazi	Pharoahe Monch
Eric Benet	Emmylou Harris	Lou Reed
T-Bone Burnett	Natalie Imbruglia	REM
Busta Rhymes	Jay-Z	Raphael Saadiq
David Byrne	Donnell Jones	Ryuichi Sakamoto
Capone & Noreaga	K-Ci & Jo Jo	Russell Simmons
Rosanne Cash	Angélique Kidjo	Sonic Youth
George Clinton	Kronos Quartet	David Sylvian
Sheryl Crow	Massive Attack	Tweet
Ani DiFranco	Dave Matthews	Suzanne Vega
Steve Earle	Natalie Merchant	Caetano Veloso
Missy Elliott	Mobb Deep	Wilco
Brian Eno	Nas	Lucinda Williams
Fat Joe	Outkast	Zap Mama

☐ YES! I want to help stop the rush to war with Iraq.
Your contribution will be used to fund additional efforts to get
the word out and to help avert a war.

Name
Address
City/State/Zip   E-mail
Make checks payable to MoveOn.org
Mail to MoveOn.org, 336 Bon Air Center #354, Greenbrae, CA 94904

"War is not the answer."
—*Marvin Gaye*

Fig. 5. A flyer distributed by Musicians United to Win Without War prior to the United States' second invasion of Iraq.

Harris, Lucinda Williams, and others count themselves members of MUWWW. Cash was one of those who felt the president confused America by shifting his focus during the war on terror. "Sixteen months ago, it was about al Qaeda and Osama bin Laden," Cash said. "I never hear the president mention that anymore. I live in New York, and I want him to stay on message with that."[22] Cash also did a Salon.com interview in which she addressed the war.

> What I'm doing now is having the courage of my convictions, which is to say I'm against it and to say why—because I really think my grandchildren are going to be cleaning up this mess and I have to face them. I have to at least be able to say, "Well, I was against it." That's the way I was brought up. My dad opposed the Vietnam War; that was very unpopular. My dad took on the Ku Klux Klan. He never backed down. You know, ultimately I have to be able to look at myself in the mirror. If you don't have the courage to say what you believe, then what good are you? As far as what active things we can do? At this point we're all a bit dispirited, but there's talk of a concert at Madison Square Garden in the next couple of weeks, to fund humanitarian aid.[23]

Of all the country artists against the war, perhaps Steve Earle has been the most virulent (though by now some may no longer regard him as a country artist). However, Earle's voice has been somewhat muffled in the din of the Dixie Chicks story. Earle broke onto the music scene with *Guitar Town* in 1986 and followed up with several quality projects before a drug problem temporarily derailed his career.

On Earle's 2002 CD, *Jerusalem*, he takes on such taboo topics as John Walker Lindh ("John Walker's Blues") and Mexican immigration ("What's a Simple Man To Do?"). In "Ashes to Ashes" Earle comments on the World Trade Center attacks, and throws in a dash of paranoia to top things off with "Conspiracy Theory."

Earle has not found much of an outlet in the American media for his views, but several Canadian and British publications have done features on the Texan's strong antiwar views. In one interview, Earle talked about his inspiration for writing the song about John Walker Lindh (the song neither endorses nor condemns Lindh's actions). Earle wrote the song while on tour in Europe with his twenty-year-old son, Justin. "That's my connection to John Walker Lindh," Earle said. "They're pretty much exactly the same age. And I became acutely aware that what happened to him could have happened to my son, and your son, and anybody's son. Nobody in my country wanted to admit that. It's one of the most American stories I've ever heard: he came to Islam by way of hip hop, which I find fascinating. He was already looking outside his culture, like a lot of American kids are."[24]

"I'm just an American boy, raised on MTV," the lyrics read,

> And I've seen all those kids in the soda pop ads, and none of 'em looked like me
> So I started lookin' around for a light out of the dim
> And the first thing I heard that made sense was the word
> Of Mohammed, peace be upon him.

Earle also responded to Keith's "Courtesy of the Red, White, and Blue." "That record embarrasses me," says Earle, "but I don't even think there's really a political component in it. It's like playing in Fort Worth and saying, 'We played Dallas last night, and it's sure good to be back in Texas.' It's pandering to an audience, but doing it in this atmosphere is dangerous. I have a fear of someone with dark skin and clothing different to what people wear in Tennessee getting hurt because of that song. It scares me. And it's really poorly written, apart from anything else."[25]

Various other country artists gave their opinion on the Iraqi conflict as it became apparent that the war would not last long. Merle Haggard, who gave us "Okie from Muskogee" and "The Fightin' Side of Me" during Vietnam, also came out with a single in the summer of 2003 that addressed Gulf War II. The Hag felt compelled to write "That's the News," a song that is more of a commentary on cable television news than a strong stand one way or another regarding Operation Iraqi Freedom.

> Suddenly it's over, the war is finally done
> Soldiers in the desert sand still clinging to a gun
> No one is the winner and everyone must lose
> Suddenly the war is over, that's the news.

Hag's newest single ends, "Politicians do all the talking, soldiers pay the dues / Suddenly the war is over, that's the news."

Ricky Skaggs gave *Country Weekly* his take on the situation in Iraq. "I really do believe there are things our government knows about Saddam Hussein that they're not telling us," he said, prior to the invasion. "I think it's watered down a lot."[26]

And Alan Jackson, whose "Where Were You (When the World Stopped Turning)" was perhaps the most commercially successful song of the post-9/11 anthems, told *Country Weekly* his feelings about the war. Jackson said he feels we have to trust the political process to take care of things, even when it's difficult to do so. "That's why we vote and put people in office. They're supposed to know how to handle that kind of stuff," said Jackson. "If they don't, then we make a change. I'm just a singer of simple sings—and that's the truth. I just don't know about all the other stuff."[27]

Notes

1. J.R. Johnson, "Entertaining Erudition," *American Foreign Policy*, April 2, 2003, http://www.princeton.edu/~afp.

2. Tony Hicks, "Hynde Rages and Rules at Warfield," *Contra Costa Times*, March 3, 2003.

3. Joe Scarborough, "Danny Glover's Supporters Start Letter Writing Campaign with Ugly, Racial Overtones," *Jewish World Review*, May 12, 2003, http://www.jewishworldreview.com/0503/scarborough051203.asp.

4. Matt Drudge, "Tears on TV: Dixie Chicks Explain Bush Bashing," Drudge Report, April 23, 2003, http://www.drudgereport.com/dixie.htm.

5. Chet Flippo, "Shut Up and Sing," Nashville Skyline, CMT.com, March 24, 2003, http://www.cmt.com/news/articles/1470672/03202003/dixie_chicks.jhtml.

6. Bill C. Malone, "Guest Viewpoint on Chicks Controversy," Nashville Skyline, CMT.com, March 27, 2003, http://www.cmt.com/news/articles/1470798/03272003/id_0.jhtml.

7. Bob Edwards, "The President and Freedom: Some Disturbing Trends," *Louisville Courier-Journal*, April 20, 2003, http://www.courier-journal.com/cjextra/editorials/ed0420_edwards.html.

8. Cliff Kincaid, "NPR's Hypocrite," *Media Monitor*, Accuracy in Media (AIM), July 18, 2003, http://www.aim.org/publications/media_monitor/2003/07/18.html.

9. Brooks Boliek, "Dixie Chicks Radio Ban on Senate Panel Hit List," *Hollywood Reporter*, July 9, 2003, http://www.hollywoodreporter.com/thr/article_display.jsp?vnu_content_id=1930521.

10. Ibid.

11. Ibid.

12. Ibid.

13. Chris Willman, "Stars and Strife," *Entertainment Weekly*, May 2, 2003, 26.

14. Ibid.

15. "Singer Travis Tritt Says Celebs Should Support Troops," *The O'Reilly Factor*, Fox News, March 18, 2003, http://www.foxnews.com/story/0,2933,81413,00.html.

16. Calvin Gilbert, "CMT News Special Explores Maines-Keith Controversy," CMT.com, June 6, 2003, http://www.cmt.com/news/feat/tkeith.nmaines.062003.jhtml.

17. "Toby Keith Reacts to Maines' Comments in Upcoming CMT.com Interview," CMT.com, December 6, 2002, http://www.cmt.com/news/display/1459027.jhtml.

18. Anne Hull, "Uncowed Cowgirls: At Tour's End, After the Brouhaha and Boycott, Dixie Chicks and Fans Still Aren't Singing the Blues," *Washington Post*, August 8, 2003.

19. Ibid.

20. Kathleen Maclay, "Researchers Help Define What Makes a Political Conservative," University of California at Berkeley Press Release, July 22, 2003, http://www.berkeley.edu/news/media/releases/2003/07/22_politics.shtml.

21. Charlie Daniels, "An Open Letter to the Hollywood Bunch," April 7, 2003, http://www.charliedaniels.com.

22. Ken Foster, "Not Every Question Has an Answer," Interview with Roseanne Cash, Salon.com, April 9, 2003, http://www.salon.com/ent/music/int/2003/04/09/cash/print.html.

23. Ibid.

24. John Harris, "My Country Is Sleepwalking," *The Guardian* (United Kingdom), September 23, 2002. http://www.guardian.co.uk/arts/war/story/0,12958,919163,00.html.

25. Chris Neal, "Tug of War," *Country Weekly*, April 29, 2003, 38.

26. Ibid, 40.

27. Ibid.

14

Country Music

A Teaching Tool for Dealing with War

James E. Akenson

Introduction

War, in all its horrific inhumanity, intrudes all too frequently into the daily lives of hundreds of millions. Thus it comes as no surprise that country music, with its propensity to comment on the trials and triumphs of everyday life, has a considerable number of songs devoted to the topic of war. Military conflicts and the events surrounding them also occupy considerable space within the kindergarten through twelfth-grade curriculum, particularly in the subject of social studies, as well as in literature. All too often, however, textbook descriptions of military conflict fail to convey the emotional, or affective, component of war or to present information in a manner that holds students' attention. Country music provides a powerful tool to engage students as they study various military conflicts.

This discussion advances examples drawn from the country music tradition that may involve students as they encounter curriculum content dealing with various military conflicts. The country music examples are combined with teaching strategies that maximize student involvement, time-on-task, and sustained focus on key content and thinking skills. The discussion emphasizes the use of factual information to achieve conceptual understanding in an ongoing interplay between the two levels of knowledge. A variety of tools ranging from graphic organizers to problem solving skills to analogical reasoning are illustrated. Each lesson described herein includes goals and objectives and addresses state and national standards that today's teachers must address. Elsewhere, the author has discussed a wide variety of teaching strategies based on country music content, including some which dealt with war (Akenson 2000). The specific teaching strategies linking country music and conflicts, such as Gallipoli and the Western Front in World War I, are not repeated in this discussion, but other examples are provided in their place. It should be noted that the voluminous nature of war commentary in the country music tradition prevents this discussion from being anywhere near exhaustive. Examples selected for this discussion merely hint at a far larger number of curricular applications than allowed by the limited space in this volume. This discussion now turns to examples that use country music to enhance the curriculum, focusing primarily on the events of 9/11, the Vietnam War, World War II, the Civil War, and the War of 1812.

Country Music over Time

Events at the beginning of the twenty-first century bring immediate witness to bear on the utility of country music for dealing with curricula addressing war. The invasion of Iraq in 2003 prompted commentary and controversy in the country music community that easily lends itself to classroom analysis. Prior to the invasion of Iraq, the author taught a lesson to eighth-grade students at Avery Trace Middle School in Cookeville, Tennessee. The lesson examined country music and war over the years, but used contemporary events both as an initial focus and as a conclusion. The lesson began with students placing the formula $DC(NEM) \times W^2 + 15\ W = C^3$ on the top of their world maps. Discussion first centered on current events and awareness of the Dixie Chicks controversy. The antiwar stance of the Dixie Chicks stood in contrast to the pro-war stance of many country music fans. Discussion also focused on the right of the Dixie Chicks to say what they thought. After the discussion the author interpreted the formula as meaning "The Dixie Chicks (Natalie, Emily, and Marti) times the second President Bush equals continuous, constant, controversy." The author then established the focus of the lesson as being one that examines country music and the genre's commentaries about war.

Upon establishing the lesson focus, the author played a portion of Johnny Horton's version of "The Battle of New Orleans" (1961), with instructions to the class to raise their hands if they had previously studied the content. Students all rose their hands, as eighth-grade United States his-

The author teaching a class of eighth-grade students in Cookeville, Tennessee.

tory examines Andrew Jackson and the Battle of New Orleans. The author indicated that the writer of "The Battle of New Orleans," Jimmy Driftwood, wrote the song as a high school teacher in order to help his students learn more about the battle. The author then explained that three additional country music songs would be used to examine the attitudes toward three separate wars. The American South, Europe, and Iraq were plotted on each student's map of the world. To guide the analysis, students used a semantic differential graphic organizer geared to the pro-war/antiwar dichotomy. Students first listened to a Civil War song, "The King Has Called Me Home," from Waylon Jennings's *White Mansions: A Tale of the American Civil War 1861–1865* (1978), and then ranked it on the pro-war/antiwar continuum. The second song dealt with World War I and the Gallipoli Campaign of 1915. Students first drew an arrow to Gallipoli within the square outlining Europe and then listened to Slim Dusty's version of "And the Band Played Waltzing Matilda" (1978). Before the third song, students outlined Iraq, drew an arrow to it, and were reminded of the Dixie Chicks controversy over the wisdom of the impending invasion. The class then listened to

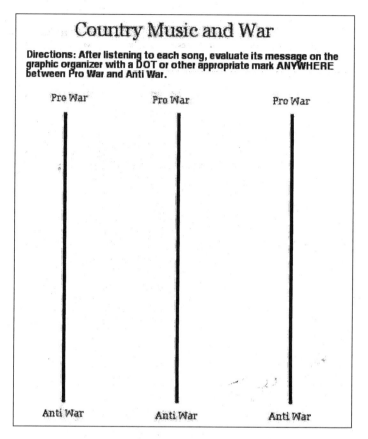

Darryl Worley's "Have You Forgotten?" (2003). After each song, each student marked his or her continuum, volunteers showed the class their rankings, and the class then discussed the evidence the students used to justify their rankings. Before the discussion, the author stressed the use of evidence from the song as well as the varied rankings that resulted from the same lyrics and melody. The author concluded by noting that four songs from the country music tradition span from the War of 1812 to the impending invasion of Iraq, that country music addresses important issues of life including war, and that controversy about war will be a constant feature of life.

Contemporary Events

Events since September 11, 2001, provide numerous opportunities for integrating country music into social studies curricula as students examine current events. The Dixie Chicks controversy involves basic issues of free speech, the right of dissent, and a controversy with Toby Keith. The overt context, the 2003 invasion of Iraq, includes a larger context, that of the response by the country music community to the events of 9/11. In an even larger context, as Ronnie Pugh (2003) and others have documented, country music artists and their fan bases tend to be conservative and in support of United States foreign policy without reservation in time of war. Numerous opportunities exist to deal with issues regarding freedom of speech and dissent. Craig Havighurst (2003) identified the basic issues of patriotism and free speech around which the Dixie Chicks controversy swirled. His article provides a basis for the initial discussion, in which students identify basic constitutional guarantees. Questions include, What freedoms are guaranteed in the first ten amendments of the United States Constitution? How many of you believe in the constitution? Did the Dixie Chicks have a right to say they were embarrassed that President Bush was from Texas? What does it mean to be patriotic, tolerant, or intolerant? Is it right to protest the Dixie Chicks' statement? Thus, the text of Havighurst's article provides an ideal springboard for dealing with the complexities of the difficult concepts associated with civic participation:

> As thousands of country fans stream into Nashville this week for Fan Fair, the country music community is wrestling, perhaps as never before, over issues of patriotism and free speech.
> Rabble-rousing songs by Toby Keith and Darryl Worley have become smash hits. Widespread radio station boycotts of Dixie Chicks music after lead singer Natalie Maines' critical remark about President Bush . . . left many thinking that country music was drawing ideological lines.

Havighurst also points out the ability of large broadcasting conglomerates such as Cumulus Media to ban the Dixie Chicks from their network of forty-one country stations. Lines of questioning highlight the complexities of the problem: Should a corporation that owns many radio stations across the United States have the right to ban the Dixie Chicks for having stated an unpopular position? Does banning the Dixie Chicks music send a message that might make artists censor their opinions? Are the Dixie Chicks any less patriotic than Toby Keith or Darryl Worley? How do you know that Iraq actually poses a threat to the United States? Since the Iraq war, has there been proof that Iraq was a major threat to the United States?

Darryl Worley's country music record "Have You Forgotten?" provides another opportunity to address subtle issues and to compare and contrast opinions in the classroom. An editorial by Karen Loew takes issue with Worley's song; she writes, "No, Mr. Worley, I haven't forgotten, and I'm offended at how you asked" (2003). Students may evaluate Loew's comments on a forced-choice agree/disagree format. Such a format requires students to take a specific position, which then allows for class discussion based upon evidence and opinion. The first statement allows students to respond to the thesis of the editorial: If you are not offended by "Have You Forgotten?" is the author wrong in her beliefs? Why didn't the author make this statement as the conclusion of her editorial instead of an opening statement? Which statements did your response agree with? Does statement 7 logically follow from the evidence the author stated in the editorial? Were the author's statements facts or opinion? How is statement 4 like statement 1?

"No, Mr. Worley, I Haven't Forgotten . . ."

Directions: Read the "Nashville Eye" editorial. Place a check mark in the Agree or Disagree column for each statement made by Ms. Karen Loew in her "Nashville Eye" editorial.

	Agree	Disagree
1. The No. 1 country song . . . offends anyone who really hasn't forgotten . . . Sept. 11, 2001.	_____	_____
2. I haven't forgotten the . . . office workers stumbling up Eighth Avenue at the end of my Manhattan block that . . . morning.	_____	_____
3. I haven't forgotten the breaths of sour smoke curling in the air for weeks.	_____	_____
4. I do remember, and that's precisely why I would say, "We don't need this war."	_____	_____
5. I haven't forgotten President Bush's oath to catch bin Laden "dead or alive."	_____	_____
6. Saddam Hussein's regime proved a much easier target.	_____	_____
7. . . . . this war . . . does not stop those who carried out 9/11.	_____	_____

Upon conclusion of the analysis, students may write a summary statement that agrees or disagrees with the central thesis and the evidence of the editorial.

Other dimensions related to the Iraq invasion and the Dixie Chicks' comments concern the motivations of participants. An initial discussion of the Dixie Chicks controversy may begin with a line of questioning regarding economic motivation: Should one take a position on an important national policy issue just to make money or receive publicity? Is it wrong to make money by making politically popular or unpopular statements or singing songs with political content? Once students have stated their opinions, they may begin to deal with a combination of fact and opinion. The "Patriotism, Profit, and Country Music" exercise may be used as a pre- and post-assessment to analyze the issues. Students complete the exercise before reading editorials and being presented factual information.

Patriotism, Profit, and Country Music

Directions: Read the following statements. The first time you read the statements place a 1 in the Fact or the Opinion column. The second time place a 2 in the Fact or the Opinion column.

	Fact	Opinion
1. Cumulus Media has a right to ban the Dixie Chicks on their radio stations.	_____	_____
2. Cumulus Media banned the Dixie Chicks in order to create interest and make more money.	_____	_____
3. The Dixie Chicks criticized President Bush to sell more CDs and have more people attend their concerts.	_____	_____
4. Destroying Dixie Chicks CDs is guaranteed by the constitution.	_____	_____
5. Destroying Dixie Chicks CDs is no better than burning books like the Nazis did in Germany.	_____	_____
6. Clear Channel Communications didn't ban the Dixie Chicks on their radio stations because they didn't want to lose money sponsoring the Chicks' national concert tour.	_____	_____
7. Toby Keith, Darryl Worley, and other country singers wrote their songs just to make money.	_____	_____
8. The only reason the Dixie Chicks protested is because they are Democrats.	_____	_____
9. Toby Keith is trying to make money by his super-patriotic album title *Shock'n Y'All*.	_____	_____

After reacting to the statements the first time, students may explain why they chose "Fact" or "Opinion." Among the questions that may be used are the following: If the statement is written factually, how do you know it is really an opinion? What evidence would you need to substantiate your evaluation or to change it? Which statements probably can't be proven regardless of how much information you might be provided?

Students then read articles and letters to the editor, which provide varied input on the controversy. Brian Mansfield's *USA Today* article (2003) includes a photograph from Bossier City, Louisiana, where fans at an event sponsored by a radio station tore up tickets to Dixie Chicks concerts, stomped on Dixie Chicks CDs, and used a tractor emblazoned with the words "Dixie Chicks Destruction" to destroy additional CDs. Jack Bowen's (2003) letter in *The Tennessean* points out the following: "In the tradition of Charlie Daniels, Aaron Tippin and Toby Keith, Worley has written a truly awful song that blindly wraps itself around the flag to make a buck. His record company can't wait to throw together an album . . . to take advantage of this latest jingoistic nonsense." The teacher points out that Clear Channel Communications, which owns over one thousand radio stations and supports President Bush, helped sponsor the Dixie Chicks national tour, which began in Greenville, South Carolina. Students may also analyze Toby Keith's (2003) Web page to determine why he would call his new album and tour *Shock'n Y'All*. Questions include, Why must Toby Keith wrap himself and his Web page in the American flag? Does this Web page prove Toby Keith is more patriotic than the Dixie Chicks? How do we know that Toby Keith isn't using a play on words from the Iraq invasion, "shock and awe," just to play on patriotism and make money? Students then rank their evaluations a second time as fact or opinion, followed by a discussion of why rankings changed or remained the same.

A final example based on events since 9/11 makes use of a Venn diagram graphic organizer for comparing two country music songs. Alan Jackson's "Where Were You (When the World Stopped Turning)" may be compared to other post–September 11 songs such as "Have You Forgotten?" Toby Keith's "Courtesy of the Red, White, and Blue (The Angry American)" (2002), or Aaron Tippin's "Where the Stars and Stripes and the Eagle Fly" (2001). The Venn diagram graphic organizer allows students to engage in factual and higher-order thinking as they examine lyrics for elements of similarities and differences. When comparing "Have You Forgotten?" and "Where Were You," note the songs' similar use of specific

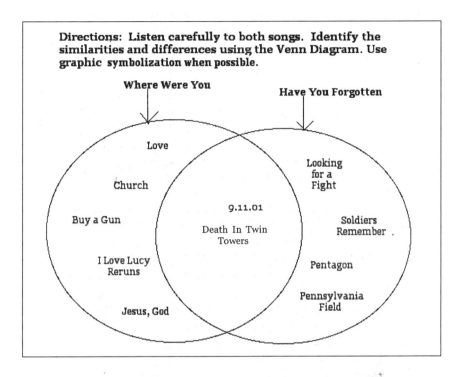

Directions: Listen carefully to both songs. Identify the similarities and differences using the Venn Diagram. Use graphic symbolization when possible.

Where Were You

Have You Forgotten

Love

Church

Buy a Gun

I Love Lucy Reruns

Jesus, God

9.11.01

Death In Twin Towers

Looking for a Fight

Soldiers Remember .

Pentagon

Pennsylvania Field

details of the attacks on the Twin Towers and the Pentagon and the deaths of innocent victims, and also note how the songs diverge, both in the events they mention and in the tenor of their comments. Alan Jackson mentions specific events and emotions, ranging from going to church and holding hands to purchasing a gun, and refers to the biblical passage 1 Corinthians 13. Darryl Worley, however, focuses on the desire for a fight and censorship, by an unnamed force, that prevented televised broadcast of any 9/11 attack footage that was deemed too disturbing. Follow-up analysis focuses upon questions such as, Why does Alan Jackson refer to God and Jesus and a passage in the Bible, whereas Darryl Worley does not? Which song is harsher, stronger in the desire for revenge? Which song would you pick to "stand the test of time" and be a favorite, a classic twenty years from now? Comparing different combinations of songs, such as "Where the Stars and Stripes and the Eagle Fly" with "Have You Forgotten?" offers various avenues of analysis, depending upon the purpose—the goals and the objectives—that a teacher wishes to stress. Venn diagrams may also involve three overlapping circles to allow for more complex comparison and contrast.

The Vietnam War

Country music provides a powerful tool for teaching about the Vietnam War, a conflict that still stirs powerful emotions. The split within the United States between antiwar activities and the "silent majority" resulted in music supportive of both positions. However, even well-written textbooks such as *America: Pathways to the Present* (Cayton, Perry, Reed, and Winkler 2002) rarely convey the intensity of emotions, despite the books' factual descriptions and photographic evidence of the split. A passage from *America*, for example, reads: "Antiwar groups grew by leaps and bounds around the country. During demonstrations, marchers chanted 'Hey, hey, LBJ. How many kids did you kill today?' In April 1967 some 200,000 opponents of the war marched in New York City" (628). In contrast, Merle Haggard's "The Fightin' Side of Me" (1970) and "Okie from Muscogee" (1969) offer emotionally charged statements that provide students an opportunity to experience the pro-war stance. Students may be directed to find statements in the texts that prove consistent with Haggard's statements and give evidence from the lyrics to substantiate their position. In addition to indicating their reactions on graphic organizers, students may be asked a wide variety of questions, such as, What specific evidence in "Okie from Muscogee" shows that the country music audience would not approve of the counter culture associated with the antiwar movement? How does the choice of Muscogee, Oklahoma, as the geographic setting for the song reinforce the set of values associated with those who would be supportive of the Vietnam War? Is "The Fightin' Side of Me" more patriotic than someone exercising their right to dissent? Isn't someone questioning the morality of our government's behavior behaving as a good citizen? Didn't our country's soldiers fight for the right of people to express their opinions even if they differed from the government's or the majority's position? Similar lines of analyses may be developed for much more obscure songs such as Buddy Starcher's "Sniper's Hill" (1966) and H.J. Dailey's "Merry Christmas from Vietnam" (n.d.).

Chad McGee (1998) developed multimedia materials to deal with the Vietnam War and the constitutional guarantee of free speech. McGee used a combination of country music songs, visual images, and graphic organizers based on word-pair polar opposites to examine the issues of freedom of dissent and freedom of speech. McGee used photos of Vietnam War–era dissent, leading questions, and a soundtrack to stimulate responses to specific statements based upon song content and free speech issues; responses were based upon word-pair opposites such as "patriotic-unpatriotic" and "agree-disagree." Songs such as Bobby Bare's "God Bless America Again" provided an introduction to the tasks focusing on freedom of speech. Autry Inman's "Ballad of Two Brothers" and Ernest Tubb's "It's America (Love It or Leave It)" (1994) provided the musical core for the presentation. "Ballad of Two Brothers" provided the soundtrack for a series of photos showing Kent State University and other protesters. Inman narrates a sarcastic appraisal of college students characterized by one brother, Tommy, who has grown a "groovy" beard, walked a difficult twenty blocks in a protest, learned that Communism provides for needs as well as capitalism, asked his parents to send more money, and, finally, asked about his brother Bud, who is serving in Vietnam. The narrative ends to strains of "Battle Hymn of the Republic," with the former protesting college student, Tommy, writing his parents from Vietnam, where he serves in honor of his brother, Bud, who was killed in action. "It's America (Love It or Leave It)," with Ernest Tubb lamenting that people no longer have respect for the law, served as the soundtrack for the section showing civil rights protests. Tubb's admonition that the protesters either love America or leave it illustrates "that's what democracy means after all." Such provocative content leads to substantive lines of questioning, including the following: Does democracy really mean you have the right to leave if you don't like something? Doesn't the First Amendment give citizens the right to question decisions such as conducting war? In what way did songs such as "Ballad of Two Brothers" and "It's America (Love It or Leave It)" reflect the values of the country music audience? Is this a conservative or liberal message? Are there songs by country artists about 9/11 and the invasion of Iraq that express the same sentiments?

The Statler Brothers' "More Than a Name on a Wall" (1988), which the author combined with the 1969 death of Private Ben Wade Stone of Whitleyville, Tennessee, provides another means of exploring the Vietnam War through country music. Students discuss evidence presented in the text regarding major theaters of operation, casualty figures, and reactions in the military and in the United States to the casualties. They then plot the location of Danang in South Vietnam and its location within I Corps area of operations. Students then discuss how they would feel if someone close to them were killed in Vietnam. Subsequently they view a video that combines the Vietnam Memorial and the setting in rural Jackson County, Tennessee, of Private Ben Wade's grave with the soundtrack of the Statler

Brothers' "More Than a Name on a Wall." Next, students read the front-page obituary, with the all-capital banner headline "PVT STONE KILLED IN VIETNAM."

> Marine Private First Class Ben Wade Stone, 20, son of Mr. and Mrs. Hooper Stone of Whitleyville, was killed in action in Vietnam on Sunday, August 10. His parents were notified of their son's death on August 13.
>
> P.F.C. Stone was killed approximately 30 miles southwest of Danang, Quan Province, while in a company-sized night defensive position, according to the Defense Department. He sustained a missile wound in the head from hostile mortar fire.
>
> P.F.C. Stone's body arrived in Nashville Tuesday night at 9:00 p.m. and was taken to his home where it will remain until time for services today, Thursday, August 21. (*Jackson County Sentinel* 1969)

The obituary also provides a history of Stone's military career from training to deployment to Vietnam, as well as information regarding his date of high school graduation, survivors, and the funeral home. In addition to plotting the progression of Stone's remains back to Whitleyville, students analyze questions relating to "More Than a Name on a Wall": How do you think Private Stone's parents felt when they first heard the Statler Brothers sing this song in 1988? Would the song have brought back specific memories of their son, his death, and the funeral service? Would they have felt their son was special and far more than a name on the wall? Would it have made them feel comforted to know that Ben Wade Stone's name is indeed on the wall? Would it have been harder on Mr. and Mrs. Stone to accept their son's death than it was for soldiers who died in World War II? How do you think Mr. and Mrs. Stone reacted to the antiwar demonstrations and the counter culture of the 1960s? How do you think Mr. and Mrs. Stone would respond to the Internet pages devoted to the Vietnam Memorial and "More Than a Name on a Wall" (http://www.angelfire.com/il2/Waynes Place/thewall.html)? The Statler Brothers and country music thus make possible analytical reasoning from a first-person perspective that is based upon both textual and nontextual information.

World War II

Elton Britt's "There's a Star Spangled Banner Waving Somewhere" (n.d.) stands out among the many country music hits that played an integral role in World War II. The migration of southern whites to urban centers to participate in wartime industrial production resulted in the spread of country music to new settings and, ultimately, to new audiences. The Grand Ole Opry Camel Caravan programs also brought country music to new audiences, as the Opry artists performed in front of troops (Malone 2002). For example, in his three-year Pacific experience, the Opry's Lewis Crook played for fellow soldiers near the front lines and for those awaiting deployment to shore in LSTs (Akenson 1984). Country music easily helps students further understand the complexities and the human dimension of the war. The author developed a video of the Draper cemetery in Gainesboro, Tennessee, which contains numerous headstones of World War II casualties, and used "There's a Star Spangled Banner Waving Somewhere" as the soundtrack. In a lesson taught in variations to fifth-, sixth-, seventh-, eighth-, and ninth-grade students, students observed the video without the soundtrack and recorded the name, rank, symbols, and inscriptions from the tombstone and calculated the age of death in combat. Students then watched the video with the soundtrack. Questions included, Do you think that the soldiers from Gainesboro who are buried in the Draper cemetery agreed with the thoughts expressed in "There's a Star Spangled Banner Waving Somewhere"? What words in the song make you think that these soldiers would really like the song? Are there any clues or references in the song to indicate that it might be about a soldier from Tennessee?

A variant of the preceding lesson focuses upon obituaries published in the *Jackson County Sentinel*. In this particular variant, students first plot their home city, then the Upper Cumberland region of Middle Tennessee, and discuss the impact that casualties would have on a small town and county. Students then read two obituaries from the *Sentinel*. The obituary for Gervous Painter emphasizes the factual, and higher-order involvement takes place. The headline for December 7, 1944, states, "Mrs. Nannie A. Painter Receives Letter from Chaplain."

> Dear Mrs. Painter:
>
> By this time you have received word from the War Department concerning your son, Gervous, who gave his life in the service of his country. I knew him, being a chaplain in his regiment, and I want to express my sympathy to you at this time of your great loss, and ours. You have many unseen friends here who are thinking of you now.
>
> Although ( ) can never compensate for your sadness, you will nevertheless take comfort in knowing that your son received the honors of a military

funeral, conducted with the full religious service of the Protestant Faith. His body now rests in a beautifully cared for American cemetery on foreign soil. American soldiers guard the grounds. Above him floats the flag he served.

It will bring you added peace of mind to know that I was with your son at the time he was killed. His death, from an exploding shell, came instantly. He was not disfigured. I was able to offer a prayer, in the presence of his friends, just as his spirit was leaving us to enter God's greater world.

I am praying that God may ease your sorrow, through the miracle of love and that He may grant you some unlooked for blessings during the days that lie ahead.

Sincerely yours.

Yoder P. Leith. Captain Corps of Chaplains. Regimental Chaplain.

Students then engage in specific tasks that require analytical thought. They examine the first line of paragraph 2 and write a word or phrase inside the blank parentheses where the newspaper left out a word. Such a task requires the use of contextual thinking and results in students suggesting words such as "I," "we," "money," and "the United States" to fit the sentiment. Middle and secondary students find and underline religious evidence in the second paragraph. Questions help identify the significance of the reference to services of the "Protestant Faith," such as, Why would Chaplain Leith mention it was a Protestant service? What have we studied earlier in American history that suggests that religious prejudice still existed in 1944? Is the South, and the Upper Cumberland, strongly Protestant with Baptists, Methodists, Presbyterians, and the Church of Christ? Has there been prejudice of Protestants against Catholics, which we studied earlier? Other tasks include underlining statements that might not actually be true. Students routinely underline statements about Gervous Painter dying instantly, not being disfigured, being surrounded by his friends, and Chaplain Leith being able to offer a prayer. One sixth-grade female asked, "Was Mrs. Painter so stupid that she would believe the chaplain could have prayed with him if he died instantly?" Analysis subsequently focuses on the purpose of the letter and the appropriateness of telling people what they want to hear even if it is not true. Finally, the lesson directs attention to "There's a Star Spangled Banner Waving Somewhere." Students react to questions such as, Would Gervous Painter have agreed with the sentiments, the ideas, expressed by Elton Britt? Would Mrs. Nannie Painter have found comfort when she heard this song? How do you think Mrs. Painter would have reacted when she heard this number 1 country music song about World

War II? A variant of this lesson begins with discussing the purpose of popular music, listening to "There's a Star Spangled Banner Waving Somewhere," determining if soldiers who served in World War II might agree with the song's sentiments, and then reading the obituaries. Country music and primary sources such as newspaper obituaries thus bring to life the abstraction of Word War II and infuse it with emotional power.

The Civil War

Elsewhere within this volume, Smith and Akenson point out the substantial volume of Civil War content, references, and symbols within the country music tradition. Civil War content may be found in curricula throughout the United States at several grade levels, including the fourth, fifth, eighth, and eleventh grades. Indeed, the space devoted to this entire discussion could easily be occupied by Civil War examples. Jimmy Arnold's album *Southern Soul,* with songs like "The Rebel Soldier," "Heroes," and "General Lee," provides an opportunity to examine controversial issues related to the Civil War. Numerous editorials address the Civil War legacy, such as Andrews's "Nashville Eye" (1997) piece "The South's Greatest Hero: Robert E. Lee." Andrews offers statements about his own childhood, when he listened "at the feet of my grandfather and his Confederate cronies," and notes that Lee's name was "greeted with the reverence usually reserved for the Deity." Andrews also provides a list of apparently factual statements and concludes that "Lee flew with the eagles while his detractors pick at the filth in the gutter with the pigeons." In the exercise, students are directed to compare the statements of Andrews with those of Arnold, and to compare them with their textbook. Students receive directions to fill out a graphic organizer with specific statements.

The South's Greatest Hero?
Directions: Read "The South's Greatest Hero: Robert E. Lee." List points made by the author. Determine if they are stated by the author as fact or opinion. Place an F or an O in the Fact/Opinion column. Indicate Yes or No if the point is or isn't found in the text. Based upon the album *Southern Soul,* indicate Yes or No if Jimmy Arnold would agree.

At the bottom of the graphic organizer, students may suggest an alternative hero since the end of the Civil War. Their responses may allow for further questions, including the following: To what degree are Mr. Andrews and

Mr. Arnold similar thinkers? Which points from the article and which lyrics from *Southern Soul* are similar? What are the limits to their ideas? Does either man take into account heroes who struggled against oppression of women or African Americans? Why does the Civil War still occupy a significant place in the minds of southerners such as Mr. Andrews and Mr. Arnold? How would Mr. Andrews and Mr. Arnold feel about our textbook description of the Civil War and its causes? Such a line of analysis brings discussion back to major issues identified by the text and the state-mandated curriculum, while the significantly different types of instructional materials provide input and variety to daily classroom events.

Another opportunity for discussion is provided by the battles for Chattanooga, a strategic objective whose capture resulted in Union forces finally having a clear path into the Deep South. Lookout Mountain, with its oversight of the Tennessee River, provided a strategic component in the Confederate defense of Chattanooga. Textbooks usually omit Lookout Mountain as part of the Chattanooga campaign; those that mention it usually provide only scant evidence and generic images of hilly topography. However, Brother Phelps's song "Lookout Mountain" (1995) provides the students with a different text and analysis. In such a context students may listen to Brother Phelps's description of Lookout Mountain and develop a list of the apparently factual events. In addition to determining the specific events mentioned in "Lookout Mountain," students may then analyze reasons for the textbook's omission of Lookout Mountain, asking such questions as, If the account of Lookout Mountain is accurate and Chattanooga is a strategic city, then why wouldn't the text mention it? To what degree do the illustrations of Chattanooga reflect the description of Lookout Mountain? To what sources could we turn to determine the accuracy of Brother Phelps's account of Lookout Mountain? Students may then examine Web sites such as "Battle above the Clouds, Lookout Mountain" and analyze the posted assertion by General Grant that "The Battle of Lookout Mountain is one of the romances of the war. There was no such battle and no action even worthy to be called a battle on Lookout Mountain. It is all poetry." Such a statement requires further questions: If General Grant said the "battle" is just poetry, what can we make of the significance Brother Phelps gives to Lookout Mountain? Don't the photo on the Web site and the photo presented in class suggest strategic significance for Chattanooga on the Tennessee River? Isn't Lookout Mountain part of the strategic hinge that opened up Atlanta to Union forces? Why would Brother Phelps record a song if

Lookout Mountain was insignificant to the strategic hinge? Do other Web pages agree with the assessment we have examined?

Such examples as Brother Phelps's "Lookout Mountain" and Jimmy Arnold's *Southern Soul* concept album point to a multiplicity of uses for country music as it relates to the Civil War. The large number of concept albums, references to the Civil War in country music, and the occurrence of visual evidence on album covers points to a rich, provocative source of perceptions that may be probed from the factual as well as the interpretive dimensions. History requires evidence and conceptual frameworks from which to engage students. The Civil War content of Brother Phelps and Jimmy Arnold suggests that the process of thinking about history and its meaning greatly enriches the teaching process of this most crucial event in American history.

The War of 1812

Jimmy Driftwood, a teacher and principal, wrote "The Battle of New Orleans" for educational purposes, and it became a major record in the career of Johnny Horton. Minimally, the War of 1812 makes its way into curricula in the fifth and eighth grades. Texts provide information, but often the coverage of material results in passive reading followed by low-level questions asked by the teacher. Crosby (1998) developed materials that resulted in middle school students engaging in sophisticated comparison and contrast of the text with Driftwood's version of "The Battle of New Orleans." Crosby began by informing the class that the thrust of the lesson dealt with the War of 1812 and "The Battle of New Orleans." He then posed a question: What do the following have in common? He listed a twenty-dollar bill, the Hermitage (home of Andrew Jackson), a bank in Cookeville, an NFL football team, a pirate from France, the 1986 Sugar Bowl, the University of Miami Hurricanes versus the University of Tennessee Volunteers, and Rum "Pickled __ __ __ __ __ __ __ __ ." Subsequently, Crosby listed vocabulary and related terms designed to orient students to the content of the lesson. Crosby and the class discussed their perception of the terms, which included "maturity," "nigh," "Jean Laffite (pirate)," "breastworks," "frontal assault," "britches," "purty," and "brambles." Students were then informed that they would first listen to Jimmy Driftwood's song "The Battle of New Orleans," record the items in the comparison chart graphic organizer, then read the account in the textbook (Weeks and Womack 1996),

---

"The Battle of New Orleans"
Comparison Chart Graphic Organizer

Directions: Listen carefully to Jimmy Driftwood's" version of "The Battle of New Orleans. Record facts and inferences in the "Jimmy Driftwood" column. Read pages 189-190 in the text. Record facts and inferences in the "Text" column.

TEXT	Jimmy Driftwood
1. 8 January 1815	1. Down the Mississippi River
2. 5,300 British	2. 1814
3. 4,500 Americans	3. Jackson enlisted aid of Jean Laffite
4. British shoulder to shoulder	4. Will whup britches off of Pakenham
5. Perfect targets	5. Met British near New Orleans
6. Americans behind cotton bales	6. French said better run
7. 2000+ British killed or wounded	7. 100 beating on the drum
8. Commander Pakenham killed	8. Stood behind cotton bales
9. U.S. casualties 8killed, 13 wounded	9. Fired gator cannon.
10. Battle took 30 minutes	10. Don't fool with Uncle Sam

---

record information given in the text, and then analyze the differences. Crosby directed students to identify the commonalities between the text and "The Battle of New Orleans" and determine which source provided more information. Finally, Crosby and the class generated a concept map graphic organizer that organized the information regarding the Battle of New Orleans. Students then placed check marks on items for which Jimmy Driftwood's song matched the text's account. Crosby then reviewed the relationship of the lesson to the items present at the beginning of the lesson. All of the items dealt with Andrew Jackson (twenty-dollar bill, the Hermitage estate in Nashville, and a bank in Cookeville), New Orleans (the 1986 Sugar Bowl, the New Orleans Saints), and the Battle of New Orleans (Jean Lafitte and Pakingham's body stored in rum). Jimmy Driftwood's "The Battle of New Orleans" thus played a crucial role in sustaining student involvement as they engaged in mastering factual information and higher-order thinking.

Conclusion

Country music lends itself to a wide variety of applications in the K–12 curriculum. As a tool for teaching about war, country music allows teach-

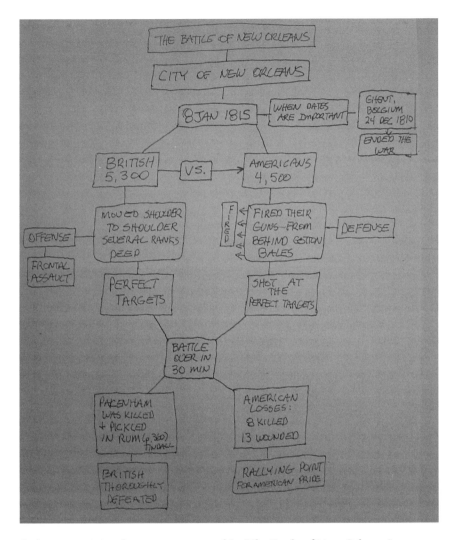

A chart organizing the events recounted in "The Battle of New Orleans."

ers to go beyond requiring rote memorization of dates, battles, and outcomes. War may be analyzed from social and political perspectives as well as military perspectives. Country music lends itself to multiple applications depending upon the grade level, specific content, and objectives of the teacher. Teachers may engage students in higher-order thinking skills, which makes use of content about war but also takes content beyond mere coverage. Most significantly, country music provides a stimulating tool that helps make the textbook content come alive and assume human proportions more clearly reflective of the flesh and blood of history.

References

Akenson, James E. 1984. Lewis Crook: Living and learning country music. *John Edwards Memorial Quarterly* 20, no. 74: 84–93.

——. 2000. Teaching country music. In *Country music annual,* ed. Charles Wolfe and James Akenson, 151–72. Lexington: University Press of Kentucky.

Andrews, Charles. The South's greatest hero: Robert E. Lee. *The Tennessean.* February 17, 1997.

Bowen, Jack. Song seems to forget who attacked the U.S. *The Tennessean.* March 8, 2003.

Cayton, Andrew, Elisabeth Perry, Linda Reed, and Alan Winkler. 2002. *America: Pathways to the present.* Needham, MA: Prentice Hall.

Crosby, Michael. 1998. Using music in the social studies classroom. Presentation to the Third Annual Fall Retreat, Tennessee Council for the Social Studies, Henry Horton State Park (Tennessee).

Havighurst, Craig. Country music in battle over patriotism, free speech. *The Tennessean.* June 1, 2003.

Loew, Karen. No, Mr. Worley, I haven't forgotten, and I'm offended at how you asked. *The Tennessean.* April 16, 2003.

Malone, Bill C. 2002. *Country music, USA.* 2nd rev. ed. Austin, TX: University of Texas Press.

Mansfield, Brian. The Chicks ruffle some feathers. *USA Today,* March 19, 2003.

McGee, Chad. 1998. Country music: Patriotism and war. Unpublished multimedia presentation. SEED 6920 Topics: Country music. Tennessee Technological University. Cookeville, TN.

Pugh, Ronnie. Political implications in country music. Paper presented to the International Country Music Conference. Belmont University. Nashville, TN. May 30, 2003.

Pvt Stone killed in Vietnam. *Jackson County Sentinel* (Tennessee). August 21, 1969.

Weeks, Terry, and Bob Womack. 1996. *Tennessee: The history of an American state.* Montgomery, AL: Clairmont Press.

Discography

Bare, Bobby. "God Bless America Again." *Country Shots: God Bless America.* Rhino R2 71645. 1994.

Britt, Elton. "There's a Star Spangled Banner Waving Somewhere." *Lee Cash Presents: The History of Country Music.* Vol. 1. N.d.

Brother Phelps. "Lookout Mountain." *Anyway the Wind Blows.* Asylum 61724-2. 1995.

Dailey, H.J. "Merry Christmas from Vietnam." Dailey Records 1005. N.d.

Dusty, Slim. "And the Band Played Waltzing Matilda." *To Whom It May Concern.* EMI SCX08037. 1978.

Haggard, Merle. "The Fightin' Side of Me." *The Fightin' Side of Me.* Capitol ST-451 LP. 1970.

———. "Okie from Muskogee" *Okie from Muskogee.* Capitol ST-384 LP. 1969.

Horton, Johnny. "The Battle of New Orleans. " *Johnny Horton's Greatest Hits.* Columbia PCG 00106. 1961.

Inman, Autry. "Ballad of Two Brothers." *Country Shots: God Bless America.* Rhino R2 71645. 1994.

Jackson, Alan. "Where Were You (When the World Stopped Turning)." *Drive.* Arista 07863-67039-2. 2002.

Jennings, Waylon. *White Mansions: A Tale from the American Civil War 1861–1865.* A&M Records AMLX 64691, 1978; A&M Records 75021 6004 2, 1989 (CD).

Keith, Toby. "Courtesy of the Red, White, and Blue (The Angry American)." *Unleashed.* Dreamworks Nashville. 2002.

Starcher, Buddy. "Sniper Hill." Boone Records 1038. 1966.

The Statler Brothers. "More Than a Name on a Wall." *Greatest Hits.* Vol. 3. 834-626 (LP). 1988.

Tippin, Aaron. "Where the Stars and Stripes and the Eagle Fly." Lyric Street 2061-64059-2. 2001.

Tubb, Ernest. "It's America: Love It or Leave It." *Country Shots: God Bless America.* Rhino R2 71645. 1994.

Worley, Darryl. "Have You Forgotten?" *Have You Forgotten?* SKG 00445-04432-2003. 2003.

Web Sites

"Battle Above the Clouds, Lookout Mountain." http://ngeorgia.com/history/batc.html.

Keith, Toby. "Toby Keith Announces New Album and Single." http://www.tobykeith.com/index.htminc=News&nws.

More Than a Name on the Wall. http://www.angelfire.com/il2/WaynesPlace/thewall.html.

Contributors

JAMES E. AKENSON is a social studies education specialist in the Department of Curriculum and Instruction at Tennessee Technological University. His current research involves integrating country music into K–12 curricula. He is also the founder and convener of the International Country Music Conference, which brings leading scholars and students to Nashville to discuss the academic study of country music and its related areas. He has coedited four other anthologies of studies in country music.

DON CUSIC is the author of fourteen books. He is currently professor of music business at Belmont University in Nashville.

WAYNE W. DANIEL researches and writes about old-time country, southern gospel, and bluegrass music. He is the author of *Pickin' on Peachtree: A History of Country Music in Atlanta, Georgia.*

KEVIN S. FONTENOT is an adjunct instructor of history at Tulane University, where he teaches Louisiana and cultural history. A student of Bill C. Malone, Fontenot is completing a biography of Jimmie Davis and has published articles and reviews in *Louisiana History* and the *Journal of Southern History.*

AARON A. FOX is associate professor of music and director of the Center for Ethnomusicology at Columbia University. His book *Real Country: Music and Language in Working-Class Culture* was published by Duke University Press in 2004.

LOUIS HATCHETT is an independent researcher specializing in the music of the 1940s. He resides in Henderson, Kentucky.

W.K. MCNEILL is a native of North Carolina who has for some years been the folklorist at the Ozark Folk Center in Mountain View, Arkansas. He has published numerous articles and edited numerous collections of traditional songs. He is the former editor of *Old Time Country* and writes regular columns for *Ozarks Mountaineer.*

RANDY RUDDER is assistant professor of English at Nashville State Community College. He received his graduate degrees in literature and creative writing from Tennessee State University and the University of Memphis. He has been a freelance music journalist for fifteen years.

ANDREW K. SMITH is an educational statistician who manages statewide literacy and numeracy testing programs in Tasmania, Australia. He has been collecting country music for forty years, and books on the Civil War for about twenty years.

IVAN M. TRIBE is professor of history at the University of Rio Grande in Ohio. His books include *Mountaineer Jamboree: Country Music in West Virginia* and *The Stonemans: An Appalachian Family and the Music That Shaped Their Lives.* His articles on various aspects of bluegrass, country, and old-time music number well over a hundred, appearing in such periodicals as *Bluegrass Unlimited, Goldenseal,* and *The Devil's Box.*

RAE WEAR teaches political science at the University of Queensland in Brisbane, Australia. Her research interests and publications are largely in the areas of Australian state and federal politics, populism studies, and right-wing politics. She has recently developed an interest in the political messages of country music.

MICHAEL ANN WILLIAMS is head of the Department of Folk Studies and Anthropology at Western Kentucky University. She is currently working on a book about Sarah Gertrude Knott, founder of the National Folk Festival, and John Lair, creator of the Renfro Valley Barn Dance.

DAVID A. WILSON is professor of Celtic studies and history at the University of Toronto. His books include *Paine and Cobbett: The Transatlantic Connection* and *Ireland, a Bicycle, and a Tin Whistle.* He is currently writing a biography of Thomas D'Arcy McGee and preparing a book on the Fenians in Canada.

CHARLES K. WOLFE is a cultural historian at Middle Tennessee State University. He has edited or authored over twenty-three books on country and folk music, most recently *The Bristol Sessions.*